Podcasting

Podcasting

The Audio Media Revolution

Martin Spinelli and Lance Dann

BLOOMSBURY ACADEMIC
LONDON • NEW YORK • OXFORD • NEW DELHI • SYDNEY

BLOOMSBURY ACADEMIC
Bloomsbury Publishing Inc
1385 Broadway, New York, NY 10018, USA
50 Bedford Square, London, WC1B 3DP, UK

BLOOMSBURY, BLOOMSBURY ACADEMIC and the Diana logo are trademarks
of Bloomsbury Publishing Plc

First published in the United States of America 2019

A catalog record for this book is available from the Library of Congress.

ISBN: HB: 978-1-5013-2869-5
PB: 978-1-5013-2868-8
ePDF: 978-1-5013-2865-7
eBook: 978-1-5013-2866-4

Typeset by Deanta Global Publishing Services, Chennai, India
Printed and bound in the United States of America

To find out more about our authors and books visit www.bloomsbury.com
and sign up for our newsletters.

For Lio, Lola, and Monty

Contents

Interviewees[1]

Jad Abumrad of *Radiolab* and *More Perfect*. Interviewed on October 26, 2016, in Brooklyn, New York.

Paul Bae and Terry Miles of Pacific Northwest Stories. Interviewed on July 6, 2017, via Skype.

Brendan Baker of *Love + Radio*. Interviewed on July 8, 2016, in Chicago, Illinois.

Alex Blumberg of Gimlet Media. Interviewed on October 10, 2017, via Skype.

Camilla Byk of *Podium.me*. Interviewed on December 11, 2015, and May 24, 2016, in London.

Dana Chivvis of *Serial*. Interviewed on July 5, 2016, in New York, New York.

Jeffrey Cranor and Joseph Fink of *Welcome to Night Vale*. Interviewed on September 11, 2015, via Skype.

John Dryden of Goldhawk Productions. Interviewed on April 28, 2017, on the phone.

Mark Friend of the BBC. Interviewed on June 22, 2016, in London.

Fred Greenhalgh of Final Rune Productions. Interviewed on April 2, 2016, in Los Angeles, and on June 30, 2017, via Skype.

Alan Hall of Falling Tree Productions. Interviewed on July 5, 2016, in London.

Ann Heppermann of *Serendipity* and The Sarah Awards. Interviewed on October 30, 2015, in Brooklyn, New York.

Richard Herring of *RHLSTP*. Interviewed on November 18, 2016, in London.

Ellen Horne of Audible.com. Interviewed on October 27, 2015, in Newark, New Jersey.

Dirk Maggs of Perfectly Normal Productions. Interviewed on November 16, 2009, and January 5, 2018, via Skype.

Aaron Mahnke of *Lore*. Interviewed on April 19, 2017, via Skype.

Jonathan Mitchell of *The Truth*. Interviewed on October 26, 2015, in New York, New York.

---

[1] Professionals we interviewed are listed here alphabetically by last name. Their affiliations with podcasts or other entities were correct at the time of their interviews.

Jeremy Mortimer, independent audio drama producer. Interviewed on July 5, 2016, in London.

Jamie Morton, James Cooper, and Alice Levine of *My Dad Wrote a Porno*. Interviewed on April 28, 2017, in London.

Steve Peters of Storyforward. Interviewed on April 1, 2016, in Los Angeles.

Scroobius Pip of *Distraction Pieces*. Interviewed on April 28, 2017, in London.

Kaitlin Prest of *The Heart*. Interviewed on October 30, 2015, in Brooklyn, New York.

Nick Quah of *Hot Pod*. Interviewed on October 26, 2016, in New York, New York.

Larry Rosin of Edison Research. Interviewed on October 31, 2016, in Somerville, New Jersey.

Miranda Sawyer of *The Observer*. Interviewed on March 17, 2016, in London.

Julie Shapiro of Radiotopia and PRX. Interviewed on July 8, 2016, in Chicago, Illinois.

Rob Walch of Libsyn. Interviewed on November 5, 2017, via Skype.

K. C. Wayland of *We're Alive* and *Bronzeville*. Interviewed on April 1, 2016, in Los Angeles.

Helen Zaltzman of *Answer Me This!* and *The Allusionist*. Interviewed on September 5, 2016, in London.

Foreword

How do we capture the present moment yet also speak to enduring themes? For if one thing in the media firmament is ripe for such treatment right now, it is surely podcasting.

It's certainly been around long enough to have earned its own history. By which I don't just mean that, two decades or so on, we have the necessary perspective to give cogent shape to its origin story, accurately trace its steps into early adulthood, or precisely locate its place in the contemporary media landscape. I also mean—I *especially* mean—that we can start to reflect properly on the more personal stuff—on how podcasting has brought us lives spent listening in new ways and minds captivated by new experiences. As a cultural historian interested in sound, I usually sense that *this* is the stuff that matters most: what precisely we hear, how what we hear works on our imaginations, how this firing of our imaginations in turn renders intangible but not insignificant shifts in the ways we think and feel and behave. Audio is supposed to be a fleeting, spectral thing—gone the very instant it's born. But it leaves its traces. There's something about the act of listening intimately which lets the stories and voices we hear get under our skin. And podcasting certainly deploys such intimacy in striking ways.

Not by accident, of course. As Martin Spinelli and Lance Dann reveal so expertly and eloquently in the pages that follow, podcasting is emphatically an *art* as well as a business. The question arises then: what *kind* of art, exactly? Genetic links with the medium of radio are all too obvious. A neatly teleological answer is therefore inviting: we might simply cast podcasting as the latest, predestined stage in radio's own mutation. Thankfully, Spinelli and Dann resist this approach. They're steeped in the ways of radio; they both bring a rigorous appreciation of the "older" medium to bear on their latest subject matter. This gives real weight to their analysis. But they've listened carefully to enough podcasts, talked to enough of the people involved, got enough hands-on experience of making the things, and have thought sufficiently deeply about the wider "new" media environment, to ensure they always transcend their own personal comfort zones. They hear afresh and without prejudice.

What emerges from this immersive engagement is always fascinating and often hugely provocative, since the implications are truly wide-ranging. Turning their attentive ears and their critical gazes toward their chosen target, Spinelli and Dann uncover new approaches to speaking, to reportage, to engaging listeners, to telling stories. The breakout podcast *Serial*, for example, offers a kind of "New 'New Journalism.'" Other series re-structure classical narrative arcs, disrupt conventional genre boundaries, and threaten the market dominance of established media behemoths. To think of podcasting *only* in relation to radio, they suggest—to measure it *only* according to radio values and styles and then list its various virtues or deficiencies accordingly—is to fail to hear it for what it *really* is. New medium or not, it is certainly something emphatically starting to take on a life of its own which, naturally, brings its own dangers. At some stage—perhaps all too soon, they warn us—stasis will set in, a certain formulaic style will take hold, and the current creative ferment will ebb slowly away.

But not *yet*. We are, as the authors put it, in a "moment of dynamism." This timely book offers us a ring-side seat. It helps us to *feel* the moment. Better still, it has profound lessons for anyone interested in nurturing modern media's most creative impulses. In short, it helps us to understand why a "moment" such as this really *matters*.

David Hendy
Professor of Media and Cultural History
University of Sussex

Acknowledgments

Podcasting: The Audio Media Revolution would not have taken the form it did without the work of Research Assistant Joy Stacey. She not only identified essential resources, undertook close listenings of individual podcasts, and managed and conducted the survey of young podcast journalists, but was also extremely useful in helping us frame issues of diversity and sexual identity in podcasting. We also had research assistant help from Ella Gray Thomas and Joe Horton who undertook additional close listenings and booked and conducted interviews.

We are grateful for a British Academy/Leverhulme Research Grant that enabled us to: travel to, conduct, and transcribe many of our interviews; undertake our survey of young podcast journalists; and pay our research staff. The School of Media, Film and Music at the University of Sussex provided research leave to facilitate the writing of this book and was also the hothouse in which many of the arguments, ideas, contentions, and suggestions found in this book were first hashed out with students and colleagues. In particular we would like to thank Michael Bull and David Hendy for giving this book productive nudges when it was in the early outline stage, which helped make what it offers more substantial and useful to both scholars and practitioners. Nicolas Till and Sally Munt gave useful feedback on grant applications for this project, as did Paul Davidson of the University of Sussex Research and Enterprise Office. The School of Media, Film and Music also provided access to recording equipment and facilities for some interview recordings which resulted in more professional material. In addition, the Head of Media, Film and Music Tim Jordan and the Head of Media Practice Adrian Goycoolea were very supportive of this project. We would also like to thank the School of Media at the University of Brighton and particularly Irmi Karl and Helen Kennedy for their support of the work on this book.

Chapter 6, about diversity and youth podcasting, is indebted to the young journalists and producers of *Podium.me* who offered their valuable time and insights in a survey of their use of podcasts and their approaches to podcast making. While some were happy to be named, all the respondents have been anonymized in accordance with new research guidelines.

Chapter 7 details the production and distribution of the podcast series *Blood Culture* which was a product of the (often underpaid) efforts of a large group of people. We would like to thank Phil Connolly and David Wigram for developing and writing the project, Marley Cole and Simon James for their sound design (and music), Claire M. Singer for her score, Stephen Cooper and James Morris for their web work, Alan Gilchrist for his patience and humor, Kaye Tilbury and Lizzie Parkinson for their work in the studio, Nick Ware for his executive oversight, Cristina Lo Celso for her fantastic input and energy, and of course all cast and crews who put the show together with us. The University of Brighton awarded us a grant that supported our research into audiences for the *Blood Culture* podcast, and the Wellcome Trust contributed the funding that made this project possible.

Thanks goes to Ed Baxter and everyone at Resonance 104.4 FM, not only for helping with *Blood Culture* but for being some of the most inspirational and dedicated people on the UK audio and radio scenes. Honorable mention also should be given to Euan McAleece for his insightful supply of links to web articles.

In addition, we would like to thank: Katie Gallof, for careful and supportive editing at Bloomsbury; Zita Krejzl, for transcribing most of the interviews and proofing the chapters; James Clifton, Jack Jewers and Lee Gooding, for moral support; Gloria Dann, for correcting her son's grammar; and Dawn Dann and Jody De Best, for their patience and emotional support.

Obviously, we are extremely grateful to the highly accomplished and lauded professionals who gave their time and shared their knowledge with us as we were thinking through the sound, relationships, techniques, technologies, forms, and implications of podcasting. Because of their importance, they are listed separately and their interview details are also found in the References, but it would be remiss to omit broad thanks to them here. Their contributions made this book extremely valuable to future generations of audio makers and media thinkers alike. We could not have written this book without them.

While we each made substantial contributions to each of the chapters, Chapters 2, 4, 6, and 8 were originally conceived and driven by Martin Spinelli; Chapters 3, 5, 7, and 9 were originally conceived and driven by Lance Dann. This chapter breakdown is also useful for identifying the first-person passages throughout the book. The Introduction and the Afterword were developed collaboratively.

Introduction: The Audio Media Revolution

There is so much writing about the moment, and reading about the moment, and blogging about the moment, and the metrics, and the business, and the monetization, and the platforms, and the technology, and there seemed to be no discussion of content, barely none . . . . That's a dangerous place where it is all function, no form.

—Julie Shapiro (2016)

In the summer of 2014 tens of thousands of fans queued outside of theatres across North America and Europe to hear live performances of the podcast *Welcome to Night Vale*. In October of that year, *This American Life* producer Ira Glass promoted *Serial* to the roughly three million viewers of *The Tonight Show with Jimmy Fallon* and within four weeks the series could boast four million downloads per episode. In 2016, 3.6 million people were listening to BBC podcasts per month. By 2017 Aaron Mahnke's home-produced *Lore* was being serialized by Amazon, *My Dad Wrote a Porno* was selling out the Sydney Opera House, *S-Town* was being downloaded ten million times in the first four days of its release, and podcasting had moved out of its geeky ghetto into an international cultural mainstream. But, as executive producer of Radiotopia Julie Shapiro noted, all the buzz around the phenomenon and excitement around the numbers[1] of what some called the "Golden Age"[2] of podcasting risked eclipsing what was really interesting and important about this moment: namely, that new modes of expression were taking shape and new ways of generating meaning

---

[1] These numbers, their implications, and their significant shortcomings as markers of actual listenership are deconstructed in various ways in Chapters 7, 8, and 9.

[2] Berry (2016b) usefully takes up the idea of the "Golden Age" in other histories of podcasting; Bonini (2015), instead, describes the resurgence of interest as a "Second Age" of podcasting, a period in which it begins to define itself more clearly. While admittedly somewhat elastic, we think of podcasting's Golden Age as beginning in late 2014 with Apple's inclusion of a built-in podcasting app on every iPhone and the launch of *Serial* through to the time of this writing.

and forming relationships were growing around this emergent medium. Johanna Zorn, long-running executive director of the Third Coast International Audio Festival, echoed this concern in a manifesto for podcasting that included a plea that reviewers outside the rarefied world of public radio take audio's new Golden Age seriously and recognize podcasting as an art form (2016). This book is, to a significant extent, a positive answer to that call and seeks to describe podcasting as a creative medium distinct from radio, with its own unique modes of not just dissemination but also production, listening, and engagement. While we do not intend to contribute to the popular hype around podcasting, and while we do keep a relatively tight historical focus, this book should not be read as an obituary for podcasting's revolutionary moment. Instead, we like to think that it holds the door open for creative audio producers who share the thinking of Ellen Horne, former executive producer of *Radiolab*, then executive producer at Audible.com, that podcasting's real Golden Age is yet to come (2015).

In the 2005 *Radiolab* podcast episode called "Space," the astronomer Neil deGrasse Tyson notes that human beings can only detect a mere 4 percent of the matter of the universe. A similar limitation, and the sense of disappointment that comes with it, also marks this book's study of podcasting. Of the 350,000 podcasts reported to exist (Quah 2017b) it was only physically possible for us to reference a tiny handful in efforts to try to describe larger phenomena and more complex patterns—a bit like our children thinking about the cosmos by looking at the stars they can see framed by a bedroom window. We admit that our attentions were most often drawn to those that burned the brightest. Despite this restriction, it has been possible for us to draw constellation lines around similar projects, to extrapolate some larger observations about podcasting's distinctive characteristics as a medium, and to use these observations to push and probe some familiar media studies ideas: Our analysis of the editing on *Radiolab* allows us to talk about new rhetorical techniques for composed audio speech and a postmodern (decidedly podcast) approach to science journalism. Our studies of *Welcome to Night Vale*, *My Dad Wrote a Porno*, and *Podium.me* describe new and distinctive modes of audience engagement while positioning podcasting as not merely dependent on social media, but integrated into it as a new form of social media in and of itself. Our analysis of *Serial* describes a "New 'New Journalism'" native to podcasting and can be used to discuss genre formation within emergent media. Our studies of *The Black Tapes* and *The Truth* help us define the new form of "podcast drama" as a product of the unique characteristics of the medium. Two Radiotopia podcasts are used to document the particular intimacy of podcast listening and extended possibilities for media-facilitated empathy. And our close production analysis of *Blood Culture* prompts questions about new media popularity and statistics.

The critical forays supported by these case studies are all organized to make the argument for the distinctiveness of podcasting. While we unavoidably make references to radio and consider the associations between podcasting and radio, we reject the proposition that podcasting is merely an extension of radio and that the language and methodologies of radio studies are, with some tweaking, good enough for podcasting.[3] They are not essentially the same thing and they are not separated merely by a distribution technology.[4] Radio certainly intersects the podcast ecosphere and marks it in many ways—not least of which is the dream of many podcast producers to land what they imagine will be a more secure job in radio (Markman 2012)—but our aim here is to describe the unique qualities of our new medium and the experiences it engenders.

Intentions and process

All of this book's contributions to an understanding of the podcast revolution are built on our set of interviews with the producers of arguably the most popular, noteworthy, and culturally significant podcasts from this period in audio history. From Abumrad to Zaltzman, we have collected the thoughts of the most accomplished podcast makers (and related professionals) about how their craft and the medium were developing formally, functionally, and aesthetically. Given the depth, complexity, and intensity of their insights, we made their voices and perspectives central to our portrayal of podcasting's development in this moment of dynamism.

We began this research with fluidity in mind. Rather than starting with a set of fixed (and likely arbitrary) demarcations, the arguments, approaches, sets of case studies, and methodologies we deploy took shape more or less organically.

---

[3] Berry (2016a), in his extensive meta-study of podcasting across numerous articles (a work that has prepared the ground for this book), points to some of the limitations of a radio-based approach to podcast studies. Ragusea (2015), addressing American public radio professionals, demonstrates—consciously and unconsciously—some of the practical pitfalls of a radio-based approach.

[4] Podcasting is much more than a distribution system. It is not merely a new way of disseminating audio content made in the old ways for old platforms. After all, the internet has been used to distribute audio content (for radio broadcast and individual consumption) for more than twenty years now (for evidence of this history see Spinelli 1996b).

The contents do not borrow much from conceptual categories familiar to radio studies such as format, geography, programming, nationality, or the comparatively more manageable set of listening presets on your car's receiver.[5] The book was informed by our previous interests (in media-making practices, aesthetics, rhetoric, poetics, drama, audiences, and transmedia), by conversations with friends, colleagues, and students, and at conferences, and it grew out of our other research and podcast production projects. There are, obviously, large swathes of podcasting that we do not cover—most significantly, we have barely touched on podcasting's most abundant form, the "chatcast."[6] This approach is in keeping with much of the existing critical writing about podcasting as well as its coverage in the popular media. Even as Larry Rosin of Edison Research[7] reminded us that modest productions can have huge followings, he also suggests that when most people talk about podcasting they are much more likely to have in mind something produced by a virtuoso in Brooklyn than a GarageBand-using amateur in Bolton. Yet while we are admittedly less focused on projects from the deep UGC backstory of podcasting, we certainly do take up some which have evolved out of DIY approaches like *Lore* and *My Dad Wrote a Porno* (and even in some ways *Serial*[8]), as well as podcasts with aspirations for evolution like *Podium.me*.

Textual analysis of podcasts, being harder to find in other places, is a key feature of this book, and our readings of podcasts here—while not vast in number— are purposefully very granular. Close analytical listenings to episodes from *Bronzeville, Serial, Radiolab, The Heart,* and *Love + Radio* detail how particular podcasts are constructed, how they are consumed, what meaning strategies and literary devices they deploy, and to what social and exploratory ends. In addition

---

[5] However, it is worth noting here that the BBC has been working with auto manufacturers to make the driving podcast listening experience more similar to using car radio receiver presets (Friend 2016).

[6] Friends gathering around a microphone and simply chatting with little or no planning, editing, or thought to production values, narrative constructions, or podcast direction.

[7] Edison Research is an American market research, survey, and polling company whose substantial analysis of podcasting trends dates back to 2006, longer than any other annual podcasting research endeavor we could identify.

[8] *This American Life*, the radio program that launched *Serial* into the world both by supporting its original production and by debuting its first episode for its audience (2.2 million weekly radio listeners), is itself an example of a long evolution in the history of audio speech media from its radio form to its podcasting form. While space prohibits our taking it up as a detailed case study, its influence on many of the podcasts cited in this book is unmistakable. Like the clockwork scratches and tattooed welts of *S-Town*'s "witness marks," an emphasis on strong character and solid narrative structure should be reminders of *This American Life*'s contribution to the most prominent American podcasts.

to these close analytical listenings,[9] this book also offers detailed production studies that describe the pragmatic and coincidental circumstances that inform and shape the way podcasts are created, recognized, and become models for future productions and subjects of critical study.

Podcasting: The Audio Media Revolution has something to offer (we hope) to two audiences: the popular and the scholarly. While taking up podcasts familiar to readers of *Rolling Stone*, *The Guardian*, *Medium*, *The Atlantic*, and *Vulture*, it also aspires to the deep dives of more research-based media writing familiar to readers of *New Media & Society*. We hope we have managed to find a hybrid tone that resonates with a popular enthusiasm (minus some of the boosterism) combined with significant critical insight and broad-ranging theoretical scope (minus some of the conditionality and risk aversion). We have approached our subject not just as academics but also as producers and as listeners. The fact that podcasting is a part of our own everyday lives has inflected our analysis. We have attempted to write in a manner that is conscious of our subjective involvement with the form, while remaining sufficiently detached to adopt a critical attitude. We use accounts of our personal relationship to the medium as reflective tools or as entry points for discussion; these passages should be read as asides that color, corroborate, and sometimes question the issues being addressed.

Revolution and other terms

What, exactly, is "revolutionary" about podcasting—a term reputedly coined only to hit a publishing word-count target?[10] Clearly our descriptions of podcasting are laced with words from old and other media: we talk about seasons and episodes, borrow "cast" from broadcasting, and we still edit "tape" (albeit on our computers). Culturally, politically, and socially, it is easy to

---

[9] This practice of close analytical listening is obviously facilitated by two of the most distinctive features of podcasting: the ease of back-scanning and repeat listening. In practice, close analytical listening means pausing the playback every few seconds to note what is going on at the level of language (who is speaking, what they are saying, where they are saying it, and to whom), how the audio is processed and edited, how the elements are being composed into a narrative and where that narrative turns or suspends, the reactions I am having as a listener and what associations and connections I am making, and how music and sound are being deployed to invite ways of listening and subsequent meanings. See Bernstein (1998) for insights that informed this practice.

[10] It is unclear to us whether this is apocryphal, but it is the assertion made in the BBC Radio Four program, *Podcasting: The First Ten Years* (2014).

dismiss podcasting as just another over-hyped and over-sold emergent medium buoyed by egalitarian but ultimately empty rhetoric.[11] Podcasts, as some argue (Morris and Patterson 2015), are really just another example of "people-catchers" which aggregate and commodify listeners for producers, advertisers, and corporations; and our devices are little more than consumption facilitators. There has also been appropriate suspicion around the idea of "newness" itself. Bottomley, for example, argues that "there is little about podcasting that is truly new, when the full range of radio's history and forms are taken into account" (2015: 180). While Lacey, more specifically, invites us to question the novelty of podcasting as offering integrated multimedia experiences (2014: 71). These readings, often powerfully informed by Frankfurt School ideas, force us to keep in mind that podcasting is inextricably intertwined into much larger media, social, and economic systems. Yet, useful and necessary as the work of these critics is, a tone of labored pessimism often dominates which can seem at odds with the perceptions of the producers we interviewed. Part of this problem, if it is a problem, is that our current critical frames of reference (most of them inherited from radio studies) might simply not be a very good fit for podcasting. Too often when looking for a component or a technique that will mark a podcast or podcasting in general as a "success" we refer to old forms.[12] For example, McHugh (2016) is largely supportive of Markman's suggestion that podcasting will succeed not so much because it is a disruptor of radio but because it "has breathed new life into established, and in some cases largely forgotten tropes and forms" (2015: 241). Conversely, many of our interviewees have lost patience with efforts to make sense of podcasting by listening backward. Abumrad, for example, is exasperated by the fact that his *Radiolab* is still considered "new" despite having been in production for more than a decade (2016).

It seems reasonable to assume that the simple fact of a person's age will influence whether that person frames podcasting in terms of radio or is hungry for revolutionary models. Edison Research's "Infinite Dial" (2017)

---

[11] For a history of democratic claims masking the neoliberal forces within emergent media, see Spinelli (1996a).

[12] Throughout this book certain podcasts are referred to as having been "successful," and this success will normally be contextualized with reference to the particular concept under discussion. This could be audience reach, engagement, cultural impact, or serving a socially beneficial purpose. In Chapter 9, for example, we argue that in a freemium economy perhaps the greatest marker of a podcast's "success" is its survival. "Success" in this book, as it is in the larger media ecosystem, is a fluid term.

shows podcast usage as consistently skewed to younger consumers. Podcasting represents a tantalizing opportunity for a new generation to draw a line under all of audio history in order to invent and reinvent, discover and rediscover, audio experiences and relationships on their own diverse terms and in their own diverse ways. Whether we describe that approach as naive or bold, the chance to reimagine drama, journalism, science, philosophy, sex, spirituality, and even humanity, is rare and refreshing and should be seized without apology. Why would Millennial media makers and consumers want to carry 100 years of broadcast history with them into podcasting? Why would we want to transfer 150 years of journalistic rules and codes into podcasting? Why would anyone dutifully accept that baggage? And crucially, we must ask, why should postmodern producers and listeners be burdened by the tired modernist mantra of "make it new"—constantly forced to refer to past work in order to describe their own as "innovative"? Simply put, podcasting *is* new for many of its producers whether we can trace its history through Bell, Edison, Marconi, Reith, McLeish, Shepherd, and Plowright or not.[13]

With these competing currents in mind, and in order to help chart a straight course to something that might be called "podcast studies," we offer here a clear and consolidated list of the eleven major podcasting features and concepts that we explore and detail in the rest of the book:

1. Consumption on earbuds encourages an interior and intimate mode of listening. This is qualitatively and conceptually different from radio speaker listening (and even listening on open headphones) and facilitates a different kind of relationship.
2. Podcasting is primarily a mobile medium. Podcasts move with the human body and are consumed in urban spaces, while in transit, in the streets and in other public places.
3. Podcasts offer more listener control. It is extremely easy to replay a podcast and listen to it repeatedly. Similarly, we can back-scan a podcast to listen to a section multiple times; this allows for different production practices and modes of shaping content.

---

[13] Also crucially, none of this diminishes radio. Its own distinct advantages are clear—chiefly its "liveness" and its ability to deliver breaking events in real time. Whatever podcasting is, it is not "live." This is not something likely to change and none of the people we interviewed considered it inevitable. Even as podcasting garnered media buzz, radio continued to have vastly larger audiences in terms of numbers (Rosin 2016 and Edison 2017), particularly in cars where radio is consumed more often by a factor of ten (Friend 2016).

4. Podcast listening requires more selection and active engagement on the part of the consumer in choosing listening options. It is a push-pull technology: listeners pull to discover and, if they subscribe, a feed pushes them new material. Discovery happens in a different way than on radio and, arguably, opportunities for serendipity are reduced.
5. Podcasts can thrive on niche global audiences. They are less rooted in material communities, regions, and countries (an advantage and a disadvantage).
6. Podcasts are interwoven into social media and as such have a heightened capacity to enhance engagement with, and activate, an audience. The same mobile devices used to participate in social media are the devices used to listen to (and in some cases produce) podcasts and there is ready and easy overlap between these uses.
7. Podcasts can be produced and distributed without the approval of a commissioning editor, program controller, or gatekeeper. This means that creators are often working with great freedom and little support.
8. Podcasts are usually distributed as part of a freemium model: there is no charge for the core product and income is earned through a variety of secondary means.
9. Podcasts are "evergreen," available (theoretically) in perpetuity and face greater obstacles in achieving "liveness" than other media.
10. There is no fixed or definitive text of a podcast episode or installment. Mistakes can be corrected, apologies added, advertisements rotated, and sound remixed.
11. Podcast do not have the timing and scheduling constraints of broadcast media. They can be as long as they need to be and released whenever desired.

While, as we have noted, it is certainly possible to find traces (and even full-throated embodiments) of these individual characteristics and opportunities on radio and in other places, we find them more native to podcasting. Taken together, they encourage us to find a distinct discourse or vocabulary for appreciating and studying podcasts. Podcasting deserves its own language.

In spite of the fact that podcasting is audio designed to be delivered through a borderless internet, our interviews and observations revealed significant differences in podcasting cultures worth mentioning. Many of our interviewees had a sense that the general momentum in the English-speaking audio world had shifted from the grand façade of the BBC's Broadcasting House to the hipster cafés of Brooklyn.[14] This shift has also been influenced by the broad political currents of recent years that have had an effect on the very idea of public service broadcasting: it is a move from a reliance on a license fee or state or institutional support into an environment in which everyone has had to be much more canny (some might say "crass") about getting money from sponsors and listeners. This is a model American producers have been familiar with for decades.

These changes have influenced sound and style. Many of our interviewees (Prest, Baker, Sawyer, Hall, Shapiro, Heppermann, and Zaltzman) noted, and sometimes lamented, that what they hear as a chatty, familiar, personal, fluid, intimate, or even "American" tone has come to be associated with podcasting in general in the public imagination. This was often contrasted with a more "European" style of audio production frequently described as sophisticated, anonymous, musical, sound-rich, crafted, and even male.[15] Interestingly, this style also tended to be associated with radio rather than podcasting.

Podcast forms

While our chapters invoke broad, familiar media studies frames such as formal analysis, production analysis, and reception/engagement analysis to better understand podcasting, they are built around particular case studies. We take the position that larger ideas are only reliably generated and expanded through a close examination of specific podcasts. This specificity is particularly important in our chapters on podcast forms. For example, Chapter 5, "Don't Look Back: The New Possibilities of Podcast Drama," examines particular structures, practices, and levels of investment on *Bronzeville*, *The Black Tapes*, *The Truth*, and other fictional podcasts. It locates the emergent form of podcast drama as a subset of audio drama, one that is determined by the modes in which the work is produced and consumed. Historically audio drama, and radio drama in particular, has been created to be listened to either informally and disposably or as sonically demanding, immersive experiences. Our case studies show that a new generation of podcast drama producers is creating works positioned in the

---

[14] Rosin (2016) emphasized this new location of energy and was very alert to the assumptions this has generated inside and outside of the podcasting ecosphere.

[15] McHugh (2016) makes similar observations, hearing in the "European feature" style a "strong authorial choreography" similar to that associated with film directors.

sweet spot between these poles, serials that are narratively sophisticated while being sonically stripped down. These works are designed to be experienced as a secondary activity that does not expect an audience to engage in the immediate and, possibly distracting, task of creating location, character, and action in their imagination.

Earlier attempts to grapple with and identify a similar "ideal position" for podcast audio in relation to listeners have been useful if somewhat stymied by imprecise or underthought case study choices.[16] By contrast, the case studies taken up in this book are by and large produced with the specific and distinctive forms and characteristics of podcasting in mind. We contend that material produced with this awareness engenders a different kind of listening. Two such examples are *Love + Radio* and *The Heart*, both discussed in Chapter 4, "In Bed with Radiotopians: Podcast Intimacy, Empathy, and Narrative." While it is still difficult to use the word "typical" when describing podcast genres, these Radiotopia offerings are very sympathetic to the formal characteristics we have identified in podcasting. This chapter casts their producers as "empathy artists" through their careful use of interiorization to engage the intimacy of podcast earbud listening. In the end, it suggests that certain subjects might have an affinity for podcasting, such as sex and psychological play and manipulation. Achieving these effects often relies on a high level of skill in sound design, which invites and encourages repeat listening.[17]

Podcast production

The chapters that focus on podcasting production suggest that an awareness of podcasting's distinctiveness has opened the door to creative practices (and dilemmas) not found on radio. For example, the lack of a fixed broadcast schedule allows for more and different kinds of integration of listener ideas and voices. Also, the lack of a permanent (or "once broadcast") audio text in podcasting means that nearly everything is updateable and reframeable rather

---

[16] Nyre (2015), for example, found that listening to "podcast" content while moving through in urban environments engendered responses quite similar to listening to "live" radio content. The podcasts he chose to sample were not emblematic of the form as we now describe it. For his "podcast" material he selected evergreen radio content of an "educational" nature merely repackaged as podcasts.

[17] Interestingly, we have found that sound art projects that are more "pure"—that are more decontextualized and less dependent on narrative—have not yet made much of an impact in podcast culture.

than static. While certainly a creative and editorial opportunity, this malleability is contentious terrain for many of the producers we interviewed, particularly as it relates to the framing and managing of advertising. The issue of advertising in general continued to dog many of the practitioners we spoke to and is also prominent in a range of other interviews with podcast professionals currently available. Like many of the other podcasting issues we seek to place in context, this one also appears marked by generational and cultural divides. Hall (2016) and others (cited in McHugh 2016) remained concerned that ads diminish the experience of podcast listening, and responses to the issue range from tense ambivalence (Abumrad) to creative engagement (Prest and Baker), to an almost complete lack of concern about it as an issue (many of the young producers of *Podium.me*).

Several of the practitioners who feature in Chapter 9 frame this issue of advertising in terms of how it might intervene in the integrity of the podcaster's relationship with their listener—one in which a sense of authenticity is a key component. The viral success of independent podcasts such as Aaron Mahnke's *Lore* and Scroobius Pip's *Distraction Pieces* can be ascribed to their homebrew qualities and the directness of their communication. These projects, created without exterior oversight, are not part of a marketing scheme or programming schedule; they tend to feature content that is a product of the producer's interests and their intuition about what their audiences will appreciate. This relationship becomes clouded once sponsors and advertisers are introduced into the process and can create the perception that a host is no longer telling their audience something because they want to, but because they are being paid to do so. Alex Blumberg's Gimlet Media attempts to position itself as a response to this conundrum, as proof that, in Ira Glass's words, "Public Radio is ready for capitalism" (quoted in Greiff 2015). The chapter notes that the issues of advertiser funding and authenticity have by no means been put to rest by Gimlet; this was evidenced by the audience outcry that followed the network's cancellation of Starlee Kine's highly praised but fiscally unwieldy investigative series *The Mystery Show*.

Our production analyses are not limited to professional projects defined by familiar ideas of quality or those that have the goal of making money. Most podcasts are marked by other social, personal, political, or cultural agendas; their study provides unique insight into different production practices with far-reaching implications. Chapter 6, "A Utopian Moment: *Podium.me*, Diversity, and Youth Podcasting," profiles *Podium.me* as a proactive and progressive youth media project and frames diversity in terms of experience rather than quotas or access. It examines *Podium.me*'s practice-based approach in contrast to other, more institutional approaches to issues of diversity. Further, it suggests that the understanding of mobile audio technology has been remarkably one-sided, focusing almost exclusively on its functions for listening rather than recording. *Podium.me*'s focus on the phone as a recording device (even before it is a listening device) allows us to rewrite an important piece of script about mobile media.

In terms of production and dissemination, *Podium.me* is not only thoroughly interwoven into social media but is so enmeshed in an environment of exchange and response that it can function like a social medium itself.[18] As noted, an integration into social media is another key aspect of podcasting, and, as we see in Chapter 7, "*Blood Culture*: Gaming the Podcast System," the actual relationships of social media can become artistic material themselves. This chapter positions the audio drama series *Blood Culture* in terms of practice as research. It details the development, production, and distribution of a project that integrated podcasting as part of a multilayered media experience comprised of film, games, and audio as well as social media. *Blood Culture*'s approach to the larger media ecosystem is presented as an attempt to address a podcast's problem of existing in a potentially limitless "sea of free audio" (Shapiro 2016) and the challenges of discoverability faced by even the most prominent of podcasters (Friend 2016). This chapter presents not just the production process of an award-winning podcast, but the means by which social media, transmedia techniques, and a covert knowledge of Apple's algorithm for deriving its podcast charts can be deployed to develop a following within a community of dedicated audio drama fans.

Podcasting engagement and reception

The engagement that happens through podcasts, not just how they are received by an audience, but the relationships they invite between multiple combinations of makers, listeners, and subjects, is where we find podcasting's most distinctive characteristics. Through these relationships different kinds of meaning can be accessed. Brendan Baker, the producer on *Love + Radio*, was particularly

---

[18] This situation is clearly enabled to some degree by the fact that the same phones and devices are used interchangeably to engage in social media as well as to record, edit, and upload audio.

useful here when he described radio as "information getting transmitted," and podcasting as more "abstract" and open to multiple engagements and perceptions (2016). For him, radio was for clarity while podcasting was for subtlety.

Among the podcasts committed to working with this subtlety, *Radiolab* is perhaps the most accomplished and the most well-known. Chapter 2, "Splatters of Shit: Story, Science, and Digital Speech on *Radiolab*," presents *Radiolab* as a new form of postmodern podcast science journalism and enquiry that incorporates perspectives not conventionally associated with traditional science reporting. We argue that this approach is facilitated by a dense, sculptural, authentically digital manipulating of audio speech that does not pretend to be real conversation. One of its other particularly postmodern aspects (mentioned above in other contexts) is its natural and easy acceptance of the impermanence of its episodes. On *Radiolab* there is no urtext; after installments are released they can be changed online for editorial reasons. This chapter examines, for example, the Yellow Rain segment from the 2012 "Fact of the Matter" episode which is altered not just for an apology but for an extended discussion of the editorial thinking that led to the initial misstep. While this aspect of podcasting makes for more a vibrant and responsive engagement with updated relevance, it does present some new challenges for scholars used to referring to broadcast audio material using time codes that can then be used by other listeners. Many of the hundreds of essays written about the 1938 Mercury Theatre on the Air broadcast of the *War of the Worlds* rely on the definitive timings of the broadcast event (see Spinelli 2009); the relative ease of identifying, accessing, and discussing specific moments of that broadcast text has helped make it arguably the most studied and most famous in radio history. When conducting the close analytical listenings in this book we can only reference time codes for the version we have downloaded (these are noted in the References). Rather than being unsettled by this lack of a definitive text and its implications for conventional scholarship, we take from this a reminder that *a podcast is more than a mere audio text*, it is a relationship invited through an audio text between people involved in making and listening to that text and beyond.

Therefore, while *individual* listening might be the moment in which a podcast "happens" in some sense, it is possible, and indeed necessary, to consider larger formations of podcast *audiences*. Chapter 3, "You Are Not Alone: Podcast Communities, Audiences, and *Welcome to Night Vale*," examines how social media is and is not used in audience formation. We describe the podcast audience as much more "knowable" than the radio audience, and the interaction (particularly the fandom) as more intense; this is evidenced by engagement at live performances of the podcast *Welcome to Night Vale*. Joseph Fink and Jeffrey Cranor have created a work that possesses a rigid and clearly articulated story world, but one that is also creatively porous, providing a space that is open for their audience to playfully share art, costume design, memes, and fictions. This transforms the listeners' relationship to the text from being individualized and semiotic to being producerly and communal.

While specific and highly committed listeners are easier to identify and their engagement is easier to document, larger configurations of audience remain quite abstract and difficult to quantify because the very numbers themselves are extremely slippery: As Davies (2014) pointed out, downloads do not equate to listeners, or even listens, and in an age in which it is possible to game the data around a podcast by buying downloads through click farms (as we document in Chapter 7), all listening figures should be taken with a generous pinch of salt. Data from podcast- or network-specific listening apps like the BBC iPlayer or NPR One, listener surveys, and even more anecdotal investigations[19] are proving more reliable than numbers from aggregators and platforms. These increasingly suggest that audiences are straining beyond familiar demographic categories and are forming around harder-to-predict niche tastes that often overlap in unexpected ways. Perhaps for this reason many of the accomplished podcast makers that we interviewed repeatedly focus on making work that they themselves find interesting rather than channeling creative energies into anticipating the interests of some abstract audience. The fact of producers building podcasts around their own enquiries, pleasures, and curiosities without a clear demographic in mind is often the route to astounding success in podcasting. While *Serial*'s impact was certainly supported by a myriad of promotional and external factors, it would not have made the waves that it did without the commitment and creative risk-taking of its producers. Chapter 8 about that first household-name in podcasting, "The Truth About *Serial*: It's Not Really About a Murder," describes it as bringing into the mainstream a new kind of podcast audience engagement and a new set of postmodern rules for journalism unique to podcasting. In that chapter we argue that the presenter is the main character of the production and *her* change and evolution should be seen as its real focus. Through *Serial*, we suggest a New "New Journalism" finds its native medium in podcasting, and, podcast journalism—itself the real subject

---

[19] See, for example, Ganesh (2016).

of the series—is shown to be much more open ended and dependent on listener interpretation than approaches taken in previously established radio versions of true-crime programs.

Listening forward

Podcasting: The Audio Media Revolution endeavors to capture a transitional moment in the history of audio making and listening. It is a moment in which marginal, DIY, UGC practices bursts into the more popular consciousness and begin to be taken seriously as more than just a subset of an older medium. It is a moment of energy and passion and commitment and creativity and investment, but is also a moment in which established practices are finally beginning to crystallize. Yet even as podcasting begins its adulthood, it remains a media scene of substantial risk-taking and innovation in which tremendous dedication to a niche idea or an artistic vision can find purchase with thousands and even millions of sympathetic or curious minds.

As the earlier allusion to *Radiolab*'s "Space" reminds, our scope in this book can only ever be very limited. This may well be the first and last book to attempt to deal with podcasting writ large and we would very much like to see other books about the medium take up, in more specific and precise ways, elements of podcasting that we were only able to reference in passing. These contributions might include: more detailed studies of podcasting as a vehicle for diversity and for conversations within and between minority communities;[20] more systematic examinations of amateur podcasting—which fill the vast majority of the podcast ecosphere; surveys of non-English-language podcast cultures; analyses of the particularities of music and sound in podcasts; studies of podcasting as a public relations vehicle for small companies and large corporations; studies of how new and diverse methods of funding and monetizing podcasts influence and condition the character and creativity of those podcasts; investigations of the literary potential of podcasting beyond being a vehicle for audiobooks; surveys of podcast-specific language, rhetorical devices, and manipulations of speech; podcasting's use in education; forecasts of how podcasting might change the missions of large national broadcasters; and exposés of the mechanics and

---

[20] Sarah Florini's research (2015) on podcasting's "Chitlin' Circuit" would be an excellent starting point.

algorithms of podcast placement and promotion within podcast aggregators and platforms. Other viable ideas will certainly come to the fore as the study of the medium develops further. Through these future ventures we hope that, with a critical foundation laid and arguments about what podcasting is or is not put to one side, a more robust culture of review and analysis of specific podcasts (the audio and the relationships) might be built that would offer us regular deep dives into the medium, similar to those that we enjoy with film and television.

2

Splatters of Shit: Story, Science, and Digital Speech on *Radiolab*

I think the world exists as a big splatter of shit . . . a big network of stuff and
we create stories out of that. So there is some . . . fundamental distortion that
we do when we tell stories. But I think it's a necessary one.

—Jad Abumrad (2016)

I was an early fan of *Radio Lab*[1] when it first aired on WNYC in New York more than a decade ago. What I found most captivating was its unusual pairing of what would become two of its most well-defined elements: an ambitious and dynamic or "unnatural" approach to speech editing (an approach I call self-consciously "digital") and a deep commitment to well-developed narrative. While I had previously heard (and attempted to enact in tentative ways in my own projects[2]) radio and audio experiments that deconstructed and reassembled speech in order to explore new possibilities for meaning, and while I was very familiar with the renaissance of reflective radio storytelling on programs like *This American Life*, *Radio Lab* was the first listening experience I remember which consistently combined the two. This chapter examines how *Radiolab's* dynamism around speech editing on a micro-level, and its commitment to keeping parallel narrative frameworks in tension on a macro-level, helped make it a benchmark series for podcast science journalism.

Another key objective of this chapter, following out of the first, is to use *Radiolab* to expand the project of cataloging—in a precise way—the different literary and rhetorical devices that can be realized through a self-consciously digital approach to handling audio speech—a project now more than a decade old (Spinelli 2006b). It studies some of the most significant editing practices throughout the

---

[1] The name would eventually be amalgamated to *Radiolab* as mentioned later in context.
[2] See "*Engaged* Magazine" (1998) and *Radio Radio* (2003).

seasons of *Radiolab* and uses them to explore the unconventional (often musical or sculptural) way the producers conceived of audio speech. Looking at how *Radiolab* has evolved in context since 2002 tells us two things: that the tropes of the digital handling of speech that might have been difficult for listeners to absorb and make sense of fifteen years ago have now been somewhat domesticated; and second, that these techniques are deployed to enhance, rather than disrupt, the larger narrative experiences of the episodes. To help with this project I rely not just on interviews, but on close analytical listenings to episodes from across *Radiolab*'s run; among these, the 2005 "Space" episode is the most referenced because, as executive producer Ellen Horne suggested (2015), it marked an early transitional moment in which the series began to find its mature identity.

Radiolab is particularly useful in helping us chart the history and development of podcasting because it began shortly after Apple made its first iPod. Also, it existed as a radio program well before podcasting as a means of audio distribution broke into the cultural mainstream and it has continued as one of the most popular podcasts since. Its run spans the nine-year lull between 2005 when "podcasting" was the OED's Word of the Year through the 2014 launch of *Serial* when the medium found a more sustainable critical mass (Bonini 2014), and through the euphoria about the "Golden Age" of podcasting which echoes to this day. It is perhaps unsurprising then that when Jad Abumrad, the founder, cohost, and co-producer of *Radiolab*, traces its evolution alongside the evolution of podcasting itself he tells a more glacial story (2016). We are not really witnessing, he says, a second golden age as much are we are a medium finally grown-up enough to have created its own identity, its own aesthetic modes and relationships. While resisting much of the "newness" implied in "Golden Age" thinking, he is certain about the medium's distinctiveness from radio and calls the podcast version the "purest expression of *Radiolab*" in terms of listening experience. And further for Abumrad, as for McLuhan, there is an understanding that the structures and forms of podcasting are embedded in, and condition, any message that might be conveyed in his podcasts. Put simply, he knows that the unique way podcasts are produced, delivered, consumed, shared, and discussed, and the kinds of relationships they facilitate, will influence how we generate meaning through his programs.[3]

---

[3]   Other major podcasting figures also share this awareness. For example, Glynn Washington, host of PRX's *Snap Judgment* has put it even more succinctly: "When you have a shift in a delivery system, that shift often times changes the content itself" (quoted in Murtha 2016).

This chapter's survey of *Radiolab* details and builds on this awareness in order to investigate some key podcasting concepts that are developed in later chapters. These include the following:

1. How *Radiolab* came to relate to its audience in some natively podcasting ways, such as including listeners in the process of narrative construction and remodeling audio texts in response to listeners.
2. How *Radiolab* models a progressive listening practice and offers examples of listening to listening.
3. How *Radiolab* offers a new, distinctively podcasting approach to audio science programming (and, by extension, much nonfiction features programming), an approach in which an authoritative tone has been replaced by a fluidity of, and tension between, interpretive frames.
4. How self-consciously digital explorations in speech editing have evolved over the course of *Radiolab* and what those explorations reveal about the evolution of our expectations for speech audio.

Understanding a bit about the early history of *Radiolab* offers useful insights and a good foundation for thinking about the eventual changes that podcasting would visit on the way we experience audio. The series began as *Radio Lab* in 2002 as a loose set of programs dropped into various holes in WNYC's schedule and then into the schedules of other networked public radio stations. Initially, the programs were a potpourri of independent and public radio features sewn together with innovative continuity material composed and produced by Abumrad (Horne 2015). *Radio Lab* would sometimes fill the slot of the NPR interview program *Fresh Air* when its host, Terry Gross, was on vacation; Abumrad remembers the most common feedback the programs received during this period was some version of "Where's Terry?" (Abumrad 2016). Both Abumrad and Horne credit Dean Capello (WNYC's Chief Content Officer) and Mikel Ellcessor (WNYC's Program Director) with an early commitment to the program that often seemed misplaced given its lukewarm reception (Horne 2015 and Abumrad 2016 and 2017). Capello thought that Abumrad's riffing in between the documentary segments was often the most interesting part of the show and encouraged an expansion of that material (Murtha 2016).

The early programs were often more inconsistent and made for more demanding listening than the other programming that surrounded them. As

Horne describes it, they wanted *Radio Lab* to be something of a countercurrent against the bulk of rather formally conservative public radio talk programming:

> We were on a mission to make something that wasn't out there in the world before we started. We thought that radio was missing a big opportunity to use sound, and that was kind of the starting place. We were really interested in trying to tell stories that used sound better, and we were interested to have stories that used conversation better. (2015)

Perhaps because of these commitments to sound-craft and innovation *Radio Lab* struggled to develop a sustainable audience. It was not until Horne borrowed the "Shark Week" marketing idea from the Discovery Channel—stripping their programs as a themed specialist-interest offering in the same slot for an entire week rather than peppering them seemingly at random throughout a larger schedule—that the series gained a bit of traction with NPR stations (Abumrad 2016).

But even after the shark-week-style branding and other tinkers like streamlining the title to the single word "*Radiolab*" in 2004, some essential characteristics of the program still made it feel somewhat adrift in schedules and puzzling to radio audiences. Interestingly, these were some of the very characteristics that Berry describes in a thorough 2015 retrospective article as much more native to podcasting than to radio as it was conventionally understood. He describes radio as "low demand" on the part of listeners—it is a "pull" medium of choice restricted to the selection of one station among a handful which, he argues, consequently does not often ask for much concentration (2015a: 12). Radio is typically, at least in this distilled characterization of its mainstream form, a medium of consistency and familiarity.

Radiolab struggled on radio for two reasons that any program would struggle on radio: it often appeared inconsistently on schedules, and its production style, one of finely crafted, minute sonic detail—a style that would sometimes take thousands of hours to realize (Horne 2015)—occasionally made somewhat unconventional demands on its listeners. While these aspects were handicaps on traditional public radio, they positioned *Radiolab* extremely well to exploit some of the potentials of the new medium of podcasting when its initial surge came in 2005.

Both Horne and Abumrad appreciate the serendipity of having podcasting arrive precisely at the moment when their finely wrought program was poised to take advantage of it. Horne in particular suggests that the most listened-to podcasts are typically the ones with the highest production values.[4] She was hearing in podcasting in general, and in *Radiolab* in particular, a fulfillment of a desire for "heavily loved things, the things that are well made, that are actually saying something new in the world where there is lots of editing and research" (2015).

In the end, as *Radiolab* (and our means of accessing audio programs) has evolved since its initial launch, Abumrad has come to think of it as a program with two distinct personalities and two distinct audiences. The podcast iteration, he says, is the "more undiluted expression of what we are doing" and he emphasizes the point that "we are not beholden to radio forms." The radio iterations of *Radiolab*, which he sometimes refers to now as "collages" of other material, are packaged with the requirements of radio in mind. Interestingly, Abumrad notes that within the past several years their full embrace of podcasting's conceptual models and a podcast way of thinking has caused the radio version to loosen its hold on some standard radio structuring devices. They have, for example, recently abandoned a strong attachment to "themed" programs because at a certain point this practice came to feel like "self-flagellation" (2016).

Tension: Stories, frames, and engagement

I always want a podcast to have character, plot, ideas . . . . I'm very attached to story because I think that's how our minds work . . . you have to construct meaning to make sense of all the chaos.

—Ellen Horne (2015)

The enemy is writing.

—Jad Abumrad (2016)

No matter how ravishing the sound or how sophisticated the editing on *Radiolab*, both Horne and Abumrad saw verbal storytelling as the creative linchpin of the series. While other tropes, techniques, and devices support, accentuate, and streamline larger parallel stories, and while these tropes, techniques, and devices can be enjoyed on their own as playful small-scale moments, they almost always

---

[4] It remains difficult to make more than an anecdotal case for this. It should also be noted that the most listened-to podcasts are also generally now the ones with the most robust promotional machines behind them. This idea is covered in more detail in Chapter 9 on the podcasting industry.

work with the narrative architecture rather than against it. Adhering to classical narrative principles, Abumrad adopts a mesmerizing tone when he emphasizes, "It's the beginning that you create" (2016). But almost as those words are still ringing in the air he backtracks, he wants to reiterate his point in the epigraph to this chapter: he knows or worries or suspects that the application of narrative always obscures as much as it can ever reveal. With his more familiar directness he says that story "is just total bullshit; but it's like the bullshit we all want and we all need." He needs "story" but he also needs to identify that story as "bullshit" on some level. He is so adept at story and so robust in his critique of it that we might reconcile the dichotomy by calling him a fine scatological artist. This attachment to a "both/and" positioning around the idea of story can be read as a template for the approach that guides most episodes: the creation of "tension" between plural framings of the same phenomenon. Later in this chapter Abumrad describes this explicitly as their essential principle in handling the more obvious content of *Radiolab*.

But for now I want to focus on simply this strong commitment to story and how it has evolved in contrast to other nonfiction media. Abumrad says:

> I read a ton of fact-based journalism where it is not story-shaped, it's just sort of lists of facts, and I can't remember them, somehow that shape doesn't get it into my brain, so there is something about the story shape that just sticks. (2016)

This is a common response to such material. I recently asked a class of MA International Journalism students (most of them aspiring to do some form of political reporting) to give me their off-the-cuff thoughts at the mention of science radio programming. Their responses were fairly consistent and fairly negative: "dull," "boring," "condescending," "would rather read it than listen to it," "not really important to me," and so forth. This informal survey is, obviously, not necessarily representative of the broader listening public, nor does it have implications for all other science programs; we certainly hear genuine curiosity, engagement, conversation, and even narrative in many other popular science podcasts (e.g., *The Guardian Science Weekly*, *The Science Magazine Podcast*, *The Naked Scientists*, *Astronomy Cast*, etc.). That said, my students' slight sense of alienation seems understandable and Abumrad's appeal for greater "story shapes" to confront it seems reasonable. A criticism of much science journalism more generally[5] is that it lacks an awareness of the human relationships and

---

[5]   See, for example, Borel (2015).

connections that drive scientific work and that shape the way people experience science. This issue arises when raw data comes to eclipse relatable context. Put another way: if audio science programming too often leaves listeners overwhelmed by reams of abstract numbers—or, worse, leaves them feeling themselves reduced to digits in a data file, preprogrammed genetic machines, or insignificant specks adrift in a universe as we will hear in the "Space" episode—then Abumrad offers a solution based on a desire to creatively and generatively engage with that material through story.

The issues of a didactic tone and a lack of relatability in science programming that the *Radiolab* approach hopes to counter have a long history in broadcasting more generally, dating back at least as far as the 1930s when Rudolf Arnhiem hoped that radio would "hammer" education into the head of "the dialect-speaking mountain-dweller" of his time (quoted in Spinelli 1996a). It is a problem felt to this day in charges of "elitism" against publicly funded public service broadcasting around the world. While the step into podcasting with its necessarily more familiar and personal tones (see Chapter 6 on intimacy) has reduced this mode of address, and while the more popular science podcasts are now less likely to get stuck in it, this tone continues to linger. Perhaps less surprisingly, the assumptions implied in this mode of address still mark academic analyses of science podcasting; we see this most clearly in the way they often segregate listeners. In their study of the conversations generated around science podcasts, for example, Birch and Weitkamp borrow the language of religious hierarchies to make the distinction between "lay listeners" and scientists (with deference offered to the latter). It is worth noting that the Birch and Wietkamp study does include an analysis of the kinds of science discussions generated by *Radiolab* in online forums; *Radiolab* does not score well by their metrics (2010). It is also interesting to note that when *Radiolab* divides its imagined audience it is part of a move usually done to efface (rather than reinstate) privilege and segregation. Take, for example, the opening stargazing scene of "Space" when Abumrad says: "Some people go to therapy. Some to church. Others come here—to the Northwest corner of a parking lot on Fire Island, where most nights you'll find a handful of people looking up" (00:53). A single line of choral music beds the mention of all three categories and undermines any sense of hierarchy among them while suggesting a similar feeling exists within each of the three frames.

It seems important to observe that *Radiolab* had consistently been the highest ranked podcast in the iTunes Science & Medicine chart of those surveyed by

Birch and Weitkamp.[6] The fact that *Radiolab* was (arguably) the most listened-to podcast while generating the least online forum discussion invites us to think about what kinds of communication experiences most podcast listeners are seeking. An impulse to generate online conversations does seem a laudable (if perhaps token) way of breaking down the hierarchies of privilege mentioned above. But even if cohosts Abumrad and Krulwich spend comparatively little time in discussion with their listeners on Twitter,[7] their popularity means that they successfully engage with an audience elsewhere. Perhaps the best place to look for this is in the mode of delivery and style of the programs themselves, which are, in numerous ways, more genuinely and thoroughly "conversational" than most things likely to occur on Reddit. Obviously, the cohost form relies on dialogue and conversation; there are also the synthetic conversations realized through the editing. But beyond those, there is a much larger conceptual conversation that is taking place between the different framings of the same material. That enticing balancing act of perspectives, that "tension" that Abumbrad repeatedly returns to as *Radiolab*'s guiding principle, enacts a deep, respectful, and egalitarian dialogue that is appealing—it is also a model for human engagement beyond podcasting.

To get a fuller picture of the role of this tension in *Radiolab* and to appreciate its consistency throughout the run of the podcast, close analytical listenings are essential. We undertook close listenings of numerous episodes, many of them referenced here. The 2005 "Space" episode (S02E05) offers particularly clear access to this tension and is extremely valuable to this chapter for a variety of other reasons as well: It is the first episode that mentions *Radiolab* explicitly as a podcast (of those that remain available in the archive of *Radiolab*'s website). It is the first episode in which Robert Krulwich appears as a formalized cohost.[8] And, most beautifully, there is also a particularly apt resonance in terms of the episode's content: the Voyager space probe and its golden disk of hopeful communication with extraterrestrial life seems to mirror *Radiolab*'s humanizing approach to science journalism.

---

[6] We looked at US data in detail from 2013 through 2015 on iTunesCharts.net and found that *Radiolab* always outperforms the Birch- and Weitkamp-surveyed podcasts and is usually the top performing podcast in its category; occasionally it reaches the first or second position on the overall podcasting chart. Going further back, detailed data is less available but these results seem to be consistent.

[7] See Chapter 3 on the podcast audience for more detailed analysis of *Radiolab*'s social media engagement.

[8] Krulwich did appear as a "guest" on previous episodes, but this is the first one that sees him presented as a "cohost" ("*Radiolab*" *Wikipedia* 2018).

In terms of both concept and production values, "Space" is one of the gems of this first formalized season of *Radiolab*, and in it Abumrad's tension of multiple frames is on full display. The three major ones we hear in balance are a classically scientific frame, an artistic human frame, and an interpersonal romantic frame. As with most of the episodes since, keeping different frames in play does not mean constantly leveling the playing field or preventing a given frame from asserting authority. Individual frames are allowed to develop with the cohosts presenting and questioning different facets and actually thinking through the implications, always suggesting them as "perspectives" or ways of seeing. Sometimes the interviewees' own words and the editing of them make the perspective explicit enough and the balance is then achieved by simply moving into a different frame. For example, when, at 30:18, the astrophysicist Neil deGrasse Tyson (who had, earlier in the episode, described humanity in "speck"-like terms) separates scientists from "the public" the episode very quickly shifts frames to a perspective that prioritizes human experience: The artist Dario Robleto begins speaking in much more melancholy ways about his installation of photographs of tomato plants grown from seeds rescued from a previously lost, long-duration space probe. Robleto's language, explicitly referring to life and hope and death and disaster, is more poetic than forensic and is utterly different from Tyson's.

"Space," like many of the episodes that would follow, does not seek to hide this framing work from its listeners. At numerous points in the episode we hear gestures toward, meditations on, and open considerations of the framing process (of the constructing of perspectives as perspectives) and we are invited to appreciate the tension between those frames. At 36:24, for example, Krulwich reflects on the constructed conversation between Tyson and Robleto: "It seems like its art's job to say that we are special, significant, glorious, and its science's job to say, no we're not." While this debate is not resolved, more importantly the lack of resolution does not seem a source of anxiety for the hosts: Tyson and Robleto are balanced in terms of tone, reception by the hosts and simple amount of allotted podcast time (7:46 for Tyson and 7:10 for Robleto). In this context, the suggestion that the universe is a big and frightening place and that humans are insignificant in it is offered as a narrative that requires consideration and engagement for its completion in exactly the same way as the narrative of the tomato seedling photographs and the beauty and power of human expression. This tension (and the listeners' involvement in maintaining that tension rather than merely seeing it resolved) is perhaps *Radiolab*'s greatest contribution to science podcasting. Crucially though, the way it insists that science is considered in relation to human context and significance is never intended to diminish science. *Radiolab*, here and elsewhere at its best, surrounds science in the same wonder as art. *Radiolab*'s popular success as a science podcast comes, in large part, from the way it probes, humanizes, and softens the certitude of scientific language and determinations.

When we hear Robleto contextualize the seedling photography project he begins by recounting the explosion of the space shuttle Challenger and the deaths of seven astronauts, and then the hopes of the school children (now disinterested adults) who proposed sending seeds into space; he sees them all evaporating into insignificance. Yet the willful creative act of the artist, like the willful narrative act of the podcast producers, resurrects them. In a sense, speck-like death is upended via storytelling that culminates at 44:12:

> [Abumrad:] If you willfully invest in the illusion of a photograph, as Dario does,
>   this stage means that the seeds and everything that they represent—the lives of
>   the crew, the hope of a class of school kids—is frozen.
> [Robleto, edited in:] Alive again, forever.
> [Abumrad:] Forever.

In moments like this—and perhaps because he is something of an outsider in the professional discourse of science or feels that this discourse has become culturally dominant or overbearing—Abumrad does seem to invest more in these humanizing frames. His perspective and project, after all, are more similar to Robleto's than they are to Tyson's: In contrast to Tyson's suggestion of the insignificance of humanity in the face of the vastness of the universe, Robleto's words suggest that the universe would not exist without humanity to perceive it. Existence, at least podcasting existence on this particular episode of *Radiolab*, is defined by perception and, by extension, molding that perception into a story shape.

While the orchestration of tension in some of the early episodes of *Radiolab* might be heard as prescriptive or even manipulative to a critical ear, episodes from later seasons (e.g., "American Football" (S13E04)) seem to have recognized these risks and often explore subtler approaches to engage listeners. The Yellow Rain segment from the 2012 "Fact of the Matter" episode (S11E01) is a useful point of reference in this evolution for two reasons: First, the producers seem momentarily to lose their grip on the value of balanced plural frames in tension and revert to a more traditional style of journalism. Second, Abumrad and Krulwich self-consciously include this error of imbalanced framing in the pod-cast in the hopes that their listeners will hear the consequences of it—in doing so they remind listeners that producers are fallible and mistakes in judgment can and do occur. Ultimately though their faith in their audience to charitably process their mistake as it happened is misplaced; the quite sophisticated anticipated audience response the producers have in mind was at odds with the actual responses they received. This scenario, even in the hostility of responses it received, is evidence of a podcast series (and perhaps a medium) prepared to take risks and still very much exploring the dynamics of the listening relationship.

The Yellow Rain segment tells the story of the Hmong people of Laos: allies of the United States but abandoned by them in 1975, the Hmong are subjected to horrendous chemical weapons attacks (described as "yellow rain") as they flee allies of the Viet Cong. In this segment we hear contemporary scientists making a very compelling case that the yellow rain was simply bee droppings and was therefore a very specious reason for President Reagan to initiate an American chemical weapons program in retaliation. On the other hand, Eng Yang, one of the Hmong who fled into the jungle, offers grisly eyewitness testimony to the plant, animal, and human effects of the yellow rain. The problem, Abumrad acknowledges, was that *Radiolab* was too insistent on that decontextualized scientific perspective in both the interview with Yang and in the editing of the original version. But, he says:

> We realized that was happening and put it on the air as an example of [a bad production decision] which maybe again putting too much faith in the audience that they are going to see us as "good guys" when we were being assholes . . . .
> I think we were putting it on the air because we were being assholes and we wanted to say, "Oh shit, we are assholes." (2016)

The episode was amended a week later to include an in-studio discussion apologizing for Krulwich's persistence in the interview with Yang and for some insensitive comments made. In addition, both Abumrad and Krulwich offer recontextualizations and explanations on the *Radiolab* website afterward, with Krulwich's being the one most open to the audience about *Radiolab*'s work in (and responsibility for) sculpting stories:

> I should have listened harder, and been more compassionate.
> I am especially sorry in the conversation following to have said Ms. Yang was seeking to "monopolize" the story. Obviously, we at *Radiolab* had all the power in this situation, and to suggest otherwise was wrong. (2012)

While Abumrad does continue to regret this incident and is aware that it is certainly possible to ask too much of an audience, he resists arguments for simpler, less reflective storytelling with clear good guys and bad guys (whether they are the Viet Cong or Ronald Reagan). Abumrad says, "I think where we made a mistake is we tried to insist on one truth in a way that was hurtful, and you heard that hurt on the air." This experience ultimately strengthened his commitment to a plurality of truth: "Every story we do now has some element of that—where you hear truths smacking into each other. And I feel like it's increasingly our job to be the people who struggle to hold both, you know?" (2016)

Clearly there is a temptation, particularly post-2016 in which the real damage of media misinformation was so keenly and broadly felt on both sides of the Atlantic,[9] to insist on demonstrable "facts" and to make those the point of departure for any serious discussion. When pressed on this point though Abumrad was adamant that demanding consensus on facts first only leads to more acrimony, entrenchment, and the spurious generation of alternative facts: "Facts don't fucking matter anymore, like they just don't matter. What has to matter is that you hear people struggling to step out of their own lens and see through someone else's" (2016).

While the examples above detail moments of tension in the specific content of *Radiolab* episodes, ultimately Abumrad intends to explore the creative and narrative possibilities of a broader, more general tension. This is not a rudimentary tension between "Science" and some more metaphysical way of approaching life or the world, but a tension or a relationship between things or the universe or "splatters of shit" and the ways we perceive them, represent them, narrativize them, and derive meaning from them:

> The balance is between taking some sort of vaporously complicated thing and infusing it into the form of a story. The story being the thing that can actually hold it. So I think that's the balance I would say, it's the irreducible complexities of things versus the definable story shapes that we can use to tell those things . . . .
> I don't think that there is a resolution to that tension; I think it just always is. (2016)

This awareness on the part of Horne and Abumrad of the tension between raw material and story shapes (and the unavoidable impact of representation on what is being represented) is quite sophisticated in the world of podcasting. This is particularly true in the area of science programs where there seems to be a much greater faith in the neutrality and transparency of language and

---

[9] My interview with Abumrad happened one week before the US election of November 2016.

communication contexts. An attachment to that transparency even seems a key original element of the branding of some podcasts: aside from the visual pun that might be conjured in our minds, when we hear the podcast title *The Naked Scientists* we are invited to think of science unadulterated, stripped of accoutrement and context.

Through the self-conscious narrative work of *Radiolab*, that framing of science as an abstract, transparent superhuman perspective is now itself contextualized, dissected, and put into fair contest with other ways of seeing. Far from being frightening or destabilizing, this is an exhilarating prospect for Abumrad; he explains this with reference to a *Radiolab* segment on the metamorphosis that happens inside a chrysalis:

> They grow into their thing and liquefy into soup, and then come out a whole new creature, and there are memories that can persist from the caterpillar into the butterfly. Like how the fuck does that work! That's very quickly not just a science question but a question about metaphysics, a question about religion, a question about . . . the permanence of the soul, like all of these things flow through that, and for me that's what's interesting about science, that it is one way to attack very deep questions, but increasingly I can't have it be the only way. [*Radiolab* is] in search of multiple truths. (2016)

Radiolab then is not so much about science in a conventional sense as it is about larger, philosophical ideas and the practice of narrative.[10]

Narrative practice: Listeners included

While solid story structure is extremely familiar now on much popular nonfiction public radio programming in the United States (and has been at least since 1996 with the national distribution of the *This American Life*[11]), one of podcasting's advancements is a more regular and more obvious unveiling of the story-making process and apparatus. *Radiolab* episodes in particular regularly remind us that

---

[10] In fact, over the years the program has had a fluid and elastic relationship with science explicitly. In the beginning of its run, the "lab" component of *Radio Lab* referred to sonic experiments and experiments in nonfiction radio documentary (Walker 2011). By the time it began to conceive of itself as a podcast, its center of gravity had shifted more explicitly to science where it has remained in aggregator categories.

[11] Interestingly, *This American Life* was originally titled *Your Radio Playhouse*. It is useful to keep in mind the clear attachment to conventional dramatic structures and techniques implied in that name, as well as the holdover nomenclature for the "acts" that divide each episode to this day.

"shit" seldom comes in a story shape, and that structures of perception must be built around it in order for it to make any sense at all.

While there are plenty of unstated cues within the editing of *Radiolab* to remind an audience that they are listening to a narrative construction (which I study in the next section), here we take up the explicit mentions (in Borgesian fashion) of story making within the narratives of the programs. Peppered through the seasons of *Radiolab* we hear, over and over again, reminders of the process of story making.[12] This is done, in large part, to develop a sense of trust with an audience. Krulwich says it is simply more honest to "let the audience hear and know that you are manufacturing a version of events." This exposing of the artifice lends a credibility to the entire project; as Abumrad says, "It's consciously letting people see outside the frame. I think those moments are really powerful. What it's saying to the listener is: 'Look, we all know what's happening here. I'm telling you a story . . . .' We all know it's happening—and in a sense we all want it to happen" (quoted in Walker 2011).

Beyond simply mentioning the word "story," *Radiolab* uses other large devices to reveal to an audience the work of their storycraft. Originally devised by Horne as a way of helping a producer leave behind the hopelessly wooden delivery of her voice-over recordings (Abumrad 2016), the practice of interviewing a reporter or producer about the story as a way of telling the story also underscores narrative constructions for an audience.[13] In this device we often here the cohosts prodding the producer back onto a clear narrative path and reminding them not to digress. This technique also has the added benefit of pushing the storytelling as far off-script as possible, making a segment utterly conversational. Abumrad says of it:

> There is a very particular language game you get into when you're on the page . . . . And then there is a very particular language you're in when two people are across a table, right? *Radiolab* lives in that second space but it wants the structure and the architecture of the first space. (2016)[14]

A conversation between Abumrad, Krulwich, and a producer is highly engaging; it also models a kind of relationship that *Radiolab* might seek to cultivate with

---

12 Two easily accessible examples are: the "Ice Cold Case" episode (2013 short), in which the process of narrative building is alluded to throughout, and which actually concludes with a hypothetical scene of fiction offered as necessary to the story; and the opening of the "Things" episode in which we hear references like "bringing the narrative threads together" (S12E08, 13:44).

13 This technique was later adopted by many other podcasts including *Reply All*, *Invisibilia*, and *Love + Radio*.

14 The best podcast "writing," he says, "happens in the space between two people" (Abel 2015: 121).

it audience (more about this in Chapter 6 on intimacy); but it is important to recognize this technique here as a peep-hole through which the audience can glimpse that narrative architecture Abumrad mentions.

A model for podcast editing

Then suddenly [I] had to go back and learn tape! I just remember being like, "Fuck, what is this thing again?" You had like coat hangers with strings and you're like "which one is this again, which one is that?" I'd regularly stitched them together and one would be flipped over so you would hear like "whoop—whoop—whoop—whoop—whirr." The tools were so limiting in some sense, but I did like the way you could actually touch it.

—Jad Abumrad (describing an experience
with analog tape to edit audio) (2016)

Ola Stockfelt, writing in the Danish journal *SoundEffects*, says of the composition of voices in the seventeen-second opening audio signature of *Radiolab*: "[It] implies 'a hidden speaker,' who is using these voices to address us, who is acting 'between' these voices and us, but who is hidden and unheard" (2012). This section explores that "hidden speaker," details the work it does at the level of language through close analytical listenings, and locates that work within changes in production technology which then influence practices of and assumptions about speech editing. It begins to describe a set of production conditions and a way of thinking about audio speech much more native to podcasting than to radio.

It can be hard for some audio producers who began work after the turn of the millennium to understand the changes that occurred when we shifted from editing our features, documentaries, and interview programs using reel-to-reel two-track tape to producing them in the wholly digital environment of the computer. Indeed the very word "digital" when applied to media today can seem a bit anachronistic—which of our media now would not fit in the category "digital"? But while the reality of this shift was obvious in the purely technological sphere—hard drives instead of tape, cursors instead of razor blades, clip boundaries instead of china pencils, and so forth—how that movement into a digital world invited changes in semantics (the ways meaning can be generated through speech), and changes in the ways projects were conceived and built, remained unclear. While I took some early steps into these areas just before the first podcasting surge, the second flowering of podcasting in general and the techniques refined by *Radiolab* in particular offer a new opportunity to catalog these innovations and devices.

When I use the terms "analog" and "digital" here it is important to recognize that these terms do not refer to specific technologies per se, but more so to the sets of assumptions and practices that have grown up around them, assumptions and practices that are not *necessarily* tied to any configuration of circuitry. In simpler words, it might be useful to think of "analog" and "digital" as aesthetic or figurative categories rather than sets of equipment. I use the terms here as technological *metaphors* for different kinds of practice and engagement, rather than essential descriptions of the way different mechanical devices produce or shape language.

For "analog," I generally refer to practices of *subtraction*, the elimination of extraneous material—as we did when we cut (out) tape on reel-to-reel machines—in an effort to create a seamless linear *simulation* of conversation as it might exist in the world; these are practices that most often hope to transparently convey information. This linearity was a defining feature of radio in a macro sense.[15] Various distinctive features of podcasting—chiefly listener playback management—mean this radio concept need not necessarily be broadly extended onto our new medium. Further, the brief editing examples from *Radiolab* that follow show that analog linearity need not define podcast listening at a micro-level either.

For "digital," I generally refer to practices of *addition* that are distinctly audible, which are self-consciously *not* conversations as they might exist in the world, and which need not be largely linear experiences; these are practices that are not transparent and audibly play with acts of communication. What I want to describe here is a slow movement into digital practices and semantics, a movement that is clearly more advanced in the pages of scholarly journals than it is in everyday audio production practice and thinking.[16] My point of departure is the observation that the vast majority of today's digitally produced radio and

---

[15] Berry (2015a: 10) describes this radio mode as "a linear stream of content that is heard synchronously by listeners."

[16] When I historicized this trajectory at much greater length more than a decade ago (Spinelli 2006a and b), I located the beginnings of a digital audio consciousness in the work of early twentieth-century Futurists. It is also important to note here that while the techniques under consideration have a much longer mainstream history in audio art, pop music, and radio advertising, public service speech radio has largely resisted them.

podcast content is still steeped in analog methods and modes of thinking. These, unconscious as they may be, serve largely to prop up assumptions about the realness and naturalness of audio speech that no longer seem tenable; these are also not the home of our "hidden speaker."

As a way of getting started, it may be useful to point to three relatively simple examples of this hidden speaker and describe the way they resist that analog linearity and transparency. Perhaps the easiest technique to grasp—and a technique sometimes heard in older forms of radio production—is the breathless edit: two pieces of recorded speech edited unnaturally close to create the sense of an interjection (hurried, earnest, angry, or passionate). We do not hear a breath where we would expect to hear one in a real conversation; the editor's decision is audible and we cannot help but be confronted by its mediation or manipulation. There is a clear example of this at 04:12 in "Space" when Krulwich asks a question in studio and an interviewee's response zips in without a beat. Next, the quick dense montage (looser versions of which also dot older forms) is a technique for conveying a multiplicity of similar sentiments or ideas expressed in similar language. A quick dense montage is heard in "Watching Me Watching You" (S14E07) when, at 05:48, we hear a tight range of opinions about surveillance and bugging. The third, quite closely aligned with *Radiolab*'s practice of reminding listeners of its editorial decisions, is the interjection of mutilated speech fragments. This we hear clearly in the introduction of Professor Bus in "The Bad Show" (S10E05) at 00:58 and it serves as a reminder that (from the beginning) the editors are constantly engaged in processing, selection, inflection, and manipulation. It is a producer's way of flagging that the renditions of the world we will hear on this episode are all first and foremost mediated.

Beyond what we hear in *Radiolab* episodes, it is clear that Abumrad has more than an intuitive grasp of how evolutions in our production technology are changing not just our ways of making audio but also our ways of conceiving it, experiencing it, and making use of it. Referring to Wittgenstein's *Philosophical Investigations* he says, "The hammer changes the hand. I feel like the tools have fed back on our sensibilities and now we expect more edits, we expect more layers, it's just somehow part of the vernacular now . . . . [In recent years] we have moved completely into a sort of digital world" (2016). Here he supports my assertion that the tools we have been using for the past twenty years to construct and consume audio language have changed our perception of that language and the way we listen to it. This is equally true for the set of tools we used for the sixty years prior to that.

In much the same way that *Radiolab* borrowed narrative structuring elements from *This American Life*, it borrowed some editing techniques from film and television. Abumrad cites Walter Murch, the famous film editor and sound designer, as a key influence and *Radiolab* is often described as "filmic." Even more profoundly though its editing style is influenced by Abumrad's study of music.[17] While his fraught relationship as a student to mid-twentieth-century avant-garde music pushed him to the comfort and security of those familiar narrative devices, he admits to occasionally getting frustrated with the fact that "our stories have to be relentlessly engaging, like every moment has to pull you forward" (2016). He finds some relief from this in "dreamy soundscapes pierced by bursts of noise" ("Jad's Brain" 2012). Horne and others also describe the musicality of Abumrad's editing broadly as perhaps the most distinctive feature of the podcast. The most digitally ambitious moments of this editing practice, like *Radiolab*'s dense and frenetic seventeen-second opening signature montage, resonate with the larger principles of offering equally positioned alternate frames of meaning. The Danish music, media, and art scholar Ansa Lønstrup hears in that opening signature montage a "listening sound practice" in which "all utterances are semantically open to more than one interpretation and meaning" (2012: 127).

One of the difficulties in this approach to editing for listeners new to podcasting is the loss of what Alan Beck called the "point of listening" (1998). Beck charted the way audio drama directors sidestepped the potential confusion of simply "hearing" dramatic elements—merely perceiving disparate pieces of sonic information—by constructing a clear and consistent "point of listening" for an imagined listener in a given extended scene. This stable sonic reference point is often absent on *Radiolab*, flitting as it does between in-studio interviews, archival audio, phone interviews, Skype-to-cohost conversations, and tiny fragments of inserted presenter voice-over. This can be disconcerting to a listener who is most familiar with older radiogenic audio feature forms with their lengthy introductions of speakers, their consistent and often elaborate handoffs between presenters and reporters, and between studio voices and those recorded on location, all focused on a fairly clear and central point of listening. But, as I hear it, this abandonment of a perceptual center of sound (or

---

[17] See Walker (2011) for references to Murch. For references to the filmic quality of *Radiolab*, see Stockfelt (2012: 116). For additional filmic references and for discussion of how Abumrad positions himself creatively as more of a musician than a journalist, listen to "Jad's Brain" on *How Sound* #35 (2012).

the abandonment of an imagined listening body or ear within an audio scene) allows for a more efficient and even greater focus on narrative. This particularly digital handling of speech enhances the narrative speed and momentum. Descriptions and information necessary for a listener to imagine a scene or to make sense of a story are now not delivered through digressionary asides but through the surgical insertion of tiny fragments of the presenter's disembodied voice used to annotate longer more fluid passages.[18] Perhaps the most apt metaphor then for the *Radiolab* approach to podcast editing might be to call it sculptural, or even cubist—the lack of a fixed vantage point allows producers to offer a distilled essence of a narrative. The resulting listening experience is one of a shifting centers, multiple centers, no center at all, or at least one in which listeners must do some work to situate themselves in their own ideal position in relation to a segment's voices.[19]

The listening voice, digital listening, and digital tropes

While *Radiolab* is now heralded by people like Ira Glass as having "invented a new aesthetic for the medium," one that is often appreciated only on the fourth or fifth listen,[20] its awareness of the new characteristics of podcast listening and possibilities for podcasts making is certainly not universal. The story of how *Radiolab*'s podcasting aesthetic evolved is peppered with battles with "radio people" who saw all the time, effort, and resources implied in its development as an insane waste (Walker 2011).[21] Horne in particular remembers how they were mocked for producing the "Fabergé Eggs" of audio (2015). While the straightforward linear delivery of most radio content has meant that it is often seen as ephemeral (even disposable), the higher engagement associated with podcasting means that podcasts like *Radiolab* can be produced with a different intension. The podcasting characteristic that enables this is an odd sort of "plastic

---

[18] For a nice example of this go to 05:48 in "Watching You Watching Me" (S14E07).

[19] See Nyre (2015) for another perspective on positioning in podcast listening.

[20] Horne speaks of the "Time" episode (S01E04) as continuing to be rewarding even after eighty listens; she compares the experience to repeated listening to a pop song (2015). While this might be an exaggeration, there is certainly a good deal of truth in the fact that certain podcasts reward repeat listening.

[21] Horne says that some episodes require thousands of hours to produce (2015); Abumrad said in a fundraising segment that some single episodes cost in excess of $100,000 to make ("Oliver Sipple" 2017).

permanence."[22] Podcasting's delivery system, built on archives and aggregators that facilitate the repeat listening and sharing of programs, opens the door to a shift in not just production concepts but also aesthetics. Put another way, the producers of *Radiolab* intuited very early on (or perhaps fortuitously stumbled onto the idea) that shifts in *listening* can invite shifts in *making*.

The reverse is also true. Stockfelt attempts to explain this circuit by reminding us that soundworks never exist in isolation (2004); they are always situational and rely on their context and reception for completion and meaning. For him, listening itself is a sort of compositional practice. Extending this idea, Lønstrup argues that in *Radiolab*'s signature montage we actually hear a "listening sound practice" (2012: 131–33); we hear voices "listening" to other voices and being modified and altered through that act of listening.[23] I argue further that moments like these on *Radiolab* model for us a kind of listening that we are invited to adopt as its audience: It is a kind of listening in which we are open to change and through which our own frames can slip and our established lines of thought can blur in a plurality of voices and perspectives.[24]

As Horne noted, the kinds of production values often needed to invite these effects are difficult to achieve and face institutional challenges. But there is now substantial evidence that shows podcast listening is qualitatively different from listening to other forms of audio[25] which can be used to

---

[22] I use the word "odd" here because podcasting's permanence is one we can edit: there is no original iteration of a *Radiolab* episode to which we can definitively refer (because different versions can be simultaneously released on different platforms), just as there is no final and authorized iteration. Horne speaks of reediting episodes more than a year after they originally aired. The most significant feature of the Yellow Rain segment we discussed earlier, for example, is the fact of its reediting.

[23] This resonates significantly with Lacey's notion of "listening out" (2013).

[24] Lønstrup's analysis certainly supports this reading and even offers a metaphor explicitly about political participation and communication. She hears in the composition of *Radiolab*'s signature a "'democratic' staging and dramatising of different articulating voices. Every voice is heard; everyone 'gets a voice' . . . and I might, as listener and a potential active voice, easily join them" (2012: 131). This ultimately resolves in the questions "'Is anybody listening?' 'Will anyone listen?'" that have a beautiful resonance with one of the subjects of "Space," the Voyager space probe's golden disk of hopeful communication. As Ann Druyan (the professional then romantic partner of Carl Sagan) describes the recorded greetings on Voyager, first mentioning the sound of a mother's kiss, the disk itself comes to sound like a metaphor for one side of the relationship formed around *Radiolab*'s listening voice (also with a slight reference to political participation): "It was a sacred undertaking, because it was saying: 'We want to be citizens of the Cosmos. We want you to know about us'" (06:50-07:22). There are also striking connections to *Radiolab*'s commitment to frames in tension in "Space": first, science slips into a love story as Druyan and Sagan decide to get married; second, the manifestations of that love are rendered by science into empirical data (e.g., heart rates, REM information, and brainwaves); and finally, that data (included on Voyager's disk) appears as a tentative effort to communicate something of one particular human's framing of her existence.

[25] Quirk (2015) notes that podcast listeners describe themselves as "highly engaged" from beginning to end of a podcast and McKinney (2015) found that 93 percent of listeners to other high-production values podcasts always gave it their full attention.

rebuff critiques from older quarters of radio that the production values on a series like *Radiolab* are unwarranted. Podcast listeners listen closely and are potentially more engaged with their experience. This kind of intensified engagement is also aided by the fact that podcasting can and does typically pursue more highly defined and niche audiences than radio. But there are consequences for this that pose ideological challenges for *Radiolab*: the fact that podcast listeners, with ever greater control and precision, curate their own listening experiences and engagement according to their own tastes and assumptions about the world certainly contributes to contemporary concerns about media-siloing (i.e., the self-selecting of media sources that confirm our existing assumptions). The fear is that podcasting in general might encourage a withdrawal from interaction and engagement with ideas that are not already a part of a listener's worldview.[26] With this in mind, Abumrad's efforts to foster an appreciation of different framings of the same phenomena and to model a listening voice might be seen as cutting against the problem enabled by podcasting of social isolation and withdrawal. It is certainly possible then, in this context, to view *Radiolab* as struggling to address a problem that has been enabled to some degree by podcasting's form.

The digital production values that Horne notes in *Radiolab* extend beyond the self-consciously digital handling of speech we hear in each episode. These digital values also imprint the research, development, and construction of the programs more broadly, and further support the argument that *Radiolab* marked a significant advancement in speech audio. The practice of the "braindump" (Abel 2015: 121–23), for example, was a step forward in the generation of their particular style of presenter language. Instead of a more traditional writing process (a single producer in front of a computer producing voice-over tracks which are eventually auditioned for an editor and then massaged for conversationality), the braindump conceives of writing as *conversation in the first instance*. Abumrad, Krulwich, and often other producers will sit in a studio and talk through their ideas of an evolving segment. Those conversations are recorded as sound files which are then later parsed, marked up, often redrafted, and reassembled to find and refine elements of narration that are used in the episode as it is heard. Abumrad says the fluidity, flexibility, and speed of the final presentational style would be impossible to achieve working without their vast

---

[26] This concern resonates with Morris and Patterson's research (2015) that critiques podcasting's privatization ("appification") of experience as embedded in and supporting a neoliberal value system.

digital scratchpad of marked-up and constantly evolving sound files (2016). The volumes of raw material and the detail in which that material is processed would not generally have been viable with earlier forms of radio production. Soren Wheeler, *Radiolab*'s Senior Editor, noted that forty-five minutes of braindump recording might produce only a few seconds of ultimately usable material (Abel 2015: 123).

While using the braindump in this way begins by conceiving of language as real conversation, the conversations we hear in the episodes would rarely be described as "real" or "natural." If an analog or old-school radio aesthetic most often produced replicas of seemingly "authentic," linear speech and conversation, then podcasting's digital mode (at least to the extent that it works on *Radiolab*) produces pure simulations of conversation with no intention of being considered "real." In the episodes, large amounts of improvisational energy are fused with audio annotations which streamline and accelerate the larger narrative. Into this frenetic acoustic environment other more self-consciously artful digital handlings of speech and sonic experiments are slipped in without feeling particularly jarring. A very accessible example of this is heard in "Things" (S12E08) at 05:10—Krulwich's descriptions of a flag case are interlaced with a location recording of a conversation between himself, his wife, and the curator at the Explorers' Club in New York.[27] Again, techniques like these have the effect of streamlining narrative rather than disrupting it.

Earlier in this chapter our close analytical listenings of "Space" and other episodes allowed us to begin describing some common, self-consciously digital, and self-consciously "podcast" tropes for handling audio speech and some of the effects they invite. Building on this foundation, in conclusion I return to our original close listening of "Space" in order to flesh-out this catalog of tropes as many of them will offer useful points of reference for material covered in other chapters and (I hope) for future podcast making and study. Again, while many, if not all, of these tropes were realizable in older production settings and had

---

[27] The fact that on *Radiolab* tropes like these have become domesticated marks a deviation or evolution from my earlier proposals (Spinelli 2006a and b) about editing techniques that sound self-consciously digital. Originally I argued that the value of digital speech techniques, at the moment in history when we were transitioning out of an analog mind-set, was in their ability to disturb and disrupt an analog way of listening and thinking about speech. Here on *Radiolab* they become (almost ironically) "seamlessly" integrated into a project in which they fit aesthetically without disruption, and in which editing and processing techniques are used to enhance the meaning of words. Interestingly, Horne notes that there has been some reconsideration of some of these techniques on *Radiolab*; the fact that these techniques have become familiar has led her to wonder whether or not they were verging on self-parody (2015).

clearly been heard on radio,[28] they are much more common on, and native to, podcasting because of the particular ways podcasts are consumed and hence produced.

While obviously in use well before we started editing in a wholly digital environment, the trope of creatively including fragments of outtake material became a much more recognizable feature of podcasts during *Radiolab*'s development. The brief inclusion of slips, gaffs, mistakes, or conventionally "unwanted" audio material into an otherwise smooth linear flow serves again to remind listeners of the continuous editorial selections being made and the power and control that implies; it can also serve to invite alternative readings and meditations not offered elsewhere more explicitly. Near the start of "Space" (03:48), for example, Krulwich begins his contribution to an introduction about the enormity of the universe with the lines: "And in this hour we discover how bi—oh sorry we—And in this hour we find ourselves in space; we discover how immense, how huge space is." His (possibly intentional) tiny verbal "slip" invites a brief reflection on the conscious editorial decision not to use the word "big" and what that decision might suggest.

Another trope familiar to *Radiolab* listeners might be called the "sonic synecdoche"—an illustrative sound becoming a metaphor for a larger, more complex idea. The example of it from "Space" begins at 20:28 when Krulwich is discussing stages of human civilization. As Krulwich is making the point that humanity will likely become extinct before any other intelligent life in the universe might find the Voyager space probe, we hear a female voice saying, "Step one," followed by an interjection of fake chimpanzee vocal sounds. After Abumrad laughs and questions the device the voice says, "Step two," and we hear a snippet from an old Chesterfield Radio Show which signifies postwar modernity. At "Step three" we hear screaming and explosions which signify the end of the world. Throughout the rest of this segment these tiny bursts of sound from these sonic vignettes are then used to stand in for the corresponding moments in human social evolution: at 20:55 the Chesterfield music replaces Krulwich talking about media culture and then again at 21:28 the chimp sounds stand in for a mention of primitive civilization without other explanation.

---

[28] Similar devices are certainly heard more often, for example, on high production-value programs produced by European public broadcasters. For more on this see McHugh discussing the "European style" of immersive audio documentary as described by Leslie Rosin, Commissioning Editor of Radio Features at WestDeutscher Rundfunk (2016: 73–74).

At 23:06 we experience a "missing interview": extraneous and unidentified mike-check material from mathematics and physic professor Brian Green crops up as the information he has provided is discussed by the cohosts. We are given quite extensive context for the questions to be put to him while progressively larger chunks of that cohost gloss and contextualization demand more and more of our focus and the mike-check material completely disappears. In the end however we never hear any conventional actuality material from the interview with Green. We are thus made aware of how the information was sourced and we have been presented with the credentials (and even the voice) of an expert without ever getting to hear him speak meaningfully about the content under discussion.

The repeat iteration, perhaps one of the oldest and easiest digital handlings of speech to enact, is now (for precisely that reason) heard less on recent *Radiolab* episodes. At 23:56 in "Space" Abumrad's voice is heard repeating the words "There is no end" twice clearly from two separate takes. Because there is no other occurrence of this technique nearby in the program, the importance of the idea of endlessness is dramatically emphasized.

In spite of the fact that these devices have become more common or domesticated, they remain most effective on a backdrop of very carefully produced and familiar audio storytelling, usually in service of a larger narrative, and often with explicit reflection on them by the hosts. That reflection is very often accompanied by direct appeals from the hosts to listen intently and carefully at particular moments and to listen out for particular things that will invite engagement. Beginning at 54:55 of "Space," for example, Abumrad tells us that when we listen to 1960s recordings from space missions, "you *hear* the real reasons for committing to space." As we tune our ears past the static on the recordings of astronauts whooping with delight and marveling with awe in their voices, Abumrad reminds us that we are "hearing" something real rather than simply being told that it is or was significant. The editing in this passage is relatively gentle, certainly something that could have been realized easily through older technology, and it perpetuates the nebulous sense of reverence the producers have worked to invoke throughout the program. The astronauts, in their tone and in their words, seem aware not just of their own place in history, but also of their own place in future narratives. They seem humbled by a shared purpose and having participated in a hugely significant human endeavor; there is no trace of triumphalism. The two-and-half-minute montage ends with samples from the last recorded transmissions from the moon before Abumrad, after a reflective pause, says, "We are now podcasting." The "we" in this sentence might refer equally to the collective human spirit that launched people to the moon as it might to the *Radiolab* production team and its listeners. In a gesture that is coy and slightly whimsical, podcasting (and *Radiolab*) is here made a part of the same story of technological evolution as the moon landing. But, as with the astronauts, Abumrad's tone is one of vague and slightly uncertain wonder.

3

You Are Not Alone: Podcast Communities, Audiences, and *Welcome to Night Vale*

It's a Saturday night, sometime in October 2014, and I'm walking through London to meet a friend in Islington, but I'm going to be late. I've come across a long line of unusually dressed people snaking out of a music venue. I stop and stare. They are mostly young, in their teens and early 20s, clad in capes and robes, make-up and gowns, some are hooded, others have their faces painted. The colour purple predominates. There is a nightmarish, carnivalesque quality to this crowd, as if the queue for a Comicon event has been transplanted into Northern London on a damp autumnal evening. I ask what they are waiting to see, they tell me Welcome to Night Vale, *a live performance of an audio drama. The crowd is excited, it is their first performance in the U.K., there is a buzz, an energy and communal enthusiasm that is reminiscent of the line outside a music gig, rather than for an "old school" radio drama.*

That queue outside the *Welcome to Night Vale* gig can be read as a sign of how podcasters have successfully transformed the passivity of listening into the engagement of fandom. With funding drives, live events, social media chatter, T-shirt sales, fan art, and Reddit posts there is now a constant and active interchange of ideas, communication, and capital between audio media producers and their audiences. Podcast websites feature merchandising pages that resemble those of a rock-band's fan-site. A visit to the *This American Life* online store allows you to purchase three different T-shirts, a custom USB drive (with the show logo etched into the plastic) loaded with thirty-five hours of *TAL* episodes, a *Serial* Notebook (fashioned after the classic 1920s detective's evidence pad), and a pack of public radio temporary tattoos. You can also carry a Phoebe Judge's *Criminal* tote bag, drink from a David McRaney's *You Are Not So Smart* mug, and pull on a Dan Carlin's *Hardcore History* T-shirt. These items are not just products associated with a program, they are the banners of fandom, material signifiers of the wish to be identified and recognized as the follower of a media text.

Traditional speech-based radio broadcasting, in the UK at least, has spawned none of these accoutrements. BBC Radio Four does not offer any *In Our Time* T-shirts bearing Lord Melvyn Bragg's face; there are no *Call You and Yours* temporary tattoos, and certainly no *Money Box Live* live tours. This is a symptom not just of these programs' different audience demographic, but of the contrast between the financing of public service broadcasting in the UK and of digital media. Podcasting is funded through the "freemium" model, where the primary product is distributed without charge, and income generated through secondary sources. These are centered on direct advertising and sponsorship, and supplemented through a raft of fan and audience-based support including crowdfunding, merchandise sales, and live events. The latter is seen as being of growing import; Julie Shapiro, the executive producer of the podcast network Radiotopia, describes their "live event strategy" as being something that will "make a lot of money for the network" which will "not just trickle down, but will pour down to producers" and allow podcasters to "go in other directions, before resorting to a paywall" (Shapiro 2016). Contained within Shapiro's statement are the pragmatic realities of the podcasting ecosystem. There are limits to what can be achieved through reliance on advertising alone; income generated from a highly engaged listenership is essential for podcasting's freemium model to be viable.

This fiscal underpinning of the relationship between podcast producer and fan follower is made explicit in the use of funding drives and digital donation platforms such as Patreon, Kickstarter, and Indiegogo. The impetus for an audience to make crowdfunding contributions is essentially altruistic, with rewards serving as markers of support that are not commensurate with the value of donation given. These include mentions on the show or on websites, access to exclusive materials or, for higher donations, copies of scripts, meetings with hosts, or appearances on the programs themselves. Six-figure sums have been garnered through online donation drives: in 2015 Radiotopia's Kickstarter campaign raised $620,412 and the podcast *99% Invisible* (the network's "every day design" podcast hosted by network founder Roman Mars) raised $375,193 in 2014 and $170,477 in 2013. His success in this field places Mars as an outlier, and the finances raised for podcasts through crowdfunding tend to be more modest. The podcast comedian Richard Herring discusses how only 3 percent of his audience of 150,000 would give "even pounds" toward the productions of his shows (Herring 2016), while Jad Abumrad opened a funding drive in 2017 by admitting that only 0.72 percent of *Radiolab*'s audience contribute toward the podcast's production costs ("Oliver Sipple" 2017). This low level of participation is not particular to podcasting, or to these program makers, they are an example of Shirky's long tail of digital engagement (2008), in which only a very small proportion of an audience is responsible for any interaction or direct support. This minority of listeners, the power users or superfans, need to be catered for, to be validated and energized by the podcasters to such a degree that they are drawn in and are willing to support a show.

This represents a change in the value of publics, and a fiscal realization of the social capital of networks. Fans across media have gained in status; they are no longer "eccentric irritants" (Hills 2002: 36) but are now "loyal consumers," the courting and nurturing of whom is essential to the funding models implicit in the free distribution of digital media content. The UK feature maker and producer Alan Hall describes this difference as being between the "one-to-one" communication that is the convention of traditional broadcasting and the forging of a "community" of podcast listeners. "Podcasting is like talking to a little club . . . they are not all listening at the same time, but they are recommending and communicating, and you have to be conscious of that" (Hall 2016). The pleas and begging messages that launch shows during podcast funding drives are laced with inclusive language: "*We* have to do this," "This is *our* great show," "Let's do this *together*." The message is that "You," the audience, are not supporting "Us," the producer, but rather "We" are creating something together—a show that we are all part of and we all own. The audience must feel that their fandom is acknowledged and that they are somehow an essential part of the production.

Podcasters can do this because there is something about the form, the mode of address, the manner of distribution, and the topics covered that successfully recreates listening as an active and involved experience. When I first listened to *Radiolab* with my then nine-year-old daughter, after just a few hours of judiciously chosen content she asked: "I love this show, where can I get a T-shirt for it?" What was interesting here was not how quickly the child of a media academic bonded with a key text in the field, but how she knew, at some intrinsic level, that this was the sort of program that one could buy a T-shirt for. This chapter will discuss how podcasters are able to redefine their listeners as fans. Whether this is the result of direct strategies, using events and social media outreach, or if there are essential qualities to the form that engender heightened levels of audience engagement? It will ask whether those costumed fans of *Welcome to Night Vale* were willing to queue in the cold because of something that the podcasters were doing, or whether it was something they chose to do among, and for, themselves.

The loneliness of the podcast listener

The podcast listener is alone; both spatially and temporally they are isolated. Headphone listening is inherently a solipsistic experience that draws the listener away from others, constructing "their own individualized sound world wherever they go" as "sound transforms public space into private property" (Bull and Back 2003: 9). Podcasting itself is an orphaned media, delivered asynchronously and consumed individually. Load a podcast and press play, and you know that you are engaging in an experience that is unique to you in that moment of time. Even if it was May 28, 2017, and you were binge listening to *S-Town* as it was released, or it was December 18, 2014, and the final episode of *Serial*'s first season was playing in your earbuds. It would be extremely unlikely that someone else was having precisely that experience, in that very moment. You also know that the Sarah Koenig or Brian Reed were not talking to you, not then and there—a podcast is a recording of something that *has* happened rather than of something that *is* happening. You are listening to an event, rather than being part of it. Nick Quah, editor of *Hot Pod*, the industry newsletter for on-demand audio, explains: "That thing that we'll never get from podcast is the notion of 'live' and the thing we'll never get from podcasts is the sense of timeliness of being 'live' or being on the ball of where we are in any given point in time" (2016a).

Liveness haunts broadcast media, for it is this essential quality that makes the experience necessary and bonding for its audience. It is the great paradox of radio that "although its audiences may be counted in the millions, the medium addresses itself very much to the individual" (Crissell 1986: 13). When the microphone channel is opened, the broadcaster engages in an act of communication that owes the imperative of its existence to its "liveness," its presence, the sense that there is something new, vital, and alive, for that audience, in that instant. It is what radio artist Gregory Whitehead characterizes as a game, a play that unfolds between "far-flung bodies unknown to each other" (1992: 254) and Neumark terms "a whole affective or emotional microclimate and locus of encounter where listeners may feel themselves to be part of a listening community" (2006: 214). This is an imagined community, vast and unknowable (Anderson 1991), but harmonized and stabilized through listening, psychologically bonded by the knowledge that they are joined in a shared act. They are listening together, to the same works, to the same person, at the same time.

Douglas locates the acts of listening in preliterate oral cultures—sat round the radio or sat round the fire—the listener is part of a tribe, sharing a common experience of a common voice. Interacting through their shared reactions, recreating them as an aggregate entity, "whether or not they all agree with or like what they hear" (Douglas 2004: 29). This is what the isolated, headphone-wearing podcasting listener is not able to engage in, at least not directly. They are not part of a live listening community and cannot benefit from those intangible bonds. There are live events associated with podcasts, which include the *Welcome to Night Vale* shows, multimedia performances by *Radiolab*, sold-out shows of *My Dad Wrote a Porno* at Sydney Opera House, and *Wooden Overcoats* gigs in theatrical venues across London. These are not listening parties, not in the manner described by Lacey as having taken place in the 1920s and 1930s (2013: 15) or as Dana Chivvis discusses having occurred during the height of *Serial*'s success (2015). Nor can they be compared to Nina Garthwaite's *In the Dark* listening events; site-specific audio experiences that are held in blacked out locations across London. Podcast performances are not a sonic experience, and neither are they about spectacle. They offer a paired down and unaugmented reversioning of the text that to the objective observer represents a reduction of the original work. The *Guardian*'s Charlie Lyne described *Cast Party*, the 2015 live event that involved several leading shows, as being a form of podcast production that was lessened by its being performed on the New York stage. He observed that "the propulsive conversational style" of the Gimlet Media podcast *Reply All* was "reduced to the spectacle of two men reading awkwardly from lecterns while a third sits behind a laptop . . . . And each evidently well-meaning host is reduced to a wannabe comedian, desperately trying to impress at the end-of-year talent show" (2016). Although there are shows that offer more, *Radiolab* live tours have featured animatronic dinosaurs and live bands, and *The Heart*'s "Wedding Ceremony" of 2016 served as a piece of performance art, but what most podcast live shows are is an act of communal engagement rather than one of communal listening. The fans are there to support the show, *their* show, and to publicly express their fandom. What this represents is a real-world manifestation of a set of relationships that had previously only existed in online space.

Podcasting and the use of social media

There has been a yearning for radio to develop as an inclusive and two-way form of communication since its first development as a media form. In 1932 Bertolt Brecht expressed a desire that radio expand from being merely a "distribution system" to being a "communication system," and prefigured the growth of the internet with his vision of a vast network of pipes" joining the audience and allowing them to "receive as well as to transmit" (1932). Bonini traces the development of this relationship between the audience and the broadcaster through various stages across the twentieth and twenty-first centuries. He highlights the development of SMS and mobile technologies as a point when these communications become more fluid and immediate (2015: 11), but these developments were always mediated by a host who oversaw and controlled the discourse. The rise of social media has not broken the broadcaster's hegemonic control over communication; a tweet or an email to a radio station is still filtered by assistants, approved by a producer and channeled through the voice of the presenter. What it does offer the audience is a greater awareness of one another, and of their position as part of a greater community of listeners. They can listen to and partake in a form of collective listening to sound and speech in a virtual space (Lacey 2013: 155).

As I write this chapter the name "Helen" is trending on Twitter. An hour previously Helen Archer, a character in BBC Radio Four's perennially popular soap opera *The Archers*, finally turned against her violent ex-partner Rob Titchener. The denouement of an emotionally tense eighteen-month story arc has resulted in a burst of online activity. As the argument between the characters rolled on, the audience interjected, Tweeting advice and support. "Helen!!!!! Helen!!!!! Helen!!!!!" "Hear that mother LIONESS Roar!!!! #thearchers she really did it!" "OMG! Helen, you were awesome! #FightBack #TheArchers"; alongside the endlessly repeated missive "Go Helen." Redolent of an Elizabethan audience hurling insults and shouting support at players at the Globe, this is the audience communicating not with each another, but calling out together. This is a moment where their personalized, interior "semiotic" relationship to the form (Hills 2013: 136) is transformed into "enunciative productivity that's bound up with a particular moment of broadcast, and immediately switched into the textual productivity of 'narrowcast' (if not actually broadcast) digital mediation" (Hills 2013: 136). The audience's relationship to the media text is transformed from the personal to the public, and in that moment the community of engagement is no longer one that is "imagined."

The podcast, with its associations with the development of social media technologies, would appear to be perfectly placed to exploit the bilateral communication potential of the web. Across the broad range of interviews carried out for this book, podcast producers rarely discussed their work in terms of it being part of a fully integrated body of social media outputs. Rather, it was an afterthought, or an addendum to the main event: the audio. Dana Chivvis described *Serial*'s social media policy as consisting of "basically Emily Condon, and sometimes myself, sending out a Tweet or doing something on Facebook, but it was the barest bones of what you could do" (2015). Producers of *The Black Tapes*, *Radiolab*, *The Truth*, and others were not disdainful of social media, but they did not approach its use in a highly coordinated or premeditated fashion. The minimalism of their social media strategy was counterintuitive given the success of their shows[1] and the intensity of their audiences' engagement.

To determine how different podcasters are using social media to engender support and to communicate with their audience, we carried out an analysis of the Twitter output of ten podcasts and podcasters. The intention of this exercise was to determine how podcasts and their hosts engage with their audience, whether they participate in an active two-way discourse, or simply use social media as a digital bulletin board on which they post information and messages. Twitter was chosen because of its ubiquity, particularly among podcasters, and because of the ease with which qualitative data may be drawn from it. The decision about which podcasts were selected for analysis was determined by which podcasters we had interviewed at that time, with the exception of Roman Mars's *99% Invisible*.[2] Tweets from both the hosts and series producers of the podcasts were gathered to determine whether a distinction could be drawn between the manner in which a podcaster speaks with their audience as an individual and how the show they work on addresses its public. The most recent 500 tweets were harvested from each source, and then coded to determine the balance of communication. The categories used were as follows:

1. Publicity—marketing of the show, news of episodes, and information about other podcasts if part of a network.
2. Merchandising—marketing of events and merchandising items.

---

[1] When I discussed this "hands-off" approach to audience relations with a UK radio executive he looked shocked and told me "Well they're doing it wrong!" To which my reply was to wonder how *Serial*'s attaining (then) over 100 million downloads could be "doing things wrong"?

[2] The intention was to gauge the online behavior of podcasters of a variety of types of shows; a more extensive study would also sample a greater diversity of podcaster's backgrounds.

3. Show Topics—tweets referring to elements of the show either broadly or with specific reference to an episode.
4. Engagement—a written response to tweet from another Twitter user.
5. Retweets Audience—retweet of audience comment.
6. Customer Service—response answering technical issues related to the podcast.
7. General Topic—a tweet about an issue that is not directly related to the podcast.
8. General Retweet—retweet of a message on a topic not directly related to the podcast.
9. In World Tweets—tweets from within the storyworld of the podcast (this is applied to *Welcome to Night Vale* only).

The results are presented and analyzed below:

Radiolab and Jad Abumrad

Radiolab was one of the largest podcasts surveyed in terms of profile and Twitter following (Figure 3.1); it also featured the least direct interaction with its social media following. In January 2017 *Radiolab* had 262,000 Twitter followers, and the 500 tweets analyzed had been made over a four-month period. *Radiolab*'s Twitter output is characterized by a large number of retweets made of its followers' messages (a retweet is the reposting of another's tweet into your own timeline and serves as a form of affirmation and recirculation of a comment or a link). Thirty-seven percent of *Radiolab*'s Twitter output were retweets and of those the majority contained praise for the show or for the presenters ("RT @huwjordan: I know this sounds a bit over the top but listening to @Radiolab restores my faith in humanity, so is badly needed at the end"). These tweets serve as a way of allowing the show to be publicized and presented with a degree of hyperbole, without the makers themselves delivering the praise. "RT @_toriwhitley: This episode kicked me in the butt and everybody needs to listen to it. Thank you, @onthemedia & @Radiolab." There were also a large proportion (26 percent) of tweets that were retweets of messages about science and technology-related issues that could not be directly associated with a particular episode but would be broadly interesting to followers of the show ("RT @guardianscience: Knotty professors: chemists break world record to create tightest knot ever made"). Direct interactions with the audience were limited (less than 10 percent of

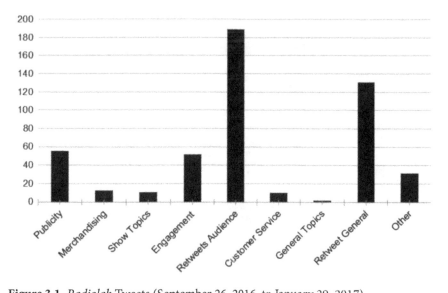

Figure 3.1 *Radiolab* Tweets (September 26, 2016, to January 29, 2017).

all communication) and most messages sent back to the audience were either thanks for comments ("@scheuster Thank YOU Tim!"), short bursts of positive affirmation ("@SorenWheeler @cwillyard Woo!"), or information about when future episodes are going to be released ("@ajvsell More episodes are coming! We're working on Season 2 now").

Jad Abumrad maintains a separate Twitter account that is distinct from the show he hosts. *Radiolab*'s Twitter profile states that "Radiolab is a show about curiosity from @WNYCStudios" while Abumrad's personal account bears the simple headline: "I make Radiolab and some music too. When I tweet it's just me." Abumrad tweets rarely from his personal account, (Figure 3.2) even though he has 25 percent more followers (320,000 in January 2017) than *Radiolab*. In his interview he described how he had previously used the platform extensively, but now mostly "stays off" for his "own health" (2016). His circumspect relationship to the medium is reflected in his output, which is eclectic and ranges across themes and ideas that resonate with the show's content and output, but it gives no insight into his personal life. He does not tell us about where he ate his dinner, what he thinks of a movie, how his training regime is going, or any direct insight into his personal politics. Abumrad does not frame his identity as a celebrity; his account is focused, professional, and distanced from the audience, though very occasionally acerbic ("@vegank8 language use changes as a result of 'popular trends.' deal with it"). Direct personal communication forms a very small

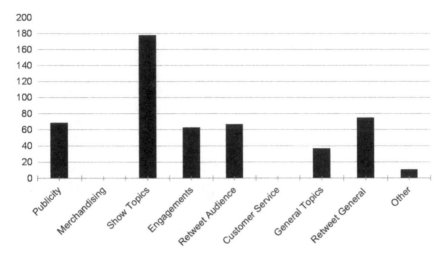

Figure 3.2 Jad Abumrad Tweets (June 11, 2015, to January 26, 2017).

proportion of his discourse; over the course of nineteen months he was involved in personal communication with other Twitter users forty-seven times.

99% Invisible and Roman Mars

If *Radiolab*'s Twitter interactions are limited in terms of direct communication, the podcast *99% Invisible* makes barely any use of the platform at all. Its account has 21,600 followers (Figure 3.3) and it has only issued 181 tweets in the two years following its launch. Those tweets that have been made are very informational and broadcastive in their nature. They are focused upon informing listeners about an episode or about a topic that ties in closely with the themes and ideas around which the podcast is centered. This is indicative of the fact that the strength of the show's following, as evidenced through the success of its Kickstarter funding campaigns, has not been built through its social media activity.

The host of *99% Invisible*, Roman Mars's output on Twitter is open, abundant, and personally discursive. In the decade leading to April 2017 (Figure 3.4) he tweeted 21,000 times to his 73,300 followers. His comments are light, flippant, positive, and in stark contrast to Abumrad's more distant output. He offers insight into the minutiae of his personal life ("Reusable gift bags are the greatest Christmas innovation since plastic ornaments"), caustic asides ("This rain can just fuck right off"), humorous anecdotes ("I passed Robert Reich while

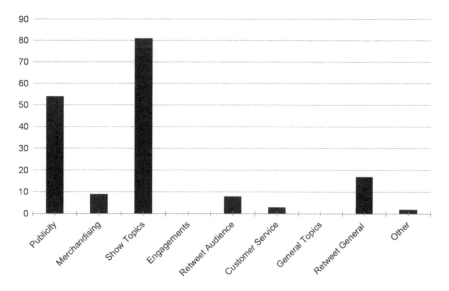

Figure 3.3 *99% Invisible* Tweets (October 23, 2015, to January 27, 2017).

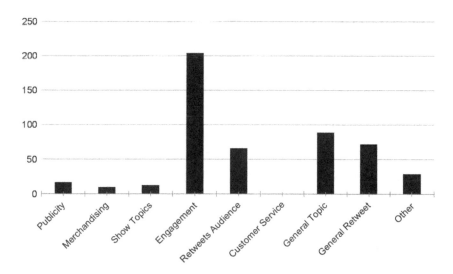

Figure 3.4 Roman Mars Tweet (December 6, 2016, to January 25, 2017).

getting lunch in Berkeley today. Managed to not ask him to hold me and tell me everything will be all right"), and details of the ephemera of his existence ("The only thing good about cold weather is I can keep my Coke Zeroes outside and don't have to squeeze them into the fridge"). Mars uses social media to talk with both his audience and other podcasters, and judiciously interspaces this material with announcements of funding drives and merchandising offers. His output is reminiscent of that of celebrity, gifting his followers with insight into his day-to-day existence, chatting with them and giving them brief affirmations, while never quite letting go of the financial basis of his relationship to them.

Lore and Aaron Mahnke

There is a simple format to the podcast *Lore:* each episode is hosted by Aaron Mahnke who tells stories of historical myth and urban legend in calm and measured tones. His words are not accompanied by sound design, interview footage, actuality, or re-enactment; rather there is just Mahnke, with some minimal musical backing, crafting story and homespun truisms from tales of vampires, murderers, secret rooms, and ghostly sightings. Within months of its March 2015 launch the series was a prodigious, almost viral, success resulting in over 100 million downloads across its seventy-six episodes (Mahnke 2017), a multi-book deal and the adaptation of the series by Amazon Video.

Mahnke developed and launched *Lore* independently and without capital investment, he saw it initially as a promotional tool for his work as a self-published author and blogger.[3] His Twitter use demonstrates an individual who works with and understands social media, deploying it as a tool both of promotion and engagement. By April 2017 (Figure 3.5) he had tweeted 43,300 times to his 16,000 followers from his personal account, and 8,000 times to the 35,000 followers of the *Lore* account. Online he is verbose, the 500 tweets from his personal account analyzed were made in thirty-one days (Abumrad's 500 tweets were made over nineteen months).[4] Neither the *Lore* account nor his own account are particularly focused upon the content of the podcast, he rarely offers further insight into the stories he covers or supplementary links and materials. His messages contain minimal details of his personal life, rather they are focused on his professional work and give updates on his creative process: "Managed to write another 1,400 words . . . episode 55 is DONE." Alongside this material are occasional insights into his views and position on political issues ("Let's stop calling stuff 'political

---

[3] A full account of the launch and growth of *Lore* is given in Chapter 9, "The Lucky Strike: Success, Value, and Independence in the Golden Age of Podcasting."

[4] Mahnke discusses how he believes he tweets too much saying that he should be "writing more often" and that he has apps to lock himself out of Twitter prior to 10:00 a.m. "but I don't know what happens, I just find myself there!" (Mahnke 2017).

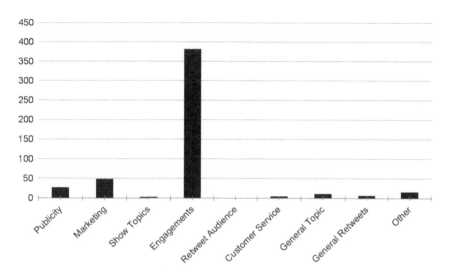

Figure 3.5 *Lore* Tweets (November 18, 2016, to January 30, 2017).

correctness,' and call it what it *really* is: human decency, maturity, and 'the right choice'") and judicially placed marketing information related to his show.

Mahnke engages with his followers, or at least attempts to, and a large percentage of his Twitter output from both his accounts consists of rapid responses made to audience comment and praise. The most frequent of which, comprising 52 percent of tweets sampled from his personal account, is simply the word "Thanks."[5] He has maintained a level of contact which is at once outward facing and depersonalized as *Lore*'s audience has grown (Figure 3.6). This is one person talking with 35,000 and he is trying to maintain some level of approachability in his discourse, even if it has been reduced to typing the same six letters repeatedly. He regards the relationships he builds on social media as being reciprocal:

> My approach to social media is treating it like a bank . . . that you deposit funds into this bank by being useful . . . . Nothing sales-related or promotional-related because when you promote on social networks you are withdrawing from that account, and I feel like the more you promote your thing, the more you take out of that bank, and when you get to zero or you're overdrawn then you've over-stayed your welcome. You're asking more from the people who follow you than you are providing to them. I try to treat social media as this thing that you have to balance; you have to give while taking. You can't just take. (Mahnke 2017)

---

[5]   It should be noted that Mahnke announced that *Lore* was to be serialized by Amazon Video during the period under analysis and he was responding to praise and congratulations from his followers.

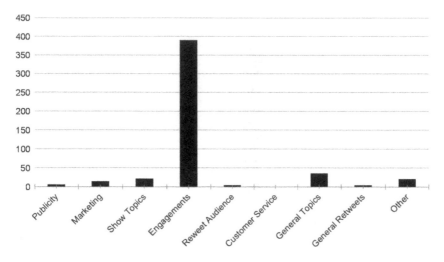

Figure 3.6 Aaron Mahnke Tweets (December 30, 2016, to January 30, 2017).

For Mahnke social media is a tool, one that he learned to use prior to his becoming a podcaster, and that he deploys judiciously to create a direct relationship with the audience. This is a necessity because *Lore* is scripted, and Mahnke rarely speaks with his audience without using a prepared text. He maintains a performative mask that he does not drop, even when he thanks his supporters and Patreon donators, the written form always underpins his address. Social media gives him a mode of directly talking to his fan base and his community of listeners without having to do so during his show. This is a technique used by producers of podcast drama, who need a means to directly engage with their audience without the necessity of their performers having to break the fourth wall.

We're Alive and K. C. Wayland

Between 2009 and 2014 K. C. Wayland wrote and produced 143 episodes of the zombie survival drama *We're Alive*. An independent production that did not benefit from a significant marketing budget or a celebrity cast, the show grew a following organically until it had been downloaded over eighty million times. In the years after its last episode Wayland has extended the storyworld of *We're Alive* through multiple series, drawing funding from Kickstarter and garnering support through the maintenance of open and active relationships with the show's fan base. Of the podcasters analyzed, *We're Alive*'s Twitter stream

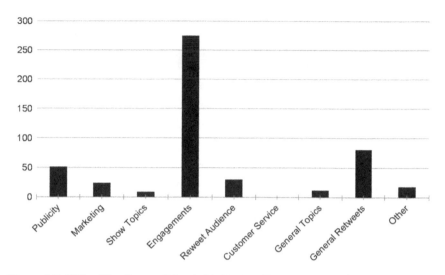

Figure 3.7 *We're Alive* Tweets (March 22, 2016, to January 27, 2017).

was the most open and discursive; (Figure 3.7) 55 percent of tweets made by Wayland through the *We're Alive* account were direct replies to listeners. These tweets consisted of discussions about the plot, answers to questions, and acknowledgments for listeners' support—it represents a realistic attempt to communicate with the show's audience.

We're Alive does not feature a narrator or a presenter who does more than announce the cast and credits. There is no direct communication in the show between Wayland and his listeners, and social media provides a bridge for the divide between the two. Like Mahnke, Wayland describes this relationship as being reciprocal: "It is a two-way road because they are giving you their time, which as a producer you should never take advantage of" (Wayland 2016). From this communication discussion builds, community grows, and both Wayland and his audience benefit. Wayland is not a podcasting or radio drama native; he was introduced to the possibilities offered by the form through his work in animation or more specifically through the studio recording of voice parts for animations. He initially used forums set up as part of *We're Alive's* website as a sounding board for his ideas. "I was able to get everybody's response week after week after week. One of the great things that helped me sort of hone my skills set is to figure out when ideas didn't work" (Wayland 2016). Wayland learned his craft in front of his audience, and used social media to gauge their response and develop his techniques.

As the audience for the series has grown, he has inevitably lost contact with the broader expanse of the listenership, about which he says he has "no idea how to communicate with." This reflects one of the key findings of this research, which is that for the podcaster benefiting from greater audience exposure, or from being part of a network or broadcast station, social media serves as a performance space or a notice board for their activities. They do not have to listen back to their followers to engender their support, because it is there already. For independent podcasters, such as Mahnke and Wayland, social media represents an important and actively used channel through which listeners may be drawn in and involved with their projects. Once their audience grows this communication becomes difficult, distracting and focused on a "small community" who are active, communicative, and involved in all his projects. These are the enunciative fans (Fiske 1992) whose relation to the media text has developed from a personalized "semiotic" discourse to an expressive and externalized one. These fans are not merely regular consumers of a particular product, rather they translate their relationship into cultural activity: sharing, discussing, and creating community (Jenkins 2006: 21). Fiske identifies a third tier of fandom, the "producerly" fans who produce content and texts in response to the subject of their devotion. They create wikis, write fictions, produce fancasts, and populate the net with illustrations and maps. Wayland describes the relationship with these fans as being mutually beneficial; the text itself is distributed for free and in return the active and the producerly fans generate content and raise the profile of the podcast. "They are working for you when you're not creating or producing anything. Having an active fan base is the exact same thing as marketing" (Wayland 2016). These are the power users, or Jenkins's "forensic fans" (2006) who form an intense and personal bond with the media text.

Welcome to Night Vale

The fans of *Welcome to Night Vale* are, in Fiskian terms, producerly: creating swathes of images, fiction, craft pieces, films, mash-ups, cut-ups, and costumes to wear on cold autumnal nights in North London. Unlike the fandom of *We're Alive* and *Lore*, their engagement cannot be directly ascribed to the use of Twitter as a form of bilateral audience/producer engagement. The podcast uses the platform extensively (Figure 3.8); it has tweeted over 6,000 times in five years and has 350,000 followers, but they are not communicating *with* their

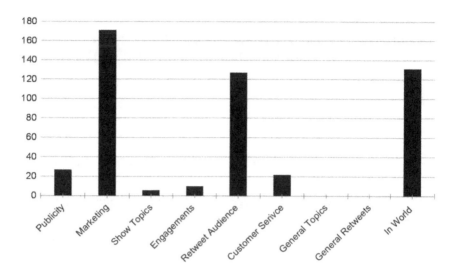

Figure 3.8 *Welcome to Night Vale* Tweets (October 24, 2015, to January 27, 2017).

audience, rather they are broadcasting communications out *to* them. A third of *Welcome to Night Vale's* tweets are given over to discussion of the franchise as a wider entity, serving as a means to advertise merchandising, book launches, and events: ("Hey, Belgium. We just added a show in Leuven. 24/09. You in? Tix on sale Thursday; other Europe dates on sale now.") These missives are combined with a steady stream of humorous and ambiguous messages that seem to originate from the town of Night Vale itself: "It is standard to tip your dentist 10% of your remaining teeth." "Stop and smell the flowers. Then whisper your darkest secrets into them. Then wait for federal agents to arrive." "Don't worry someday you'll find that person who is perfect for you. They can't hide. We have satellites."

Welcome to Night Vale's success was not born of an active social media policy or an attempt to reach out to its audience, at least, not in terms of direct one-to-one communication with fans. It proliferated online because there is something very familiar and very spreadable about its content. It utilizes a mythology and cast of characters that are familiar figures in twenty-first-century American media. It takes these elements, which reference the works of Stephen King, the writing of Poe, the plots of the X-Files, and a swathe of horror movie clichés and represents them in consumable and sharable packages through both its host's on-air pronouncements and 140-character (and later 280-character) tweets. These messages are perfectly packaged for social media, succinct bursts of paranoid surrealism that will slot into a timeline already laced with references to alternative facts, subjective reality, and surveillance culture. They are not intended for an audience outside of the series' core fandom, and should be read not as a marketing tool but as one of a range of story and media devices that the series creators deploy as engagement tools.

Welcome to Night Vale: A case study in engagement

Night Vale is a town where every conspiracy theory is true, and people live with that.

　　　　　　　　　　　　　　　　　　　　—Jeffrey Cranor (2015)

Welcome to Night Vale is a bi-monthly drama podcast written and produced in Brooklyn, New York, by Jeffrey Cranor and Joseph Fink. The program consists of local information broadcasts from the titular town's community radio station, presented by the earnest, energetic, and otherly host Cecil Palmer. It is at once darkly comic, willfully disorientating, and quietly reassuring. There is a knowing familiarity to the terrors that stalk the town of Night Vale, and there is a cast of lurking horrors and tentacled monstrosities that have been lifted from the post-Lovecraftian canon of the American gothic. Faceless figures, ominous "glow-clouds," multiheaded dragons; nightmares presented with an indifference that reduces them to the banal. These Eldritch horrors are combined with edicts and pronouncements from the forces that govern Night Vale, a coldly indifferent technopoly, the City Council, that combines with the Sheriff's "Secret Police" to survey and control the population and maintain an otherworldly status quo:

> The City Council announces the opening of a new dog park at the corner of Earl and Somerset, near the Ralph's. They would like to remind everyone that dogs are not allowed in the dog park. People are not allowed in the dog park. It is possible that you will see hooded figures in the dog park. DO NOT APPROACH THEM. DO NOT APPROACH THE DOG PARK. The fence is electrified and highly dangerous. Try not to look at the dog park, and, especially, do not look for any period of time at the hooded figures. The dog park will not harm you. ("Pilot" 2012)

What cuts through the darkness of this material is the warmth, familiarity, and naive insouciance of Cecil Palmer, who offers the warmest of radio voices as the world slithers and tumbles around him. His presentation, when combined with the podcast's episodic format, is reminiscent of Garrison Keillor's NPR staple *A Prairie Home Companion*, which broadcasts news from the fictional town of Lake Wobegon "where all the women are strong, all the men are good looking, and all the children are above average." Andrew Bottomley concludes that Night Vale is a remediation of radio drama "along with local community radio and other fringe categories of talk radio" (Bottomley 2015: 186), but this does not completely take into account the show's roots. *Welcome to Night Vale* was not born of radio, or audio, but of the emergent traditions and forms of off-Broadway and off-off-Broadway theatre. The single narrator, addressing an audience directly and intimately, owes as much to the works of New York performers and companies such as Radiohole, Elevator Repair Service, The Collapsible Giraffe, and Spalding Grey as it does to the tropes of American public radio. Fink and Cranor, along with a number of the *Welcome to Night Vale* cast, had previously been part of Neo-Futurists, a New York theatre company. They were drawn to podcasting because it offered a mode of production that was "cheaper than the theatre" (Cranor and Fink 2015). They saw podcasting as a way to address audiences beyond the "few hundred" who would visit one of their "critically well received but hugely costly" theatrical shows. They describe their investment in the early Night Vale productions as being extremely minimal: $85 for a USB microphone, a $5 hosting subscription, and free audio software.

The growth of the series is emblematic of how digital media texts expand and spread online. In the year following its June 2012 launch *Welcome to Night Vale* was downloaded 150,000 times (Cranor and Fink 2015), giving the podcast an audience base of approximately 6,000 listeners per episode. During the summer of 2013 memes began to appear on the blogging platform Tumblr that combined quotes from the series with images drawn from the NBC horror show *Hannibal*. Fans were making connections between the two texts, and finding a common sensibility between the franchises. Both are ostensibly concerned with depictions of horror and pain, but framed with irony and accompanied by "knowing winks" to an audience that is allowed to feel that they are part of a joke. The spreading of the show on Tumblr allowed its audience to grow; this was a period when the platform was in vogue and inhabited by the early adopters and influencers of the internet. Later in 2013 the podcast hit a tipping point and its audience began to be measured in first millions, and then tens of millions.

Welcome to Night Vale is part of a wider form of hybridized media fandom that encompasses Cosplay fans, Creepypasta devotees, Bronies (male fans of the Hasbro toy and media franchise *My Little Pony*), and the followers of indie game phenomena such as *Undertale* and *Fright Night at Freddy's*. Instead of clannishly settling and identifying themselves with particular texts, these fans cross over, intersect, and morph content together. A Google search for Bronies and *Welcome to Night Vale* (inevitably) brings up cartoons of purple ponies sitting before microphones uttering gnomic statements. *Welcome to Night Vale* has harnessed the shift in distribution of media in what Bonini describes as a move from "diffusion to circulation" (2015: 15); Fink and Cranor recognize that the franchise's fandom is "more about the fans than it is about us" (Cranor and Fink 2015). *Welcome to Night Vale's* live performances are as much communal gatherings as they are shows or spectacles. On stage the format of the podcast is recreated, and Cecil faces the audience from behind a microphone and delivers the show. It is not an extension of the audio experience, but rather a recreation of it. There is no make-up, no costume, no set. The cast enter and leave clasping their scripts and wearing their daily clothing, while it is the fans who are garbed in costume and prosthetics. It is their shared appreciation of this cult text that is as much part of the experience as what is happening on stage. Fans are brought together in a shared social space, and they are actively encouraged to acknowledge and register one another as a significant part of the performance:

> Everyone in the audience was already looking around for someone that they thought might be a murderer, now they looked past those people that they came with or with people that they already know, because they foolishly trusted those people. No no no, they sought out the eyes of a complete stranger and when they made eye contact with that stranger they locked in, staring at that person and only with that person, one of them thinking, "Yeah . . . that person could be a murderer" . . . and each one of them pointed at that stranger and each said, "You could be a murderer" . . . and then slowly they lowered their pointing fingers and each one of them said out loud, "I have my eye on you, suspect." They would remember the face of that stranger because they knew it would be important through the evening. ("The Investigators," *Welcome to Night Vale* Live Performance (2016))

Marshall (1997) suggests film stars are distanced and associated with an image of the live crowd facing in one direction. *Welcome to Night Vale* is perfectly pitched to work in an era of multimedia synergy, a world where there is an overabundance of contact, the audience face toward the performers who then direct them to be aware of one another when they are online, they are listening, or in the performance space. This is digital fandom made real; the imagined community no longer imagined.

As a text, *Welcome to Night Vale* deploys a rich mix of knowing references and in-jokes to engender a closed and cultish relationship with the audience. The repetition of the familiar, the returning characters or mimetic references to the fearful "dog park," the "faceless old woman," or the "five headed dragon" who stands to be mayor. These are the components of a private world the recognition of which bond the audience together. Umberto Eco's analysis of cult films texts, quoted by Jenkins in *Convergence Culture*, argues that works must come as a completely furnished world so that its fans can quote characters episodes as if they were aspects of "the private sectarian world" (in Jenkins 2006: 97). Night Vale repurposes and repositions the familiar, creating a cult experience that can be quoted because, as Eco argues, "it is made from quotes, archetypes, allusions and references drawn from a range of previous works" (in Jenkins 2006: 98).

There is an essential openness to the world of Night Vale which invites contribution from the listeners. The cult text according to Eco "must provide resources consumers can use in constructing their own fantasies" (in Jenkins, 2006: 98). What Fink and Cranor provide is the scaffolding of the world of Night Vale, the story, and the character, but no physical details. No visual information about locations, characters, or costume. Just one image that represents the entire series—a huge eye that hovers in a purple sky above a water tower and telephone line. It speaks of the themes of the series, of omnipresent observation, of mystery, of the open plains and sparse towns of the American west, but little more. The only other information we are given is that Cecil is neither "tall nor short" and that Carlos (Cecil's lover) has "magnificent hair." Without significant visual information or description everything is left up to the audience, who are given the freedom to create the world for both as a phenomenological and imaginative experience or, physically, by drawing and constructing images online which they have done in their tens of thousands.

These fan art creations are not just copies of the original texts that may be reduced to being acts of mimetic textual productivity (Duffett 2015: 137) because the fans have been given nothing to copy. They create their art from a blessed position because their imagining of a character's appearance cannot contradict the iconography of the official canon, because there isn't one. Any drawing of an element of the series has no lesser or greater status than any other. While this was initially the case, a style guide has organically developed online— and a search through images uploaded demonstrates that various visual tropes and elements have begun to ossify. The crowd seem to have concurred that the Cecil has white blonde hair, glasses, and sleeve tattoos, and Carlos does indeed have magnificent hair. Cranor and Fink are respectful of audience creations and outputs, and admit to using the fan-built *Welcome to Night Vale* wikis to "check in what episode certain things happened" and "the names of the interns who have died" (Cranor and Fink 2015). They never actively engage with any of the works that have been created based on their series:

> We want to be able to have our own ideas, and our own story without bleeding into their world, or having their worlds bleed into ours. At the shows people often show up in costume, and even if that's not necessarily what we thought the characters looked like, it doesn't really matter because it's what they thought it was, and it allowed them to build this sort of creative expression through our world, which is cool. (Cranor and Fink 2015)

They have created a digital playground, a space that is open and sharable but that, ultimately, they do not engage with.

Cranor and Fink's work could be read as a textbook example of how to create a cult or transmedia text; Francesca Coppa described it as something that could have been invented by an artist trying to "imagine Henry [Jenkins]'s definition of transmedia's best self" (Coppa 2014: 1080). Its creators repeatedly insist that this was not a conscious decision or part of their process. At its inception there was a refreshing naivety about how they developed *Welcome to Night Vale* as a storyworld and as a merchandising franchise. They describe how the project started as a "hobby with no particular listener in mind"; they just happened upon a blend of content, of techno-paranoia, of wry humor, of openness and social liberalism that precisely chimed with the needs and sensibilities of a Gen Z or Millennial audience. "Trying to write for a particular demographic is poison for creativity. If you had got Jeffrey and I together it would be like 'write something that would appeal to a 13-year-old girl.' We would have no idea where to start because we would be trying to write down to someone . . . . Rather than just being like 'I'm just going to write something that works for me,' and then if it appeals to someone it does" (Cranor and Fink 2015).

This element of authenticity is at the heart of the show's appeal and of podcasting more broadly. More than anything it is the sense that the creators are producing the work they want to create, and the audience is making an active choice to consume it. It is a relationship that is fragile and that must be treated with respect; the works of Hills, Duffett, and Jenkins all make it explicitly clear that contemporary media fans are highly aware of their status and of the potential that they are being exploited. Cranor and Fink were resistant to selling the film and TV rights to *Welcome Night Vale*, principally because they want to be sure that something true to their vision and their fans' vision is created (Cranor and Fink 2015). That Cranor and Fink are aware of this link is indicative that they have either learned from the experience of marketing a hugely successful podcast franchise or that they were not quite so naive when they began the process.

The authenticity of engagement

If we had tried to attract those people then I think we would have failed, but by just making a thing then it determines its own demographic. It's self-select-ing isn't it, the people who like a podcast? Because why would they listen to something they don't particularly like?

—Helen Zaltzman (2016)

The strength of the relationship between podcaster and their audience hinges on an unmeasurable, intangible, and subjective quality: authenticity. This can encompass ideas of honesty, directness, and a "down-to-earth" character that borders on the amateur. The manner that podcasts are consumed, as an opt-in media that is often experienced via headphones, draws the listener into an experience that is close and private.[6] It is an active form of listening that lies between the casual experience of merely "hearing" a radio broadcast and the immersive listening required for a soundscape or montage. Lacey characterizes the difference as being between the "perception and sensation" of sound that hearing embodies, and the "attention and giving to another" required of actually listening (Lacey 2013: 17). The podcasters know this and work with it. They draw the listener in, adopting what UK feature producer Alan Hall characterized as a "folksy, friendly, and intimate" (Hall 2016) manner that counters the formalized presentation of traditional journalistic broadcasting. Jad Abumrad and Robert Krulwich's scripted interplay on *Radiolab* perfectly encompasses this approach, giving the impression that they are engaged, they are active, they are talking to "you" the listener, directly without vocal or performative shield. Michael J. Collins locates *Serial's* success in the presentation of Sarah Koenig, which he describes as being: "akin to hearing an incredible story coming from the mouth of close

---

[6] The implications of and relationships formed by the earbud listener to the podcaster are discussed in Chapter 4.

college friend—a . . . complex mélange of disturbing and intriguing subject-matter delivered with this engaging oratorical style" (2016). This informal mode of presentation—companionable, spontaneous, and intimate—is the result of script meetings, rewrites, and some hundreds of takes and retakes (Abel 2015: 96).[7] Podcasting has moved on from the homespun, UGC roots described by Berry in his 2006 paper, but intrinsic to the form is an immediacy and directness of contact that speaks of something personal and personable. The podcaster has not been commissioned or had a project assigned to them; rather it is something that they have built and created from the ground up. The listeners have chosen to listen, actively seeking out the show and choosing to experience it (Friend 2016).

Radio must serve a wider audience; it is broadcasting in the oldest and truest sense of the word, casting and scattering its content as it progresses, not knowing where it might take root and begin to grow. It cannot target niche tastes because the radio audience is heterogeneous in its make-up and focused in its interests. It is expecting a branded experience aimed at its perceived demographic needs, which must be served broadly and generically. Ellen Horne has produced *Radiolab* in both its narrowcast and broadcast formats and characterizes radio as having "to be more inclusive." "You know that people are coming across the radio who did not intend to hear what they are hearing. You have to make sure that you do not offend people who did not specifically seek this out, younger audiences, broader tastes" (2015). The podcaster controls their creative space in a manner that the radio broadcaster never can. They own it, and they invite the audience in, who are then free to choose whether to partake of the content, or not. The podcaster decides on that audience, the content, the packaging of the show, and the social media messaging that surrounds the program.[8]

At the time of writing I was also working as a freelancer at the BBC: presenting a documentary that I was surprised to have commissioned. I would not have chosen to make this show; my personal favorite, a documentary about Bronies (mentioned earlier) that William Shatner had agreed to present, was rejected because it was felt that it would not appeal to the station's core audience. When

---

7 Charlie Lyne describes how the live *Cast Party* event shattered the illusion of the hosts' spontaneity by shining "a glaring spotlight on the artistic liberties at the heart of these shows—the feigned naivety of the hosts, the micro-managed 'spontaneity' of the storytelling. I doubt *Radiolab* listeners ever really believe the show's presenters when they gasp in surprise at a story they themselves are telling, but it's especially hard to suspend your disbelief when you're watching them read out their reactions from neatly ring-bound scripts" (2016).

8 Issues of authenticity and the relationship of podcast producers to their text are discussed further in Chapter 9, "The Lucky Strike: Success, Value, and Independence in the Golden Age of Podcasting."

I began working with my producer I found myself entering an almost child-like state of dependency. I was led to interviews, sat in front of microphones, coffees were fetched for me, and questions placed before me to read. I have seen this behavior in other presenters, a wonderful detachment where you are the "talent" and the show elements are all laid out before you. The contrast to my work as a podcast producer is stark. As a podcaster I am the focus of each project, and am responsible for the implementation and running of every element. I have had to carry out interviews, find actors, brief designers, master mixes, upload episodes, check the RSS feed, select artwork, finalize contributor contracts, and engage fans. Hundreds of hours of work are required to give each podcast the life and energy they need to survive and be noticed.

Media fans are active and wary of being exploited for commercial gain. What podcasters do to foster community among their audiences is to approach their projects holistically, using social media as just part of strategy, and with at least the veneer of creative authenticity in place. The UK comedian Richard Herring expresses this relationship as a conversation: "You feel like you're part of the conversation, and it feels more real than a radio conversation, which will have more constraints on it. I think the audience are drawn in that way" (2016). Freed of the machinations of mainstream media, of the necessity to channel work through pitch meetings, commissioners, QC teams, and compliance processes, that podcaster is free to talk to their audience directly and honestly. Alan Hall identifies the key difference between traditional broadcast radio and podcasts as being this sense of the total ownership of the project. Podcasts made this way are "more complete products or productions" whereas in Europe and Australia producers do not have that relationship to their work because "we are makers who are asked to do something, and any marketing or hustle is beyond our remit" (2016). Podcasts are often made by someone who has a holistic understanding and relationship to the subject; they understand the project and they know how to "hustle" it. This is what Aaron Mahnke and K. C. Wayland are doing in their active and discursive use of social media; they are repaying their listeners' input and contributions and engaging with them in a manner that demonstrates the strength of their connection both to their product and to their audience. What Joseph Fink and Jeffrey Cranor understand is that contemporary media fandom is a rhizome, and podcasting can provide a space where the listeners can begin to communicate with one another.

4

In Bed with Radiotopians: Podcast Intimacy, Empathy, and Narrative

My ideal listener is someone who isn't multitasking, someone who's not driving, someone who's not doing their dishes; it's someone who's lying on their bed at night with their eyes closed and making the podcast their primary point of attention.

—Brendan Baker (2016)

We're sitting [recording this interview] in this little lacy booth right here with . . . this blanket I stole from the guy that I lost my virginity to when I was eighteen years old. This is basically like my bed on the walls.

—Kaitlin Prest (2015)

One of the key observations in this book is that podcasting is considerably freer than radio in numerous ways. Even the producers most attached to the radio format seem to revel in podcasting's possibilities in style, content, and engagement. The podcast edit is racier and bolder, and podcasts often contain material most national broadcasting regulators would rarely sanction.[1] Where radio might suggest and allude, podcasting is full frontal. While these moments are relatively easy to hear and catalog, they point toward other characteristics that have been much more challenging to capture adequately: intimacy and empathy in podcast narrative. These native podcasting traits are the focus of this

---

[1] For example, Alan Hall, our interviewee with perhaps the longest track record in radio, says in describing a moment in one of his programs in which an elderly blind woman was having pornography read to her: "For broadcast we weren't allowed to report her saying, 'Do you mind if I just go to the loo? I want to jizz myself up.' We couldn't say that in the broadcast but we could put it in the podcast" (Hall 2016).

chapter. In an effort to refine our understanding of "podcast intimacy," and its implications for broader human relationships, we will take up here:

1. headphones, earbuds, and the physicality and aural mechanics of podcast listening;
2. modeling intimate listening practices (opportunities *to listen to intimate listening* in action);
3. interpersonal trust in podcasting; and
4. empathy itself as artistic material for creative podcaster producers.

As primary subject material I will study the two Radiotopia podcasts *The Heart* and *Love + Radio*. At the time of our interviews and my examination, *The Heart* was produced by Kaitlin Prest and Mitra Kaboli; having evolved out of the CKUT, Montreal, radio program *Audio Smut*, *The Heart* offered an expansive set of female-driven, sex-positive, highly crafted documentary, personal essay, fiction, and hybrid-genre episodes that took up a very broad range of topics involving physical and emotional encounters of all kinds. *Love + Radio*, at the time of our interviews and my examination, was produced by Brendan Baker and Nick Van Der Kolk and offered extremely engaging, seemingly simple personal narratives and interviews dealing with a range of social themes and situations and again designed, edited, and produced with extreme skill and care. Both of these programs suggest intimacy in their very titles and push the concept further than any others I then knew.

"Intimacy," as a term, has been a familiar feature of radio studies for decades now. And, as with other aspects of podcasting discussed in this book with roots in radio, a "radio intimacy" is often invoked as evidence that podcasting is not quite the paradigm shift that some suggest. Taking just one contemporary example by way of introduction, Bottomley cautions that while an "intimate" style in podcasting might seem novel compared to recent decades of mainstream radio output, it can be heard in much of the radio drama of the mid- and early twentieth century (2015: 182). He hears the "natural and spontaneous" delivery of Night Vale Community Radio's Cecil as simply a rediscovery of that old-time radio thread. His focus on drama means, however, that he only ever hears intimacy as a contrivance, as a part of an act, as inauthentic by definition. This, however, should prompt the questions: "What, if it exists, might an authentic podcast intimacy sound like? And how is it engaged, enacted and probed by podcast producers?" But now as then, the concept of podcast intimacy often appears too messy and woolly for conventional academic sensibilities. Here I attempt to comb out a bit of that wool in order to help reduce some of the critical anxiety. Through a precise set of close analytical listenings I distinguish and describe a more tangible intimacy that occurs around and through podcasting. This is more complex than earlier concepts of intimacy and has much more potential to generate empathy and to humanize the deeply marginal; but it also holds a potentially troubling capacity for manipulation.[2] My final close analytical listening of *Love + Radio*'s "A Red Dot" episode reveals how skilled producers have creatively explored these dimensions of podcast intimacy (both positively and negatively).

A sensible first step in using these programs to help us understand and describe podcast intimacy is to place them in the context of what we have already said about podcasting and the general debates about the form. Perhaps surprisingly, both Prest and Baker were somewhat resistant to the use of the term "podcasting," often wanting to read it primarily as a delivery technology.[3] Of the several reasons they each cited to hold on to the term "radio" for their work, *money* was the most unexpected: Both Baker and Prest lived in Brooklyn and worked in the shadow of WNYC Radio; both occasionally saw a "radio job" as being more secure and more financially rewarding. But more significantly, the masses of UGC content that had defined the medium up until that point meant for them that podcasting was widely seen as radio's amateurish cousin. Radio, any radio, offered them a professional cultural recognition that was attractive:

> There's a real hierarchy in the radio scene of like, "Are you 'on air' or not?" And if you're not on air it doesn't fucking matter, and you can feel that in a conversation when you say, "Oh you know we're on air?" even in Montreal or some obscure station nobody knows about. Still people are like "oh, it's a real radio show" you know? (Prest 2015)[4]

---

[2] With this idea of manipulation in mind, there is a long-standing cultural prejudice against sound as deceptive in favor of the more static, "localizable" and consistent image. See, for example, Karatzogianni and Kuntsman, in which sound becomes a means of affective manipulation and has a troubling influence on perception because it can make us see an image in a way that we would otherwise not see it (2012: 243). Sound cannot be pinned down; it is much harder to hold it and analyze it empirically, and it is viewed as dangerous in a way that the image is not.

[3] This came through clearly in their interviews and also at their panel discussion "Narrative Sound Design" at the 2016 Podcast Movement Conference in Chicago.

[4] At another point Prest is clearly aware of the absurdity of applying radio notions of "respect" to her work. Pausing to smile, she said, "How can you walk around [radio events] and expect people to respect you professionally when the work that you're pointing to is a recording of you masturbating in a public bathroom?" (2015). It is obvious to anyone who has ever listened to a single episode of *The Heart* that it could not exist on public radio in any recognizable form; clearly then for Prest conventional forms of radio respect are not really the aim.

There was a formality and a seriousness associated with radio work, even on an "obscure station," that was validating. Similarly, Baker also seemed aware that he was caught in the same tension. Laughing, he said, "There is something that feels more 'respectable' about radio." (It is important to remember that— in spite of what might be described as early-career insecurities on the part of these producers—in very real ways *The Heart* and *Love + Radio* had earned significant markers of respectability: they had contracts with a major podcast distribution network, advertisers, enviable listener numbers, and *The Heart* had won the world's top radio prize, the Prix Italia, in 2015 for its episode "Movies in Your Head," the first podcast to do so.) But when pushed, these concerns about respectability and narrow professional recognition began to recede in favor of what Bourdieu calls artistic "position-taking."[5] Both producers hear their intimate audio work in conversation with other experiments in the history of radio art, from Pierre Schaeffer to Gregory Whitehead. They wanted to be included in the critical discourse that has grown up around radio art in recent decades. And given that the culture of radio criticism remains quite scant (as Prest noted with exasperation) when comparing it with the culture of film criticism, the thought of starting from scratch with a new genre of podcast criticism felt somewhat daunting and demoralizing.

Contributing to their apprehensions around the terminology was a sense that audio's older guard had some deep-seated suspicions around the new form and the new producers that were going to take some time to overcome. Hall is sometimes emblematic of this when comparing radio to podcasting. Radio, he says, was

> characterized by modesty, definitely compared to press or TV. It was characterized by an anonymity . . . . You could be invisible almost. It was characterized by a kind of more intelligent consideration of something. It wasn't looking at the surface, it was intended to be going deeper into something, and the stuff that really appealed to me was there was an elegance of production. Not all of those things can be applied in the podcast sphere, I don't think, because they tend not to be that modest. (Hall 2016)

Whether we take at face value Hall's suggestion of radio as "anonymous," his description of its "modesty" is more interesting for our discussion of intimacy: "modesty" suggests his radio voices were less self-aggrandizing, but also, in a

---

5   That is an effort to describe and distinguish their work with reference to a larger field of creative cultural production (Bourdieu 1993: *passim*).

rather Victorian sense of the word, more discrete. A lesser (but still significant) aim of this book is to pick through the complex intergenerational dialogue about professionalism, standards, and cultural values in audio as part of an effort to describe podcasting's potential as distinct from radio. With this in mind, does it not make sense to reclaim loaded concepts like "immodesty"? Rather than becoming defensive in the face of these perceptions and generalizations, podcasters might own them, embrace them, and expand upon them. The podcasts being considered here *are* certainly less anonymous and more personal than most radio, and this is certainly one of the keys of *The Heart*'s appeal. They *are* more immodest and more indiscrete, but this leads to an authenticity of language and a more intimate connection with a listener. They *are* less respectable in that they regularly present in detail subjects that conventional broadcasters would typically abjure as salacious or even dangerous (such as transsexuality and pedophilia). It is precisely in these transgressions that we find some of podcasting's cultural significance and social potential.

With this neither Baker nor Prest would disagree. Again, we hear in Prest's care around the terminology an artistic position-taking: the term "radio" has deep meaning for her. As she describes it, it means a "transmission," a crossing of barriers, a conveyance from one person to another. The nuance offered by this chapter is to describe *The Heart* and *Love + Radio* as conceptually engaged in acts of transmission that have outgrown the mechanics of radio waves and the semantics of radio language. The fact that both these producers cite Whitehead as a significant influence shows that they understand this. "The materiality of radio has nothing to do with sound," says Whitehead. "It has to do with the set of relationships" (in *Radio Radio* 2003). The discussion of "empathy artists" at the end of this chapter depends on this understanding.

After this artistic positioning of the producers is taken into account, both *The Heart* and *Love + Radio* are quite clearly identifiable as podcasts. Nowhere is this distinction more clear than in the handling of sex. Anyone who grew up, as I did, in New Jersey in the 1970s and 1980s, knows that sex (in various degrees of explicitness) has been a staple of radio for some time.[6] That often prurient and misogynistic approach to sex extends deep into radio's history and is typified by Mae West's 1937 blacklisting from American radio for her portrayal of a very sexualized Eve seducing a hapless Adam out of the Garden of Eden in pursuit of

---

[6] Even before radio, the history of sexual pleasure through listening was often defined by eavesdropping in which intimacy went hand in hand with scandal (Hendy 2014: 221).

her own excitement and "big ideas." In the more modern era this radio theme of sexualized women being simultaneously objectified and punished for that sexuality continued through a long line of formats. "Topless radio," "X-rated radio," and "sex talk" (Hilliard 2009: 53–57) all, in varying degrees, invited, goaded, tricked, and even bullied women into an audio version of the male gaze in which their sexuality was on display while men (from shock jocks to listeners to broadcast regulators) passed judgment. Throughout this history of humiliation the notion of "intimacy" was largely alien, and when it did appear it was, ironically, contextualized in terms of the "perverse" (Hilliard 2009: 65).

Podcasting's systemic, structural, and institutional break from radio models was an opportunity to draw a line under this unfortunate history. The independence of the form, the freedom of extremely committed producers with restricted budgets and alternative expectations, and the willingness to ultimately leave behind radio notions of "respect" meant that podcasting, particularly on *The Heart*, was able to frame sex differently and tell different kinds of stories about it. Once this past was jettisoned, producers like Prest and Kaboli could then use these new approaches to sex to explore the way a broad range of connections are made between people mediated by audio, speaking and listening. Empirical psychological evidence is now more commonplace which affirms what audio producers have known intuitively for decades: that the brain works differently (and harder) in engaging with audio stories than visual ones—this, in turn, fosters more intimate connections with the voices heard (Rodero 2012). These intimate connections around listening, both within podcasts and to them, are studied in detail in the rest of this chapter.

Audio intimacy in historical context

I think this work is important because we need a new language to mobilize, to articulate who we are as loving sexual beings.

—Kaitlin Prest (2015)

The history of the idea of "intimacy" on radio is largely one of politics and architecture, not one of bodies, minds, or hearts. Given how frequently "intimacy" is used in radio histories and listening histories, there is often a striking lack of specificity and consensus around the term. But generally, it gestures to domestic or privatized spaces rather than affective human contact or emotion. Perhaps this is because the more affective intimacy—the intimacy I locate in and through podcasting—is squarely outside of an academic comfort zone for most of us. Often, as is the case in Susan Douglass's benchmark *Listening In*, intimacy is defined by what it is not, or in opposition to something else. Early radio talks and speech were declamatory, she says, "rather than conversational and intimate" (2004: 203). Clearly the fact that it was "oratorical" rather than intimate had something to do with an awareness of its mode of distribution—an awareness that filtered through the tone and the style of radio address in the 1920s which we might characterize as a single voice communicating to "the masses."

Without doubt this mode was influenced by the simple listening technology: the sound quality was extremely lo-fi; the speakers and listening devices were clumsy; in short, there was very little radio that entered your ear without great resistance and mediation. This meant that when a perception of intimacy did come to radio more than a decade later it was framed in broad social and political terms. Loviglio argues in *Radio's Intimate Public* that twentieth-century radio should be seen as a tension between public and private communities. Radio's intimacy (supported by an evolving conversational tone) cracked open the previously private or domestic sphere to create "blurred social spaces." In considering Saul Bellow's famous reflection on walking down an avenue and hearing FDR's words come out of the radios of nearly every parked car he passed, Loviglio says:

> The open doors and windows of the cars in Bellow's recollection, like the open windows of houses in other versions, mark the site where public and private have temporarily merged to form a national community, an *intimate public*. (2005: xv) (italics in the original)

While very useful in helping us get to grips with lines between public and private spaces that seem at once clearly defined and porous, Loviglio's "intimate public" does not really consider either the physical or emotional proximity of human beings, and (at least in this example built as it is around a national figure speaking about issues of national import) we might just as easily call it "camaraderie." Intimacy is also elided with "informality" in discussing the appeal of radio personalities like Will Rogers and Father Coughlin (2005: 9); in this case it is more a manner of speaking than a manner of sounding—it is words rather than voice.

While discussions of contemporary media "intimacy" become more well-rounded (and even reference affect), they have a tendency to treat it as phony, as a con-job. O'Keeffe is a case in point; in her *Investigating Media Discourse* she describes a *pseudo*-intimacy built on the *para*-social (people sat speaking as if they were old friends). She cites a *simulated* co-presence (a presenter's referencing of surroundings), vocatives, and other rhetorical figures (2006: 90–124) in order to cast suspicion on the idea of media intimacy. While certain intimate broadcast language is marked by "a relatively complete and honest level of self-disclosure" the material distance between presenter and listener means the relationship is only ever ersatz.[7] Because the audience is always "out there," "a sustained sense of commonality must be simulated to transcend physical distance."[8]

Even more critical (and perhaps cynical) than O'Keeffe, Hall sees in this performative simulation a simple manipulation designed to monetize an audience (2016); if our audiences feel more emotionally invested they will buy more of what our advertisers are pushing. While a kind of intimacy certainly can and is used in this way to sell or to dupe, what this reading fails to take into account is that, in cases like *The Heart* in particular, it is not a strategy to some other end, but an end in itself.[9] Why else would Prest dedicate her life to recording in her closet for less than a half-time salary? Prest's creative and social missions to explore and activate intimacy are almost always more substantial than what critics of intimacy imagine. The invitations into intimacy are opportunities for Prest to develop a sex-positive feminism and a sexual expression outside of a stereotypical male gaze (Prest 2015). Perhaps because of their tone and content these explorations simply make cringe-ready academics and seasoned, hard-boiled public radio/audio producers uncomfortable. This is unfortunate because while Prest is literarily passionate about intimacy, it is for her an extremely fraught and complicated affair (as *The Heart*'s "Fu*k Love" episode testifies) that she

---

[7] This impression resonates quite well with Michael Bull's handling of Adorno's concept of the "we-ness" enabled through sound technologies which offer "the substitution or transformation of 'direct' experience by a mediated, technological, form of aural experience" (2005: 345).

[8] This emphasis on simulation is utterly different from Prest's emphasis on "transmission" which sees the technology as potentially dissolving barriers in the pursuit of more authentic relationships. The discourse of privatization then may be a useful starting point, but it does not offer a full picture of what is here evolving as a distinctively podcast intimacy. If, as Bull suggests, "iPod users both re-claim representational space and the daily 'realm of the eversame' precisely by privatising it" (2005: 354), we must now add that in podcasting this privatized space is not individual, it is intimately shared with someone else, be it Prest or Van Der Kolk or one of their interviewees.

[9] It is important to observe that there are two different frameworks at play here: seeing a podcast as a means to generate money and needing money to produce a podcast. While Prest clearly takes the second position, it is interesting to note that in her interview she suggests that the American broadcasting and podcasting funding model, in which producers are dependent on listeners to more directly fund their work, tends to increase kinds of intimacy in American audio comparatively. She says producers need to cultivate "a high awareness of how people are responding" in order to succeed; but again for her success seems like it is not principally involved with issues of revenue.

investigates with skill and insight. In anxious and empiricist times, there might simply be a fear or broad rejection of intimacy's potential because it is difficult to quantify and pin down in conventional discursive prose, and because it readily references such ephemeral states as love. Part of the problem is undoubtedly down to cultural differences in approach to these ideas as well, as Prest, Hall, and several of our other interviewees have noted (this is taken up in the next section). Our close analytical listenings to the intimate currents of several episodes of *The Heart* and *Love + Radio* later in this chapter are offered as a remedy to some of these critical misgivings.

Against the backdrop of these difficulties, false starts, apprehensions, and suspicions, it seems useful to offer here a description of intimacy as clearly as possible. When we talk about podcast intimacy we refer to efforts to create and reveal emotional experiences and personal connections in a comfortable space between interviewers and interview subjects, between the producers themselves, and between listeners, producers, and subjects. Put yet another way, for Prest this means creating moments in which people can "admit that they fantasize about having babies with someone after knowing them for one hour" (2015). This, very nicely, reveals intimacy as beyond sex. It is an experience with someone for which sex might typically be a prerequisite, but in which it is not necessarily the goal. Therefore, podcast intimacy is not all about sex. What is at stake here are experiences which traffic in openness, honesty, and authenticity—again, these are terms that make some critics see red. (But, as we will see in the concluding analysis of *Love + Radio*'s "A Red Dot" episode, Radiotopia's producers do not take them at face value either.) These are also experiences that do not end in themselves but use intimacy as a route to empathy, described by Michael Hardt as a reciprocal circuit of "touching" in which our power *to move others* depends on our openness *to be moved by others.*[10]

Cultural differences in emotional communication and narrative

The openness and type of appreciation necessary to engage intimacy, empathy, and emotion through narrative are, at least in part, culturally determined. Our

---

[10] Hardt writes in the Foreword to *The Affective Turn: Theorizing the Social*, "The greater our power to be affected . . . the greater our power to act" (2007: x).

interview material, for example, generally supports the cliché that Americans are more open than others: a wariness and unease around suggestions of podcast intimacy marked a number of our interviews with Brits while none of the Americans saw it as a particular issue of concern. Executive producer of Radiotopia, Julie Shapiro, spoke of the way some American podcasts had recently been processed at an audio event in Australia: "There was a lot of critique of the kind of heavy-handed, holding the listener's hand, telling them every little detail" (2016). "Hand holding" has been a fairly common criticism of a number of America projects (particularly *This American Life*) for some time now.[11] This idea of "hand holding" is worth considering closely here because it unconsciously links two often-disparaged aspects of an American audio production style: an affinity for personal closeness and a very strong attachment to clear narrative structures.[12] It is worth remembering that people generally hold hands for one of two often interrelated reasons: (1) love, affection, or some kind of emotional bond, or (2) giving or receiving guidance, support, security, or help. When we imagine lovers hand in hand in a park or someone helping a poorly sighted person across a busy street, neither should convey particularly negative connotations.

There are, unarguably, podcasts that over-do what McHugh calls the "American narrative style, described variously as 'hand-held,' 'spoon-fed' and 'host-driven,'" and come to feel cloying or condescending. But this is a matter of perspective, a perspective that may also be informed by resentment that American productions often eclipse those of other countries in the larger podcasting landscape and charts. Shapiro defends the Radiotopia podcasts as being sufficiently innovative to avoid these criticisms most of the time. As should become evident through our close analytical listenings, this holds true for nearly all of the episodes surveyed in this book.

Whether or not having clear narrative structures is necessarily an "American" trait can be debated, but it is, broadly speaking, more important to podcasting than it is to radio. If radio is a "flow" medium, podcasting is a "beginning-to-end" medium. In radio we speak of programming; in podcasting we talk about *a* program. It would be extremely odd to start listening to a new podcast episode somewhere in the middle, and you can listen through to the end at your leisure

---

[11] See, for example, Heffernan (2007) and Patterson (2016).

[12] Hall, expressing some anxiety that podcasting is blurring lines between fiction and documentary, cites, in close proximity, an American commitment to "story" and the production ethics of Prest and *The Heart* (quoted in McHugh 2016).

even if interrupted by a phone call or the doorbell. An awareness of this lets Prest see her work as that of a "narrative audio artist" (2015). Baker too says that strong narrative form provides him with an entry into close relationships that more abstract sound artwork would not (2016). And both *The Heart* and *Love + Radio* seem near-perfect embodiments of the connection that cultural critic Arthur Frank identifies between narrative and empathy:

> Storytelling is a practice that seeks to establish empathic relations by offering listeners a moral imagination of others' worlds, what identities are possible in those worlds, and what actions are indicated by those identities . . . . [T]o be empathetic is to know someone else's story. (2016: 151–52)

For Frank, as well as for Prest and Baker, it remains extremely difficult to access the material of empathy without story.

Prest is certainly aware of the criticisms of a rigid attachment to narrative forms in podcasts, but says that those forms need not be prescriptive. If a "formula" exists, she says, the possibilities within it are as limitlessly fascinating and satisfying as the before-and-after photograph. She acknowledges making use of McKee's *Story* (1997)[13] (a common text used for structuring film narratives), and other podcasters often cite Barthes's more complex codes (1974) (see Chapter 8). But perhaps the narrative theory most useful for thinking about contemporary podcasting was offered by Todorov who elegantly distills narrative into two, relatively self-explanatory principles: *succession* and *transformation* (1971: 39). The only thing further that need be said about succession is that the units of the story need not proceed in linear time as long as there is a progression. Transformation is more nuanced in that characters change within the architecture of the story, but the most successfully intimate podcasts invite a further empathetic transformation in listeners as well. The most familiar narrative shape, which Todorov found epitomized in the Holy Grail story, is the "quest." Indeed the high-profile podcast examples of it are not limited to those considered in this book but include a huge list of others—from *The Mystery Show* to *Limetown*, from *Things You Should Know* to *The Moth*—in which the thing being sought (by characters, producers, or listeners) is often not some sort of prize or treasure (even in a metaphorical sense), but a new knowledge or self-awareness.

---

[13] Also, it should be noted here that the current renaissance in narrative is not limited to podcasting. Sconce observes that classic narrative structures appeared as a feature of even art-house cinema some years ago (2002).

As we note in Chapter 8 on *Serial*, concern can be raised around this approach (usually by an old guard) when interviewees and producers ("real" people) come to be thought of as "characters" in a narrative. Needless to say, this is not in any way an anxiety shared by the producers of the intimate podcasts discussed here. Baker almost always refers to his interviewees as "characters" in the first instance—he views that as part of the process of crafting empathetic connections. And Prest, when questioned about her using recordings of interviewees recreating scenes from events that happened years in the past, said simply that "the emotional truth of the moment is more important than what really happened." The stories themselves exist in a real register—they are the things that are real, even if the interviewees are "characters" and the scenes are recreations.

The closeness of strangers

The *Love + Radio* episode "The Silver Dollar" offers an excellent opportunity to hear together many of the aspects of podcast intimacy discussed so far. In it, musician Daryl Davis (an African American) tells about his efforts to understand and engage with white supremacists of the Ku Klux Klan following an odd encounter with an audience member at The Silver Dollar club at a truck stop in Maryland where he was playing piano in a country band. A close listening analysis of it is particularly useful in showing the reciprocal nature of empathy as suggested by Hardt (2007).[14]

The first thing to note, as with almost all of the *Love + Radio* episodes, is that the host or interviewer presence is virtually nonexistent. Davis begins the episode with a cold-open story about how he was mauled by a dog as a child after being warned that it was aggressive which concludes with him saying that, in spite of this attack, he still loves dogs as an adult—an anecdote that will have resonance later. Van Der Kolk is only heard off-mike to illicit crucial bits of information for the audience (e.g., at 15:23 when his interjection makes it clear that Davis's girlfriend is white).[15] As he relates serial encounters with

---

[14] The times referred to in this close listening come from the version of the program found on SoundCloud. It lacked the ads at the top so the times will not correspond to the version on iTunes.

[15] In this production approach the handling of audio and sound design becomes extremely important as it must do much of the narrative signposting work of a presenter. Here this is in evidence at 04:59: as Davis is recounting his first conversation with a Klansman his voice is panned hard from left channel to hard right channel as he delivers the different sides of the story. His voice is also filtered and there is ambience reminiscent of a club; both these effects are cut when he pops out to provide us with an interpretive gloss on the scene.

various Klansmen he describes the mode of engagement that he stumbled onto: repeated listening. In first meetings he would give the Klansmen plenty of opportunity to talk. As hateful as the discourse was he would repress a visceral reaction and instead just question facts, ask for evidence and seek common ground where he could find it. He eventually reflects with a rhetorical question which gets repeated in the episode (14:58 and 18:53): "How can you hate me when you don't even know me?" His subtle attempts to get that question answered by the Klansmen are a humanizing tactic that eventually, over months and years, leads to an understated resolution rather than an answer: when the Klansmen get to know him as a real human being they no longer hate him. Through this process they ultimately loosen their grip on their racism, leave the Klan, and give Davis their hoods as tokens. Davis sums up his process like so:

> While you are actively learning about someone else you are passively teaching them about yourself . . . . Challenge them, but don't challenge them rudely or violently; you do it politely and intelligently. When you do it that way, chances are that they will reciprocate. (29:58)

What is on display here is emblematic of a broad range of intimate podcast listening: transformative empathy grows between characters only through persistent, careful, and patient listening. Davis's ability to instigate a change was dependent on his being prepared to listen seriously and nonjudgmentally to the grievances of another—not to agree with them or their causes, but to consider them.

Van Der Kolk only takes over at the very end to support Davis's gloss that consideration and even friendship are not a tacit approval of politics and to frame the episode as a Radiotopia production (36:40). But after the "thank yous" to sponsors and a promo for another podcast comes something that extends and supports our developing understanding of the kind of intimate relationship that *Love + Radio* is cultivating with its audience: Van Der Kolk invites people to call the *Love + Radio* "Secret Line" and leave a "confession" (37:42). We then hear a phone message: A woman confesses to working as an escort for a few years before she was married and became a soccer mom. Even her husband does not know her secret and "it feels good to be able to say it to people who don't know me and who hopefully aren't judging me." She then addresses the listeners directly and says, "You shouldn't judge people on their past decisions, because at the time I was a single mom and it was really easy money and it freed me up to spend lots of time with my kids." Podcast listening and engagement here become a literal confessional (as in a religious tradition) where absolution happens, in which potential judgments are negated in favor of recognizing other (more profound) human conditions and values.

Before leaving "The Silver Dollar" it is important to return briefly to its main content to reemphasize something in particular: while Davis is listening to Klansmen, we are listening to him. In that process there is a subtextual appeal for us to listen like Davis listens. This type of listening practice is necessary to empathy and Arthur Frank describes it in this way:

> People who treat others' stories as unhearable in order to hold themselves in their identity—often an identity of self-righteousness—give up on empathy, and that cost is dangerous. Other people's stories may be wrong, but forcing ourselves to hear them can bring us out of the complacency of certainty that our own named identity is incapable of such things. Giving up that certainty is an empathic practice.

Empathy then involves patient, steady, respectful work in hearing the stories that others tell about themselves in order to learn why another acted the way they did and how they made sense of those actions within the narrative logic of those stories (2016: 161–64). One could say that Davis comes to see himself as a character in the Klansmen's stories and the way he responds empathetically to them effects the way his character is ultimately written.

In the sequel to "The Silver Dollar," "How to Argue," Davis and Van Der Kolk seem to be more directly addressing the same audience that Arthur Frank has in mind: well-educated liberals at risk of falling into self-righteousness. Davis begins by saying, "You don't have to respect what they're saying, but you need to respect their right to say it" (01:12). Shortly after, he elaborates by saying that you cannot beat the hate out of someone, "but you can drive the hate out with logic and love and respect." Davis's detailed recounting of the white supremacist diatribes he listened to repeatedly is difficult, even painful, for a liberal-minded listener to absorb. In this way "How to Argue" offers us a *model of podcast listening*; Davis's willingness to enter into uncomfortable listening is a moral example of how we are meant to listen as well. But it is also a model for a broader podcast listening practice: allowing the uncomfortable into our ears is the first step in an empathetic relationship of progressive change. The episode ends with Davis describing his wedding and mentioning that a senior leadership figure of the Klan was one of his guests. A reporter presses the Klansman by asking, given his beliefs about miscegenation and white supremacy, why he would attend the wedding of a black man to a white woman (31:11). The Klansman's response was, "Because it's Daryl." Thus, following an empathetic listening practice, a human connection becomes more important than ideology, even to a Klansman.

Podcast intimacy: Lessons in how to listen

When I have sex, I think of radio.
When I have radio, I think of sex.

—Kaitlin Prest (in "Kaitlin + Mitra, Part 1" 2015)

In their interviews, both Baker and Prest assume the majority of their listeners listened on headphones. When using a search engine the meta-tags for *Love + Radio* directly advise us to "Listen with headphones." Edison Research's 2017 "Infinite Dial" (their annual statistical survey of podcast use in the United States) suggests this is plausible and shows a significant and rapidly growing majority of listeners using phones or other portable devices to listen to podcasts (implying headphones). The actual mechanics of how we listen defines, to a large extent, the nature of the relationship possible through podcasting, particularly its intimate dimensions.

Prest, in describing how headphone listening effects what they do through *The Heart*, notes:

> Podcasting is more of a one-on-one relationship . . . . [T]he tone that a lot of radio shows take is that they're talking to a big, wide, endless audience. Whereas with podcasting I think that a lot of the time it gets created for an individual . . . . [I]t's not people sitting in the car with their family.[16] (2015)

Earbuds in particular, placed as they are within the opening of the ear canal, collapse the physical space between a person speaking and the listener; the person speaking is literally inside the head, inside the body, of a listener. While earbuds, the means by which we have come to re-embody the voice of another in ourselves, are (historically speaking) relatively new to both listening and theory, headphones appear as important at several key points over the past 100 years, notably the 1920s and the 1960s (Nyre 2015: 280). What has been

---

[16] A one-on-one relationship between her and her listener is so important to Prest that she has resisted cohosting to maintain that personal intimate contact with a listener (2015).

written about earbuds so far has usually taken an emphasis very different from the one I am offering here. Earbuds, and earlier headphones for mobile devices, have been noted most often for what they keep out rather than what they let in. In Bull's significant contribution to the social science of modern listening, *Sound Moves: iPod Culture and Urban Experience*, his respondents typically describe using their headphones to create a privatized personal space of security as they walk through potentially threatening or unpleasant conditions. One such user described her experience of walking through New York streets isolated by headphones that allow her to pass "unfazed" by unwanted male attention and bland surroundings (2007: 344). The defensive function of headphones here contributes to a reclaiming of personal sexual space and establishing boundaries against unwanted advances. But the headphone function most important to our understanding of podcast intimacy is their opening us up to other kinds of advances—even uncomfortable ones.

Writing in the *Leonardo Music Journal*, Charles Stankievech offers an excellent history of this aspect of headphones and earphones by focusing on the stethoscope and its ability to interiorize the body of one person inside another. He concludes by suggesting that headphone/earphone listening dissolves the difference between "the contained and the container" and describes a connection between people that dissolves physical boundaries.[17] Because with earbuds the sound enters directly into the body, the external architecture of the torso, shoulders, head, and ears do not filter the sound. This, Stankievech observes, means that the equalization cues which source a sound's location are short-circuited (56–57), thus any acoustic sense of distance, exteriority, and even otherness becomes impossible. We could say then that earbuds allow for a hyper-intimacy in which the voice you hear is in no way external, but present inside you.

Earbuds push intimacy inside a body—they are, in very real sense, about re-*embodying* the voice. This observation cuts against a discourse familiar to media writing for nearly a century which described radio as a "disembodied voice."[18] When we listen to *The Heart* with earbuds and hear Prest masturbate,

---

[17] "For with the stethoscope there occurs a remapping of one body onto another. The interior space of the patient's body coincides with the interior of the doctor's body . . . . In this newly created space organs float in the abyss dissected by auditory exploration" (Stankievech 2007: 56).

[18] If, as Allen Weiss suggests in *Phantasmic Radio* (1995), virtually the entire conceptual history of radio is marked by the quintessentially modernist themes of the alienation of the self, the annihilation of the body and the dispersal of the disembodied voice, intimate podcasting offers a postmodern remedy and heals these wounds in remarkably un-ironic ways. As intimate earbud podcast listening regrounds us in the body, it also reconnects us with the other.

or hear characters or participants engaged in actual oral sex, the earbuds help to ground the grain of those voices in physical bodies (principally our own) engaged in physical contact.[19] This observation helps us appreciate the intimacy at play here as a physical experience rather than a metaphoric one. There is a suggestion of something similar contained in *The Heart's* logo: a drawing on a pink field of an anatomical human heart rather than the symmetrical and purely symbolic heart of a Valentine's Day card. Further, an emphasis on physicality closes the distance at both ends of *The Heart's* podcasting circuit. While earbuds penetrate our heads, Prest's position on the microphone is audibly and remarkably close. Undeniably, Prest's way of speaking intensifies this proximity. When you listen to even one episode of *The Heart* it is difficult to avoid being struck by the particular way she uses her voice:

> When I record I go into intimate pillow space, you know? I go into the feeling of the way that you feel when you wake up in the morning, and you remember that your lover is lying beside you, and you reach for them and pull them close to you, and say good morning in their ear. (2015)

While there are many other quality, well-produced, sex-positive podcasts (e.g., Dan Savage's *The Savage Lovecast*, *New York Magazine's Sex Lives*, and *Sex Nerd Sandra* on the Nerdist Network, etc.) none regularly have Prest's proximity to the microphone, and hence to us. Indeed, approached with the entirety of this framework in mind, this particular podcast series (if not podcasting itself to some degree) can stand in for oral/aural sex.

Prest's way of speaking and mode of podcast address are quite self-conscious. During the early development of *The Heart* she rejected advice from Roman Mars, the much more experienced creator and producer of the podcast *99% Invisible*, to conceive of her hosting as a "safe place for the listener" and to leave the sex, the whispering, and the intimacy to other voices in her podcasts. But Prest was not concerned about bracketing either sex or the intimacy it typically implies into segregated "safe" spaces. Instead, she says, the early mission of *The Heart* was to represent sex thoroughly in the truest way possible; so, for the microphone and the listener, she tried to "embody unbridled sexuality" while recording. While her microphone presence in the latter episodes is slightly less

---

[19] Whitehead makes a similar point in his contribution to "*Engaged* Magazine," noting that through the fila in the ear sound has unique access directly into the bones (1998).

overt than in earlier iterations of the podcast, it remained a consistent, defining characteristic:

> I'm sort of emitting like my crush on you in the show . . . . [I]n real life all of the sort of physical barriers to being attracted to somebody don't exist in [podcasting]. So you can fall in love with the voice in a way that you wouldn't fall in love with an image . . . . I want the door in peoples' hearts to eroticism to be opened when they listen to the show. (2015)

This focus on audio's (and now, in particular, podcasting's) compatibility with love and eroticism has been observed tangentially elsewhere. Williams, in her academic study of video pornography, argues that if the hard-core moving image was meant to place a viewer in a scene, "hard-core sound . . . seeks an effect of closeness and intimacy rather than of spatial reality" (1999: 123–24). *The Heart* is perhaps the most thorough podcasting example of complex explorations of the kind of intimacy described by Williams.

Earbud listening also permits routes to intimacy that extend beyond voice tone and granularity, and mike proximity. The assumption of this kind of listening allows, as Baker described, much more immersive and precise acoustic experiences which, while he says might work to some degree on speaker-based radio listening, engage much more "when the world is happening between your earphones" (2016). These include not just textured soundscapes, but tiny fragments of speech which are dropped in to the larger narrative to support, inflect, or arrest it some way. When I hear these "eardrops" while listening on speakers they usually register only as sonic interruptions, rather than speech I understand as speech; examples of this occur at 05:21 and 06:14 in "The Silver Dollar" and will also feature in the subsequent close analytical listenings of *The Heart* episodes. Baker often refers to these as "subliminal" and it is not until I listen with earbuds that I discern the language at all.

Some of these devices are so subtle that Baker did not expect a listener to absorb them on the first pass. He produced *Love + Radio* knowing that people can and do rewind and relisten—an approach he does not adopt when working in radio:

> In *Love + Radio* sometimes we're intentionally being abstract or we're counting on the fact that certain listeners aren't going to get all the allusions, and that's OK . . . . So when I'm working on a podcast I'm consciously thinking about that, like how can I hide Easter eggs or encode details or create more subtle experiences that people are going to interpret differently depending on their mood, depending on their setting, depending on their level of attention. (2016)

This native podcasting approach creates more intimate possibilities. Conversely, when working on radio Baker says his production techniques are generally less concerned with a listener's "emotional experience."

Eardrops and other accoutrements are not just puzzles for listeners to work out—encoded secrets to be unwrapped as their own reward—they instigate a heightened engagement and attention. They invite precisely the kind of intense listening mode needed for empathy to form in the podcast space—they set a listening tone. But they do not, in and of themselves, make for empathetic experiences. On *Love + Radio* and *The Heart* the producers brought about empathy very often through identity formation narratives, through a human seeking for belonging or searches for relationships that deliver a meaning or an insight. The most effective of these narratives contain actual models of empathetic listening within them—these are scenes in which the podcast listener hears, in an intimate context, a demonstration of someone or something listening in a compassionate, or at least an accepting or nonjudgmental, way. *The Heart*'s "How To Become a Princess" episode provides an excellent example of the possibilities for inviting empathy around an identity formation narrative supported by modeling.[20] In it Stefonknee, a Canadian transgender snowplow driver and mechanic, shares the story of the break-up of his[21] cisgendered, heterosexual marriage, her alienation from her children, her depression and homelessness, and her rediscovery of sex and finding deep and lasting love in a polyamorous kink relationship. The story is told gently, openly, and in detail, and (particularly the segment describing Stefonknee's new relationship, laced as it is with both tears and arousal) opens the door to quite deep empathy around human suffering and human recovery in listeners that presumably share few of Stefonknee's most obvious identity markers. Profoundly human moments like a painful break-up, a loss of access to children, and homelessness overcome barriers to empathy and dampen any reactionary judgment a heteronormative listener might have around Stefonknee's manifest identity.

Tuning in carefully to the specific sound and language of this episode allows us to witness the dynamics and larger purpose of modeled empathetic listening. At 06:56, Stefonknee lets out an audible, deep, and lengthy sigh as she begins

---

[20] This episode is also an excellent example of *The Heart*'s use of proximity effect with mike placement to create an "in your ear" or "in your head" sensation (01:10 and 02:41) as well as effective uses of sound design to support a narrative movement (01:44).

[21] The pronouns in this sentence are used to avoid confusion only. As Stefonknee recounts details of her past cisgendered life the masculine is used; when relating moments of and after her transition the feminine is used. "Their" proved too confusing in this context.

to describe entering a homeless shelter. Her despair at that moment was not absolute because, she says, "We had our babies to play with," referring to her doll Franny in particular. "You have dolls, so you're not alone. They're really good listeners too." The dolls function as surrogate podcast listeners within the frame of the story, soothing by their simple nonjudgmental presence. Particular listeners are a part of her story, comforting by their passive response; podcast listeners then are metaphorically included in the story and function in the same way. We are invited in and invited to empathize at human levels which, in some ways, transcend gender. Similarly Kaboli (narrating the story) models an "appropriate" nonjudgmental response throughout, describing the polyamorous living situation in the same sentence and with the same inflection as she describes the houseplants (08:59)—this lifestyle is so normalized as to be barely noteworthy.

It is not unreasonable to ask, as a critical listener, why Stefonknee would choose to relive such extremely painful and personal moments of her life in such a public forum. There is little for her to gain from it in terms of self-promotion, and similarly suggestions of narcissism do not ring completely true. More likely, the episode seems to suggest a desire for additional, simple human contact and recognition on the part of someone who had received little of these things earlier in life. But there also seems a desire here shared by both her and the producers: this is not necessarily or specifically to change perceptions of transgender people in society, but perhaps more broadly to increase the empathy in human interaction of all kinds.[22] This, it seems, is a key aspect of the understanding of empathy shared by these podcasters: it is not, and should not, be confined to individual stories. Instead these individual stories function, in Arthur Frank's words, to change the "moral imagination" of a broader public (2016: 156).

The podcast listener as wedding guest

One way of thinking of the network of relationships formed around and through these kinds of podcasts is reminiscent of a wedding ceremony: guests are invited to witness and participate in an intimate sharing of others. When pushed beyond a metaphor to involve guests at an actual live event, there is evidence that levels

---

[22] Similarly, Erik, the victim of childhood sexual abuse in Kirsti Melville's award-winning *The Storm* (ABC, 2016), describes the distressing interview he gives for that documentary as his "gift" to the world. It is pain offered in the hopes of eliciting some broader empathetic change in the culture.

of engagement and connection between producers, participants, and listeners—
and between listeners among themselves—increase (Edmond 2015).[23] With this
in mind, *The Heart*'s "Kaitlin + Mitra" episodes which describe how Kaboli and
Prest met, decided to work together in audio, relocated to Brooklyn, fell out,
reunited, and then got "married," episodes which include audio from the actual
"wedding" event, merit particular attention.

The first episode begins with their backstory, shares insecurities, moments of
comforting, physical tenderness and intimacy, and some inevitable professional
tension. The tone, with its naked honesty, openness, and innocence, has a gentle
child-like quality to it (while not at all "childish"). It offers a portrait of real
relationships utterly untainted by irony. The episode ends with a montage of
both Kaboli and Prest reading the break-up email that the former sent the latter.
While present in the first episode, the closeness in the second episode escalates.
It begins with Kaboli reading a fundraising announcement in her conventional
presenter voice; but it is punctuated by a barely audible eardrop whisper—which
prompted me to back-scan, increase the volume, and relisten—in which I hear
her say, "We love you. Thank you" (02:08).[24] Prest then takes over the story
and she swiftly brings listeners and guests back to her bedroom where she is
diligently at work editing programs while the outside world is dancing. We hear
an interweaving of a close-miked and tightly edited Prest having a conversation
with Kaboli in her head, the story of Prest signing the contract with Radiotopia,
and then the moment at the opera when Kaboli casually "proposes" to her. After
some deeply reflective lines on their past, Prest whispers "so moved" (12:51),
at which point we return to Prest's bedroom, the scene of so many and varied
intimacies. It is in this space of intimate resonances that we hear recordings
of Prest and Kaboli formalizing their future working partnership around *The
Heart*.

As Pachelbel's familiar wedding music sweeps in, the episode itself becomes
the intimate ritual of their wedding (held in October 2015 at a Brooklyn theatre)
and the podcast series itself becomes their marriage. The podcast then does not
merely exist in self-contained, anonymous, or discrete form; it is a manifestation
of a real, material, intimate human relationship, not confined in an audio sphere.
And, as every marriage needs formal validation, we the listeners are invited to
be their witnesses. This moment marks another characteristic particularly native

---

[23] These ideas are addressed much more thoroughly and critically in Chapter 3.
[24] On speakers, this presents as a barely audible flicker that is only just decipherable as a human voice.

to podcasting: listeners are actively invited into a world, a situation, or a set of relationships. We are invited to listen via social media and by friends as well as the hosts of other podcasts; and further, we as listeners were invited to attend Kaboli and Prest's wedding. Podcast listeners rarely wander into a podcast relationship in the manner of radio listeners surfing through channels or stations. This makes the podcasting space safer: there is an assumption of amity, and there are no wedding crashers; this makes podcasting extremely fertile ground for intimacy and makes that intimacy more viable.

Sharon Mashihi, an editorial adviser on *The Heart* and an ordained minister, officiates at the ceremony (15:30) and we hear Kaboli and Prest exchange their vows (with seemingly genuine emotion marked by sighs and sobs) in which they commit to nourishing each other's ideas. The audio scene is so intimate and we are so present with them that it is only when they promise to be good business partners that we are reminded that they are not in a conventional romantic relationship. Soothing a sore spot in their previous relationship, Prest offers the eardrop "I believe in you Mitra" at the end of this scene and again we hear the emotion in her voice (16:25). While not without its comedic moments and laugh lines—Kaboli's words at the ceremony include her saying that without Prest she would likely only "sell weed and watch cartoons" (17:10)—it never descends into parody or irony. This indeed can make the episode hard going for listeners with cultural backgrounds steeped in these modes. But even if a listener has these predispositions, it is difficult to fail to recognize the deep affect of this episode.

The service (but not the podcast) concludes with another lighthearted but genuine and non-ironic touch which emphasizes for a final time the connection between listening and intimacy—indeed, this is the emphasis of the producers' entire podcasting project: Prest and Kaboli exchanging earrings rather than typical wedding rings as Mashihi utters, "May these earrings hang from the appendages from which we listen" (Garfield 2015). The resistance to irony, I contend, is a conscious (rather than accidental) part of the way Kaboli and Prest think about their work and the kinds of relationships they seek with their audience. Irony splits an audience in two: the cognoscenti who laugh and the dupes who often get laughed at (Sconce 2002: 352). Irony then facilitates an identity formation around an exclusion of some "others" which seems the antithesis of the larger empathetic project of the *The Heart*. In fact, if irony exists at all around *The Heart*, it *might* be heard as a nudge and wink within the commercials. Sometimes the presenter might deliver advertising text over-earnestly and leave the listener wondering whether the tone signals the presenter's subtextual ambivalence to the product or service being promoted.[25]

Trust and empathy as artistic material

What happens when you're listening to somebody but you don't see them is that their words are real, their words are the words of somebody else but because you don't see them you create a visual around those words . . . . And that actual creation makes what they are saying literally a part of you. And so, what I think that does is that it allows audio to be a good vehicle for empathy because when you hear somebody talk . . . they become a part of you in a certain way. There's like a certain thing that happens that makes you understand what they're saying a little bit more internally . . . . So I think that's really a superpower of audio . . . it can actually be a vehicle for empathizing with other people. It can be a vehicle for exploring, for understanding emotional truth.

—Alex Blumberg (2017)

Trust has long been an inextricable part of the media relationship. News outlets covet the descriptor "most trusted" while virtually all advertising resorts to some kind of trust appeal. Trust has been described as a key component of podcasting which leads it to be perceived as a more genuine and reliable media form (Sheppard 2016). The importance of this phenomenon is heightened when we realize that while podcast listeners express trust in podcast presenters, hosts, production teams, and the shows themselves, general media consumers are ever more skeptical and trust appears as a diminishing resource in the larger media ecosystem. Perhaps we can account for this by noting that the podcasting circuit *begins with trust flowing in the other direction*: intimate podcast producers *trust their audiences* not just to behave well at weddings but to respect podcast content material and to process it in a "right way." They have a very nuanced set of expectations as to how it will be consumed and trust that the audience

---

[25] Around a particular food service commercial the presenter says of one of their offerings that she "has never tasted anything like it"—the likely implication being that she has not tried, and has no intention of trying, the item she is promoting. Interestingly, I do not hear any traces of potential irony around advertisements that resonate more clearly with *The Heart*'s content and ethos such as the Babeland online sex toy retailer or the *Masters of Sex* television program.

will live up to those expectations. In a radio setting, where we had armies of regulators, gatekeepers, and editors enforcing what could and could not be said, there was no social need for this bidirectional trust—the radio relationship was always chaperoned. In podcasting there is no chaperone and trust must work both ways. And as with any unchaperoned encounter, the risks are greater, as are the chances for failure, distress, and emotional damage (see, for example, the analysis of the Yellow Rain segment in *Radiolab*'s "Fact of the Matter" episode in Chapter 2). In fact the trust relationship on which podcast empathy depends is usually only obvious when it is tested, played with, unravels, or breaks down somehow.

A close analytical listening of the *Love + Radio* episode "A Red Dot," produced by Steven Jackson and Chloe Prasinos, documents a very intense instance of this trust being tested and empathy itself being used as material to instigate and explore shifting emotional currents around a podcast. While clearly inviting empathy, "A Red Dot" also exposes the dangers in allowing empathy to happen (as it usually does) uncritically or without any self-consciousness. To achieve this, the episode is extremely proficient in the way it uses many of the other invitations to intimacy and supportive narrative sound design techniques discussed earlier in this chapter. These are highlighted in the following close listening:

After a commercial and a content warning, the podcast properly begins at 01:02 with long stretch (sixteen seconds) of human breathing punctuated by some very subtle mouth sounds. This focus on the grain of the voice tells us we are about to hear another human being: the intimacy of the close-miking of "Frank," the interviewee, has primed a potentially empathetic response which will be more clearly invited in another two minutes when Frank tells us, with fear and emotion on his quavering voice, how he was violently assaulted by a man with hammers after coming home from the store one day. A small crescendo of low frequency noise (04:25) which peaks around the word "pervert" is a clue to something that will only be revealed later. I, the listener, am totally with Frank in this scene, trusting him and experiencing the assault and its strength of feeling from his perspective through the timbre of his voice. The emotion of his retelling is raw and real.

At 07:00, after another long (ten second) pause, in which Frank and I (the listener) let the adrenaline subside after the first harrowing scene, Frank asks the producers for a break because he is finding the recording "a little intense" and he would like some tobacco to calm his nerves. This foreshadows the end of his final, much more empathetically complex vignette. He also, at this point, very cordially offers a producer a warm-up for her coffee, and it is here that I experience my first tiny misgivings: his request for a break seems almost too perfectly delivered—particularly as he foregrounds the "intensity" of the hammer assault story, wanting to make sure we picked up that feeling should it not have come across in his telling of it; he is modeling the response he invites in us. There is something vaguely unsettling in his voice, but I cannot specify it.[26] While nothing is ever spelled out and while the sensations are very vague at this point, I seem to be placed on a knife's edge in this moment between empathy and suspicion; I am generally predisposed to identify with Frank but traces of wariness are also making themselves known. It is only at 07:36 that Frank formally introduces himself as a convicted sex offender for an assault on a minor thirty-five years earlier (it is revealed later that the victim was less than fourteen years old and that he was in his early twenties). Frank delivers this information in a clear and somehow friendly way, openly admitting to his sexual offense in the past, expressing regret, and suggesting that he is no longer the person he was at the time of his crime.

He then wants to offer some context for what happened, and when he frames his offense in terms of "lifestyle" and "addiction" (as if it might have been a fashion choice) that I begin to get suspicious of his words alone (10:11). When asked if the pedophile's impulses ever go away he repeats, "For me it did," twice to drive his point home. As he tells us that he cannot imagine being trapped as a pedophile, that it would be a "huge nightmare," I begin to feel that he is trying very hard to convince me, but I also feel that the extra efforts need not necessarily imply that he is lying.

Frank then describes his post-conviction life and the situation of other sex offender "registered citizens" and mentions confidential programs to keep them from reoffending. In this discussion his emphasis is squarely on the pain and difficulty it will cause perpetrators when they get caught; in terms of his own empathetic reactions, virtually none of them extend to victims or potential victims (15:20). When asked by a producer if the act that led to his conviction was consensual, Frank initially skirts the question because he does not want to speak for his victim, but when pressed he says that he perceived that she was receptive. At 17:15 he describes his thoughts of causal regret on the morning after by saying to himself "Oh man, I shouldn't have done that," as if he is

---

[26] I know about the story before I listen to it the first time so it is likely that I am predisposed to misgivings, even at the beginning of this initial listen, to hearing a trace of Sarah Koenig's "charming psychopath" from Chapter 8 in Frank's voice.

lamenting a hangover. Lots of lengthy silences (of five seconds or more) happen around moments like these which force us to consider what is being said and how it is being said; in them I cannot help but mull over Frank's agenda in giving the interview.

Amid his describing several conventional tropes of penitence (such as going into a church on the day after the incident to ask for forgiveness) I do finally hear a moment of broader empathy at 24:12—not for his victim, but for his victim's father. Frank says, "I looked at him as being justified for his rage" while being beaten by him after Frank admitted to him what had happened. Frank says that he allowed himself to be beaten because he felt he deserved it and it made him feel "unburdened" in the moment. In these words, which again have a ring of rehearsal about them, Frank is also trying to position himself as someone worthy of my empathy; but in addition to that sense of rehearsal I am also aware of the remarkably skillful way that the producers have edited the interview to both enhance the opportunity for that empathy with Frank and further, largely through the use of lengthy silences, to invite me to question any empathy that might be directed toward him as a possible product of cunning manipulation.

Frank claims that when the police arrested him they forgot to Mirandize him so his lawyer could have had his charges thrown out but that he decided instead to bare the just consequences of his actions. This incredible detail is followed by another clear appeal to empathy:

> I've done something wrong, I feel like I'm broken. I feel like I'm not human because I've done this, and now I have to carry it. And, you know, who can you go and tell? No one. No one. (25:33)

This invitation for me (a good and liberal podcast listener) to reassure him that his empathy and his regret mean that he is human and that he is not alone becomes extremely troubling: it prompts me to question the values—those humane and empathetic podcast values—I have absorbed through my listening to other intimate podcasts, to other episodes of *The Heart* and *Love + Radio*. In showing or suggesting that Frank might be carefully calculating this responses, the producers play with and problematize my own empathy, they seem to suggest that I should not hold empathy unconditionally; it should be applied with consideration and tempered by context.

When he comes to tacitly suggest—precisely while saying that he does not want to suggest—that the girl led him on and invited him into the situation, a producer interrupts, saying it sounds like he is trying to justify his actions (26:39). There is another swell of extremely low frequency shuddering noise when Frank replies by saying he wants to distance himself from the event and that "It's not who I am." At 28:20 a producer, in a response that coincides with my own (or perhaps even prompts it), says she is getting angry with him for the "excuses" that we hear cropping up through the more conventional expressions of remorse. Frank's, "So I participated," response is calm and measured but possibly tinged with a touch of dismissal.

He makes another direct appeal to our empathy when he says at 30:18 that the only way that he can forgive himself is to hear from his victim that "she is OK" and to hear that she forgives him; he then modifies this by saying that he would accept the fact that she might not forgive him as long as he hears it from her. This then leads into a much more direct story which models the kind of empathy he is seeking, not from his victim, but from the people he is speaking to (us the listeners and the larger world). Frank describes a scene at a self-esteem building workshop in which the participants were put into pairs and partners were asked to reveal to each other the worst thing they had ever done: "Being said it was a safe environment, I felt OK with letting her know. I simply said that I had molested a child. She held on to my hand, as if to say it's OK, it's OK." Then, in a move that closely resembles what is happening through this particular act of podcasting, he is put into a position in which he is asked to reveal to everyone in the whole room what he has done:

> Everybody in the room came up and held me. I was not stoned to death, and that felt good because it was about, I would say, six months after I had gotten out of jail and returned to my home.

Frank offers this story as an example of the way he wants to be treated by us. But I am left perpetually in limbo: is he suffering and wanting empathy, or does he instead like the attention that comes his way when he says he wants empathy and forgiveness?

This state of uncertainty is allowed to continue. In the midst of phrases that can have the ring of platitude ("We can live in a space of love," and "I just ask folks not to hate") he describes how his business collapsed in the wake of Megan's Law.[27] In its perfection, this story sounds somewhat contrived. But as the episode begins to near its end, Frank's stories become more clearly caricature

---

[27] Megan's Law was a federal law enacted in the United States in 1994 in the wake of the abuse and murder of Megan Kanka; it is used as an informal name for subsequent state laws. These laws required sex offenders to register with their local law enforcement and allowed the publication of their names on websites.

and cartoonish. In a supermarket Frank says someone shouted at a friend of his, "There's a sex-offender over by the vegetables!" But throughout it all he cultivates not only the persona of someone persecuted, a victim in his own right making a legitimate appeal for empathy, but also of someone aware that the empathetic circuit begins by being moved by someone else (e.g., he mentions visiting several times the man in jail convicted of attacking him with hammers).

In the final ten minutes of the podcast Frank loses his composure and any empathy I might have cultivated for him feels utterly rebuked. At his most egregious, he talks about the current persecution of sex offenders as having similarities to the situation of Jews under the Nazis. The adrenaline and the intensity reach a troubling climax when he quotes the Pledge of Allegiance, describes registrants having to sleep on buses, and talks about explosions of rage and potential mass shootings because sex offenders have been bullied to such an extent. While earlier I had been working to keep in my mind the possibility that he might be legitimately upset at the living conditions of registrants, the anger and menace audible in Frank's voice as he curses and makes threats in this moment make it extremely hard for me to maintain even a trace of empathy for him.

At 49:56 a producer invites Frank to give them (even off-mike) a clear account of what actually happened during the offense. The seventeen-second pause that follows is interrupted only by a slight and considering "hmm." Emotion now gone from his voice, Frank's tone is very analytical when he says to the producers: "This is interesting, because fear comes up now . . . . Will I become more of a demon, or will I become more human? What do you think?" He is clinically aware of his own feelings and utterly focused on managing the way he is perceived. In the end he agrees to tell the story off-mike because, he says, "I trust you guys." At that point he reveals, with some emotion on his voice, that he is "very nervous" and again asks for a bit of tobacco. It is important to note that while at the end I am much less disposed to give him the same benefit of the doubt I gave him in the first scene, I do still question to what extent he is sincere or calculating.

In the closing minutes, as he and the producers are mulling over how or whether to proceed, Frank invokes the connection that has formed between himself and the producers, a connection which presumably he sees as extending to the podcast's listeners as well:

> This is a relationship we've developed. We're in a relationship. That's hugely important. So for you to know that what I have spoken is the truth, then I need to tell the whole truth. (54:19)

In what feels like a monstrous twisting of Whitehead's assertion that the materiality of radio is a set of relationships, my place as an empathetic listener has been profoundly destabilized. Frank's words make me feel somewhat complicit in his unclear but certainly unsavory project; this, in turn, forces me to interrogate my investment in podcasting relationships writ large. I am left questioning who manages these relationships that are the real material of podcasting, who controls them and how they are invoked into being.

Frank's final question to the producers ("What do you think?") could also, tauntingly, be addressed to the podcast audience and is a version of a question other people have asked me after listening to "A Red Dot": Why was this man's story podcast? (In fact Frank *himself* questions at one point whether or not his is a story that the producers want to tell.) This prompts other questions: to what extent is this episode sensationalist and controversial for controversy's sake, or, to what extent is this an experiment in the limits of podcast compassion, empathy, and intimacy? Frank's was not a voice I wanted inside my ears, my head, my body, or my mind. The creative force of "A Red Dot" is the invitation to ponder how and why I let this man inside me to the extent that I did and, more importantly, the invitation to think critically on the very idea of podcast empathy. When I take up these reflections I come to see empathy less as an unerring human predisposition and more as a malleable artistic material; I also come to see the podcast producers themselves less as narrative artists and more as empathy artists.

5

Don't Look Back: The New Possibilities
of Podcast Drama

When there is a new form there is a real compulsion to justify it, to really explain. Why are you reading this thing? Why is this sound in your ears? There is a compulsion to justify it.

—Eli Horowitz (*"Homecoming* S01E01" 2016)

Homecoming was Gimlet Media's standout production of the autumn of 2016, billed as being their first "scripted podcast" series. When I first heard this term I found it puzzling that they had chosen this to describe what was plainly an audio drama. They seemed to want it to appear to be a new form of work, but then Gimlet exists on the knife-edge of podcast commercialization and Brooklyn hipsterdom. They probably felt terms such as "radio," "radio drama," and even "narrative audio" were outmoded for Gimlet's audiences. *Homecoming* was set up by its creators as representing the inception of a new medium, but was marketed using the familiar audio drama trope of being "like TV for your ears." The show itself was fine, though it took itself very seriously; there was a celebrity actor from the TV series *Friends* in one of the roles and there were some fantastically written and delivered phone conversations. Each episode concluded with a studio discussion where sponsors were credited, and Horowitz was interviewed about the program by his boss, Gimlet Media's CEO, Alex Blumberg. He explained why he had chosen that particular format for his work; how there is a necessity with new forms of media for the modes and means by which the audience are experiencing that media to be contextualized within the text itself. Audiences are not ready to adapt to new modes of consuming content. Early novels, he argued, were epistolary, early films mimicked the set up and form of the stage, and early dramas in podcast have often taken the form of faux-reportage, placing the microphone and apparatus of recording into the characters' hands and in the scenes. *Homecoming* would attempt to push on beyond this starting point; his series would truly break new ground. In so doing, Horowitz at once reduced the entire history of audio drama production as being a "kitschy or retro exercise" that he wished to avoid, and he also failed to register the similarities between his own work and those other podcast drama productions, from which he was distancing himself.

Audio drama is not a "new form" and its history cannot be swept aside, but since 2015 it has experienced profound changes. What *Homecoming*'s first season represented was not a watershed moment in the history of audio entertainment, rather it was an example, a well-funded and high-profile example, of the development of a subset of audio drama, the podcast drama. This chapter will discuss the qualities and identity of this form, and will detail how it is defined by the people who produce it, the people for whom it is produced, and the manner in which it is consumed. The audio drama movement is bursting with potential; David Rheinstrom, producer of the review show *Radio Drama Revival*, describes this as a state comparable to "a pre-Cambrian explosion of talent and material" (quoted in Greenhalgh 2016). Podcast drama is dominated by a small group of shows that have garnered widespread recognition and tens of millions of downloads. There is also a plethora of fan and home-produced work, a mass of comedies, genre shows, and amateur productions that speak of a vibrant and developing creative movement. As Rheinstrom's analogy suggests, the form has the potential to expand and grow beyond its current niche identity, to gain traction and mainstream acceptance. There is also the possibility that it may ossify, becoming locked and restricted by the tropes and formulas that have proven successful to date. This chapter is being written at this moment of change, and is an attempt to identify a new creative form as it establishes and gains coherence.

"The lights have gone out"

Podcasting offers the promise of the open internet (Berry 2006), of free access and the possibility of unconstrained creativity, yet producers of podcast drama stand accused of producing works that lack diversity and range. A range of academic, critical, and production commentators have suggested that there are too many genre works, too many works for a tight demographic of male, thirty something listeners (Mortimer 2016). Its creators have forgotten the history of audio drama, and in so doing have failed to realize the potential of the form (Verma 2017a); they are unwilling to experience and challenge the audience (Weiner 2014) and are not offering its audience a new experience. They are merely "remediating" the forms and methods of traditional radio broadcasting (Bottomley 2015). A survey of the top twenty podcasts of September 2017 would appear to support the last of these accusations. *Limetown*, *The Message*, *The Black Tapes*, and *Tanis* are constructed as reporter-led shows fronted by "Koenigesque" presenters; *Welcome to Night Vale* is a community radio show; *Homecoming*'s drama is constructed from "found sound"; *The Bright Session*'s drama unfolds through a series of recordings made on a psychiatrist's couch; and the first season of *Down the Wire*. Each employs a device that positions the means of recording in the drama itself, thus giving an explanation as to why the audio exists.

The first line of the first play written for radio was "The lights have gone out." Richard Hughes's 1924 production *Comedy of Danger* was the story of a group of miners trapped underground, in darkness. By placing the characters in the same visually reduced state as the audience, Hughes demonstrated that he didn't trust his audience to do the mental work of constructing scenery, creating costumes, and blocking action that is typically required in a modern radio drama. Instead the drama occurred in darkness and the audience were encouraged to turn out the lights at home so that they could share in the experience with the cast (Rodger 1982: 15). Ninety years later podcast drama producers appear to be guilty of presenting the medium in a similarly reduced form.

Historical perspectives

There has been an awareness of the potential of the web as a means by which audio drama may be distributed for over twenty years. In 1999 Tim Crook recognized that the internet offered an open and democratic platform that would allow "young writers" to produce and distribute work without experiencing the "brunt of exclusion and denial of opportunity" that the BBC's drama commissioning process presented (Crook 1999: 41). For seventy years the BBC had been the only realistic source of funding for English-speaking radio drama (Dann 2015). The costs of a full-cast production are high, not when compared to television or film, but when it is compared to other forms of audio production. Since the passing of the first "Golden Age" of radio in the United States the BBC has been the only body willing to fully fund any volume of radio drama in the English-speaking world. The scale of the BBC Radio Drama Department's output extended its influence beyond the medium of radio, making it, with over 600 works produced every year[1] and a combined audience for all its output of nearly 500 million (Imison 1991: 3), an important component of the cultural identity of the UK.[2]

There were early experiments made by the Corporation to distribute works online, including a *Drama of the Week* offering, and Jeremy Mortimer's platform for short-form audio works, *Audiotheque*. Despite this it took the introduction of RSS distribution, nearly a decade after Crook's statement, before the web's potential as a distribution platform for audio drama began to be realized.[3] What podcasting offered audio drama producers was access to an audience, but the reach was limited and the field remained specialized (a "niche within a niche" (Greenhalgh 2016)) and dominated by amateur and home-recorded productions. These provided a testing ground for ideas and writers, a space equivalent to the theatrical fringe that hadn't been available before, but the BBC remained the main source of fully costed drama budgets. Independent audio drama producer Dirk Maggs spent several years trying to set up an internet model of distribution for his production company Perfectly Normal Productions. He failed to find any investment for such a project because

> as soon as you put a writer and actors in the equation, people do not want to invest in radio ... it's just too expensive. ... Between 2004 and 2007, we were in numerous *Dragon's Den* [the U.K. version of the pitching show *Shark Tank*] situations, saying, "Listen, we can make wonderful sounding drama, put it on the net and people will buy it and we can show you figures that would ensure that in five years we get into profit," and they say, "Well, how much do you want us to invest? 250,000 pounds? Forget it. Where's our return on our investment?" (Maggs 2009)

The BBC's dominance of the radio drama as a cultural form has at once maintained it, and constrained it. The terms of the Royal Charter, by which it

---

[1] In 2017 each week the BBC broadcasts five *Afternoon Plays*, a *Saturday Play*, a *Classic Serial* episode, five short-form *Woman's Hour* Dramas on Radio Four, and a *Sunday Play* on Radio Three.

[2] There is an impressive body of writers who were given the support and resources required to start their careers: John Arden, Giles Cooper, Robert Bolt, Bill Naughton, John Mortimer, Harold Pinter, Tom Stoppard, and Joe Orton all received what David Hendy describes as "BBC Radio's institutional kiss of life at crucial moments in their careers" (Hendy 2007: 194).

[3] There were early experiments and attempts to set up online audio drama distribution companies and networks. One such was run by the Sci-Fi channel who in 2000 approached New York-based producers (myself included) to create genre works for online distribution.

is granted the right to broadcast, stipulate that the Corporation cannot produce work that is specifically intended for the web only, all works must be initially broadcast as part of the output of a traditional radio station before being made available online (Friend 2016).[4] This traditional broadcast audience is greater in number, and takes precedence over the digital listenership, with podcasting being diminished to being as a stepping stone for younger audiences, an introduction to speech radio proper (Friend 2016). This has limited the form of works; programming must fit around the listenership and the schedule, rather than vice versa. Single dramas become a necessity of radio broadcasting because of the unpredictability of the audience's listening patterns; they are not expected to follow long and complex stories across several different days. Producing works primarily intended for broadcast on terrestrial stations constrains the potential audience. Works are created to satisfy a tightly defined demographic, with the majority of dramas being broadcast by BBC Radio Four, a station that has an audience identified as being aged 45+, of social class ABC1, and predominantly female (Dann 2015). Drama projects for BBC Radio Four are bought and green-lit by a single commissioning editor for "Drama and Fiction", so effectively a very high proportion of the development of the form was directed through a single individual and intended for a single type of audience. While experimental, innovative, and challenging works were commissioned, such works were broadcast in fringe slots, in isolation, and with minimal recognition. For writers working in radio, drama is an experience that Hendy characterizes as being "akin to shouting into a deep hole. Writers live by being noticed, but radio leaves hardly any trace" (Hendy 2007: 195). The form of audio drama has not had a chance to expand and diversify because works are lost, creators are disassociated, and critical analysis has been limited. Radio drama has never had a coherent movement or recognized body of work, there has yet to be, as producer K. C. Wayland points out, a "French New Wave of audio drama" (2016) or for that matter a "Dogma" or "Mumblecore" or "Noire" or anything.

What the new generation of audio drama writers and producers have is the opportunity to develop works outside of the BBC. For the first time in seventy years the center of gravity for the field is no longer to found in the studios of Portland Place, but has shifted across to a thousand bedroom studios, lock-ups,

---

[4] Issues relating to online licensing and contracts for writers and actors also held the BBC back. Initially, when they were released to the web, dramas were only available for a week, and only produced by in-house producers (Mortimer 2016). In 2017 the BBC has a *Drama of the Week* podcast, which takes a single work from the seven or eight broadcast each week and makes it available online.

and improvised recording suites in the United States where new possibilities are emerging and being realized.

Running from the past

As Crook predicted, writers are no longer reliant upon oligopolies to have their work produced, and producers no longer need to interact with the commissioning process, or pitch meetings, or broadcast schedules. Here is, as Sterne argued, an "alternate cultural model of broadcasting" (Sterne et al. 2008) that allowed two off-off Broadway writers with a $85 USB microphone to gain a global following and hundreds of millions of downloads. Fink and Cranor, the creators of *Welcome to Night Vale*, are the poster boys (or most high-profile examples) of the limitless creative potential of UGC-derived audio drama. Their backgrounds are in experimental theatre, and their work, for all that it is an affectionate satire of the modes of speech that are intrinsically rooted in radio broadcasting (Bottomley 2015), is born of downtown New York's theatre scene. They do not carry with them an awareness of the history of radio drama, and what that form represents.

Podcast drama producers are drawn from a different set of cultural experiences and influences to radio drama producers, with film commonly being cited as the medium in which they originally trained and worked. Zack Ackers and Skip Bronkie, the writers and producers of *Limetown,* were originally independent film producers. K. C. Wayland describes how he became interested in audio fiction when he was in a studio recording actors for animated works, and learned how powerful the voice on its own could be. Eli Horowitz, a writer and editor for McSweeney's before he wrote and directed *Homecoming,* places film as "a touchstone" in the production of the series because: "We're all so drenched in movies from such a young age—it's hard to not be influenced by the scenes and beats and atmospheres" (quoted in Taylor 2017). These producers and writers can describe audio drama as being a new medium because to them it is. They don't need to push their art, or to be original, because they are not carrying an understanding of or expectations for the field in which they are working. They are making the same breakthroughs and the same mistakes as have happened before, but that does not matter to them, because the form really is new to them, and they are making of it what they wish.

By running "full tilt" from the legacy offered by the history of audio drama (Verma 2017b) they are at once recycling the forms and tropes of traditional radio (Bottomley 2015) and failing to understand what the medium offers. The imagination is completely freed in audio production (Hendy 2000: 118; Douglas 2004: 2; Crissell 1994: 6–10). The producer can stage any and every imaginable event because they don't need a stage, or a set, or special effects, or props, or actors who even look like their characters. Everything and anything is possible with this form, but when Gimlet Media, Wayland Productions, and Pacific Northwest Stories market their works as being "TV for your ears" or "Movies without pictures" they are making their audience conscious of the sense that has been deleted from the experience. Podcast drama producers, with their reliance on found sound formats and their avoidance of complex action and scenography, appear to be unwilling to trust the audience to use their imagination to compensate for missing sensory data.[5]

Tim Crook identifies access to the "inner life of characters" (1999), the freedom to seamlessly access the thoughts inside a character's mind, as being another pillar upon which radio drama is constructed. Podcast dramas feature "sleep diaries," recorded "notes to self," and pieces performed to microphone that are reminiscent of the infamous "I'm sorry Mom" monologue delivered to camera in the film *The Blair Witch Project* (1999). These are scenes where the character talks to the audience but the audience does not directly experience the character. They do not hear the world through their ears and the thoughts in their head, techniques that are long evidenced and established in radio drama works such as the BBC Radio Four productions of Hattie Naylor's *Wooden Heart* (2005), Lee Hall's *Spoonface Steineberg* (1997), and Tristian Sturrock's *Mayday Mayday* (2015).

Producers of podcast dramas are not using these techniques, because they have not encountered them, and they do not have the cultural awareness of the form that BBC producers are assumed to possess. This is not necessarily learned through academic study, or classes in radio drama, which are marginalized

---

5 In *Homecoming* there is no sound that is not diegetic, there is no voice-over or narration, and no action, because "the audio format prevented him from structuring his story around physical action" (in Hess 2016). An example of this is found in the third episode where a medical patient has a breakdown and rips another patient's tongue out; we do not hear this grisly and chaotic event, rather it is told to us the day after by another character. This is a technique used in television to avoid having to shoot costly sequences.

in most curriculae.[6] Rather there is a cultural awareness of the form that is testament to the pervasive influence that BBC radio has upon the culture of the British middle class. Radio drama producers will have heard the soap opera *The Archers* as tea is prepared, caught the ending of an *Afternoon Play* as they channel surf in the car or stabbed at buttons of cassette recorders to capture the opening bars of *Journey of the Sorcerer*, *The Hitchhiker's Guide to the Galaxy* theme.[7] Podcast drama producers have none of those expectations and none of that understanding. They are approaching the form unburdened by history or cultural expectation.

Jonathan Mitchell—*The Truth*

"They're made out of meat"

"Meat?"

"Meat. They're made out of meat."

"Meat?"

"There's no doubt about it. We picked several from different parts of the planet, took them aboard our recon vessels probed them all the way through. They're completely meat."

"That's ridiculous . . . you're asking me to believe in sentient meat."

—"They're Made Out of Meat" written by
Terry Bisson and produced by *The Truth* (2012)

"They're Made Out of Meat": A pair of disembodied alien intelligences discuss their startling encounter with intelligent carbon-based life forms, sentient flesh that communicates by "slapping their meat together." "Man vs. Nature": Three friends argue about who slept with whose wife as they float on a dingy lost at sea; "Scavenger Hunt": the relationship between two work colleagues unravels

---

6   The history of audio drama is fractured and discordant; the form lacks what Michelle Hilmes describes as being "a sense of expressive continuity" linking one work to the next (quoted in Verma 2017b). A coherent taxonomy has yet to be established through which techniques and approaches may be described. Chion's terminology was developed for the analysis of screen sound and while Crook (1999) and Rattigan (2002) have posited a set of terms they have failed to be widely adopted.

7   When I worked with Simon Jones (who played Arthur Dent in the radio version of *The Hitchhiker's Guide to the Galaxy*) in New York, I wanted to take the opportunity to tell him about the influence the series had had upon me as a child, serving as an early catalyst for my appreciation of the medium. I began to tell him this, getting as far as "Simon, I thought I should tell you—" before he interrupted me: "I know what you're going to say. That I've been a great inspiration. Yes? That we wouldn't be here if it wasn't for Arthur Dent? I get that a lot from people of your age."

as they bicker their way around a New York treasure hunt that is meant to be a bonding exercise; "Intimacy Challenge": a group of dinner party guests take an extract of the Lotus flower and secrets spill forth. The characters in Jonathan Mitchell's *The Truth* podcast are never comfortable, never certain of themselves, their lives are filled with hesitancy and uncertainty. They stumble into each other, over each other, and leave one another hanging in pauses pregnant with potential. There is a familiarity to the themes and set-ups of Mitchell's short-form dramas. It is a world of wry humor, awkward dates, and tech references that speak of the concerns and lives of white, middle-class urban America. These stories are played out with an improvised and naturalistic character that is striking and original.

Mitchell launched *The Truth* with Hillary Frank in 2009 and the show gained profile three years later when it was adopted by Roman Mars's Radiotopia network, and a piece, "Tape Delay," was featured on *This American Life*. *The Truth* presents fortnightly works, vignettes characterized by loose and flowing dialogue created through a combination of script, improvisation, and editing. The works are born of Mitchell's desire to recreate the naturalistic delivery of film dialogue and a love of the controlled free-form creativity that is found in the music of Frank Zappa. His background is in music, and his final degree submission at Mills College, Oakland, was a piece of musique concrete built from conversational speech. This process fed into his "obsession" with film, and he realized that there was an opportunity to expand his experimental works into, if not dramas, voice-led works, sound pieces that he would never have had the finances or resources to film. He wanted to explore the intonation and delivery of natural speech, which appealed to him because it was "more human" and "more expressive" than composed or scripted speech (Mitchell 2015).

Mitchell cites his time working at *Radiolab*, and his appreciation of *This American Life*, as being key to the development of how he uses narrative structure to shape and frame his audio compositions. Mitchell places a great emphasis on the role of story in his work, talking about the relationship of his characters to the plot, and of the music and rhythms of story. He discusses his shows in terms of plot points, inciting incidents and story beats. This is the vocabulary of narrative structure, yet these elements are not immediately apparent in the finished pieces. There is movement in the works, people have confrontations, they develop and learn about themselves, but there is also a looseness born of their improvised performance that serves to disguise the frames upon which the story has been constructed. They are what radio drama producer Jeremy

Mortimer describes as: "beautifully subtle, and intriguing portraits of people, places, time, and things that are not necessarily narrative driven" (Mortimer 2016).

Mitchell develops his show's material in a manner that is closer to a comedy TV show than to an arts-based audio drama. He meets a team of writers each week for pitch and discussion sessions where five to seven ideas are presented afresh, and existing scripts read and developed toward a production version. The final drafts are taken into the studio where Mitchell's actors are encouraged to learn their lines so that they can be performed by rote, as opposed to reading them from the page (as would be the case for most radio drama). They are asked to perform until they learn the scene, "then I do a few takes where they are paraphrasing it, and then I'll do things like say 'surprise each other, take as long as you need to do this scene, we can go for another half hour if you want'" (Mitchell 2015). What he is seeking is the patter and pauses of real speech, the hesitancy and unfinished sentences. The non-sequiturs and half-heard diction that he had encountered in the cinema and in the unscripted dialogue of reality television—a form that Mitchell cites as an inspiration for his search for "liveness" and "naturalism" in his production. He works with actors who are familiar with one another, often drawn from the same improv theatre company, allowing there to be confidence and informality in the performances. Recording takes place on location whenever possible, using mikes mounted on boom poles to capture actors as they move and respond to each other. This material is then shaped and crafted into coherence in the edit. Here, in a process reminiscent of his earlier experimental works, he takes unformed naturalistic speech and gives it form and structure.

The performances themselves are perfectly pitched for close earbud listening. Mitchell sights the growth of Mumblecore among his influences, a cinematic form that was defined by its unformed and at times incomprehensible dialogue. There is little place for such patterns of speech in radio drama because it is produced to be listened as a secondary activity. A traditional BBC radio play must cut through the background noise of cooking, cars, and children that are keynote sounds of their listeners' everyday lives. The muttered, unhurried, and at times half-formed delivery of *The Truth* is designed to be experienced on headphones. It is an intimate experience with the voice breathed directly into the audience's ears.

What locates *The Truth* as a podcast drama, as opposed to an audio drama, is not necessarily its content (though earlier episodes favored speculative fiction and genre-based scenarios). Rather it is the performances and production, the naturalism and found sound aesthetics, the avoidance of the non-diegetic. The audience rarely hear the inner thoughts of characters or the guiding voice of a narrator. Recording devices, or the process of recording, feature in the set-up of several stories, as if there must be an intrinsic reason, woven into the work, for it to exist as sound alone. *The Truth* borrows from film, it borrows from musique concrete, and it borrows from the music of Frank Zappa and reality TV. Very little of it feels or sounds like radio drama, but that does not matter because its audience have not grown up listening to radio drama; but they do have a lifelong understanding of the cadences and performative patterns of the cinema.

The limits of the market

Podcast drama is distinct from other kinds of audio drama because of the identity of its producers, and of its audience, but this can limit the scope and potentiality of its content. Despite the apparent freedom the podcast producer has to determine who their audience will be, the pressures of the market mean that works that appeal to particular demographics are favored. Independent podcast drama producers create works that appeal to the core podcast listening demographic, and successful projects will be born of the tastes of the audience— one that is described as being variously "middle-American Millennials" (Dryden 2017), male and under fifty (Mortimer 2016), and "geeky" (Greenhalgh 2017). Listeners are not presented with a broad range of listening because show classifications, algorithms, and the architecture of the online aggregators draw them toward the kind of work that they already know they like, or that have already been successful. This is the appification of audio media that encourages the audience to "listen in" rather than explore and "listen out" (Lacey 2014).

Podcasting exists outside of direct regulation with no procedure or policy to ensure diversity of content. BBC was built on the principles that the Corporation should inform, educate, and entertain the population. Early radio audiences had no choice as to what they could listen to; there was only one station broadcast and the feeling was that what "the audience often had to take from [the BBC] was rather like medicine: it was not altogether pleasurable, but it sometimes made them feel better" (Crissell 2002: 46). This Reithian spirit still exists within the Corporation, the sense that it is their role, as former Head of Radio Drama Caroline Raphael explains, "to lead taste [and] to create taste as well as to give people what they want at the same time" (Raphael quoted in Dann 2015). This does not apply to the podcast space where audiences can choose to listen to what they like when they like. If they do not want their "medicine" there are a thousand other productions on offer that will be more pleasing to the palette. Michael J. Collins observes that they are drawn to works that reflect the concerns of their lives. *Welcome to Night Vale* kills its interns; its audience understand this and get the joke because they are interns themselves. They are part of an emergent generation of digital natives for whom mass observation, paranoia, and conspiracy are part of their daily digital experience (Collins 2016). *The Truth* is laced with the neuroses of its young(ish), urban, technically literate audience. Podcast dramatists frequently use the issues that bond the Millennial generation as story devices: characters are overworked, they suffer sleep deprivation, are concerned about money and job security, and are made to feel powerless.

Full-cast audio drama is several degrees cheaper when compared to film and television productions, and this is often positioned as being an attraction of the form (Mitchell 2015; Wayland 2016; Bae 2017). Despite this, the cost of audio drama production when compared to other forms of speech media can be prohibitively expensive. An hour of full-cast BBC radio drama costs £22,000 to produce (BBC 2017); this will pay for project development, the writer's fee, studio hire, cast fees, a producer, a director, an engineer, a sound designer, and music rights. Most podcast drama producers, working without the fiscal support of the license fee, must strip productions down to allow them to operate on budgets much lower than this figure. Jonathan Mitchell creates *The Truth* for approximately $10,000 per hour, and can only do so by operating as a "one-man band," taking on many of the preproduction and postproduction roles, and by not properly paying himself (Mitchell 2015). Most podcast dramas operate on budgets far smaller than Mitchell's, who benefits from the profile and audience that *The Truth* has built, as well as broader support of the Radiotopia network.[8]

The potential for podcast drama to produce a rich diversity of funded works is further constrained by the requirement that commercial projects are "pre-sold" to advertisers with a guarantee of an audience before they are "green-lit"

---

[8] There have been a very small number of podcast dramas that have been produced using full industry costings; during the research for this book two shows were singled out as having benefited from budgets that are comparable to those used on programs such as *Radiolab* and *Serial*. Producers did not discuss this matter on record, but both projects most often mentioned were funded as part of a marketing exercise by a major international corporation.

(Mortimer 2016). This does not mean that risky or unusual script will not be recorded, but they will be a "harder sell" to funders and may gain limited fiscal support. Panoply's head of scripted content, John Dryden, describes how he would not necessarily turn down a drama production because he did not think it would "get to Number 1 in the iTunes chart" (Dryden 2017); he might see a project as being important to make but "before we make it we would have to go out to advertisers and find someone who is prepared to advertise in it. If it is a more niche [work] you charge less for the advertisements, you'd have fewer advertisements and therefore the budgets would be smaller" (Dryden 2017). The problem with this is that to justify investment required of a full-cast audio drama the audience size drawn to a project would have to be high. There are no fixed income figures available for the podcasting industry, but a reference point for 2017 would be $1 of income for every thirty-five listeners (Pinsker 2015). This figure aligns with what we were told by podcasters about their income during interviews and would be inclusive of advertising and crowdfunding support (but not tertiary income generated by live tours or merchandising). At this rate each twenty-five-minute episode of *The Truth* would require an audience of approximately 160,000 to justify its costs, which is close to what, in 2015, Jonathan Mitchell reported the size of his audience as being (Mitchell 2015). An audio drama produced at BBC rates of £22,000 per hour would have to draw in an audience of 924,000 per hour for it to be viable as a commercial production. Listening figures of this scale are comparable to those reported by only the most successful drama podcasts released since 2010; *We're Alive* gained an audience of 500,000 per episode (Wayland 2016), *The Black Tapes* 600,000 per episode (Bae 2017), and only *Welcome to Night Vale* with approximately 1,000,000 listeners per episode eclipses this number (Cranor and Fink 2015). For a full-cast audio drama to be economically viable it would have to be one of the most popular drama podcast that there has ever been. Eight years after Dirk Maggs's efforts to fund online audio drama were rebuffed, the same issues face producers who wish to finance their work; there is very little guarantee of there being "a return on investment."

These economic pressures can result in a conservatism on the part of producers that belies the freedom that this open form appears to offer. This is not unique to drama or to podcasting in particular; deregulation of media production and distribution can lead to standardization of content. Hendy describes how this has occurred in commercial radio where there are successive instances of the available programming increasing initially following the freeing up of broadcast rights, and then this is followed by a "concentration of formats" which is accompanied by a concentration of ownership of media companies which takes us "more or less back to square one" (Hendy 2000: 41). The same thing is happening in podcasting, where the number of media owners or influencers is being reduced and the range of formats is tightening (Quah 2016a). There is also potential for the field of audio fiction to be dominated by a single player, Audible. The spoken word arm of Amazon, Audible.com has potentially "limitless reach and limitless funding" (Greenhalgh 2017). The works produced by Audible to date have been adaptations of popular media franchises (i.e., *Aliens* and *X-Files*—both produced by Dirk Maggs) or genre works (i.e., *Locke and Key* an adaptation of Clint Hill's graphic novel horror series produced by Fred Greenhalgh) that draw in the same audiences as podcast dramas. In 2017, they signaled a change in direction when they announced the creation of a $5 million fund to produce works by "emerging writers" (Barone 2017). This fund is being overseen by a coterie of panelists drawn from the theatre with the aim of "widening the reach of emerging playwrights, who might otherwise be writing for Off (and even Off-Off) Broadway theaters" (Katz quoted in Barone 2017). Audible may be able to offer funding for projects, but whether it can offer profile and audience is questionable. The reach of Amazon is considerable, and at this moment in time they have a portion of Jeff Bezos's billions at their disposal, but they are a subscription service and not part of the wider internet. They are isolated, charging for content when there is a "sea of unlimited free audio" being offered (Shapiro 2016). Whether the announcement of the playwright's fund represents a shift in their approach remains to be seen.

Podcast drama reflects the tastes of its audience with a tendency to focus on genre works. Productions that are "difficult," "resonant emotionally," or break beyond the limits of genre are being made, but most often with the benefit of external funding. Chris Hogg's 2017 series *Rathband* played across the borders of docu-drama, personal journaling, and audio fiction in a work that told the story of David Rathband, a police officer during a killing spree in the North East of England. Simon James produces sonically rich and musically lavish works, including Neil Cargill's 2016 series *Akiha Den Den* which functions as much as a piece of extended musique concrete as an audio drama. The anthology series *Serendipity* presents striking, mature, and original works that highlight the potential of the form. These projects require public funding to be made: *Serendipity* is in part funded by the Sarah Lawrence College, *Rathband* by the Arts Council England, and *Akiha Den Den* by Creative Scotland. The strengths of the BBC, and of BBC radio drama, are that although work must be produced to appeal to a very particular demographic, strands of Reithianism remain part of the Corporation's creative DNA. This means that challenging and experimental works are still being commissioned, funded, and broadcast—not in great volume, but more than would be the case if it were reliant on commercial funding. Podcast networks, with oversight for a range of projects, may, as John Dryden suggests, begin to support a diverse range of works and approaches, but without external input it is difficult to see how marginal or unusual works would be cost-effective.

Alongside funding from advertisers and grant awarding bodies, there is a third source of production finance emerging: rights and licensing deals. It is through the licensing of *Homecoming* as a TV series that its production costs are being recouped, the indie podcast dramas *Welcome to Night Vale*, *The Black Tapes*, and *The Bright Sessions* have all also been licensed, and it was through the potential of its being developed as a TV series that K. C. Wayland's *Bronzeville* was produced.

K. C. Wayland—*We're Alive* and *Bronzeville*

Between 2009 and 2014 K. C. Wayland self-produced and distributed over 134 episodes of the "zombie podcast" *We're Alive*, casting friends and personal contacts into roles, and recording episodes during "down" time at a university studio where he worked as a technician. Strap-lined as being "A Story of Survival," *We're Alive* followed a cast of misfits in their struggle to survive the zombie apocalypse. It was released at a time when podcast drama was almost entirely limited to fan- and home-produced works. Wayland framed the project as a commercial venture seeding early episodes with advertising for businesses run by his family and friends. His intention being that this would "show the way" and highlight the potential of the form for paying clients. The first season of *We're Alive* gained less than 1,000 downloads from its thirty-seven episodes and earned "approximately $150" in advertising revenue (Wayland 2016). From this base, the *We're Alive* franchise has grown exponentially, and in the eight years since of the first episode the series has been downloaded 80 million times (Wayland 2017). *We're Alive* possesses a dynamic punch and crisp physicality, the signature of a producer whose cultural influences are drawn from cinema. Wayland admits that he "gets bored by audio entertainment" (Wayland 2017), but he recognizes podcast drama as a format through which he can tell the stories he would not have the chance to produce for television or film.

There were two external influences at play that helped support the viral spread and growth of *We're Alive* through 2010. The first was technological. There is a congruence between the increased spread of a podcast series and developments in digital platforms of distribution and circulation. In Autumn 2014, Apple included an "easy to use" podcasting app in its iPhone IoS8 software. Two weeks later *Serial* was released, the viral success of which has been ascribed to the coincidence of these events (Rosin 2016; Walch 2017; Blumberg 2017). Jeffrey Cranor and Jospeh Fink identify the spread of *Welcome to Night Vale* to a period when the blogging app Tumblr was also growing in popularity (Cranor and Fink 2015). They noted that this was the primary platform on which listeners would swap recommendations, memes, and art related to the show. Wayland associates the rise of *We're Alive* with its being featured on the now-defunct Zune Marketplace, an audio media platform run by Microsoft that was intended to be a competitor to iTunes. The series was regularly "podcast of the week," boosting its visibility when a second cultural set of influences came into play. In 2010 the AMC TV network premiered *The Walking Dead*, another zombie survival story that garnered huge TV ratings. This was the beginning of a period when the telling and retelling of a story drawn from George A. Romero's 1968 film *Night of Living Dead* would come to dominate mainstream media. There were spin-off series (*Fear the Walking Dead*), Hollywood movies (*World War Z*), comedies (*Zombieland*), videogames, RPGs, LARPs, and a host of indie movies. *We're Alive* with its back catalogue of episodes, profile on the Zune network and kinetic production values, was positioned to become the audio component of this phenomenon.

In 2016 Wayland released *Bronzeville*, a gangster thriller set in a 1930s black neighborhood. Produced by actor Laurence Fishburne's Cinema Gypsy Productions, *Bronzeville* was originally developed as a TV product. Wayland's audio series was positioned as a "proof of concept" produced in lieu of a TV pilot. Period drama is prohibitively expensive to shoot; meticulously detailed sets, scenography, costumes, and special effects raise the cost of production. An episode of *Boardwalk Empire*, HBO's gangster drama set in the same period as *Bronzeville*, is reported to have cost $18 million (Littleton 2010). Wayland's production, despite having a cast and crew of seventy people, would have cost significantly less.[9] This methodology allows audio work to access funding with the potential of there being a considerable return on investment if licenses are sold, but it can limit the form's potential. Audio drama is reduced to being a sensorially impaired precursor of the full visual production. Wayland describes having to work with both writers and performers to understand the potential and constrains of the medium, and the series's origins as a televisual script are still apparent in the final work.

Bronzeville does not sound like other podcast dramas. Scenes are set and established through atmos, effects, and dialogue. There is action: frenetic, violent, and played out in real time without the support of voice-over or narration. Actors are close-miked and give their performances from a fixed point, which results in a clear, unspoiled sound reminiscent of the dialogue replacement recordings heard in cinema. Atmos, room tone, Foley, and effects are added in post, which allows Wayland complete control over his sound. That his final mastering mixes are balanced for speakers, not for headphone listening, further accentuates the quasi-cinematic quality of the audio. This is sound designed for hi-fi listening, for headphones perhaps, but not for earbuds; it is the sonic equivalent of the intense sensory overload of the summer action blockbuster. *We're Alive* appeals to a large, mainstream audience unfamiliar with audio drama, but who are familiar with the topic and tone of the work. There is a group of characters, they need to survive, there are zombies trying to eat them; *We're Alive*'s premise is as simple and direct as storytelling can be. *Bronzeville* has a cast of forty characters, multiple locations, and with few visual reference points or supports to ease the listener through the experience. It functions as an audio drama, reminiscent of the works that Dirk Maggs produces for Audible and has previously produced for the BBC, but is distributed as a podcast. While Verma praises the series as possessing a "'kaleidoscopic" style, which shifts between a number of shallow scenes across a social geography relatively rapidly" (Verma 2017a: 8), it perhaps struggles to succeed as a podcast drama. It is an immersive experience, demanding all the listener's attention, and is therefore difficult to fully engage with when on the move, in the car or listening on headphones when walking through a city's streets.

---

[9] For several decades the BBC has used audio production to test and develop program ideas for television, particularly in the field of comedy. The TV series *Little Britain*, *League of Gentlemen*, *Flight of the Concords*, *Mitchel and Webb*, and *The Day Today* were all trialed as radio series before transitioning to the screen.

Divergent phenomenological states—
podcast drama and urban listening

Listening to *Bronzeville*, episode four, on headphones while walking through the streets of North Brighton, England. A (sub)urban listening exercise:

<*I turn from the school gates having dropped off my son. It's 9 a.m. I slip my headphones on. Press play. I start walking*> Narrator, male American, sounds as if it could be Laurence Fishburne. An announcement. "Bronzeville April 6th, 1947" <*Suburban houses around me. I look up, judge cars, cross the road*> A new voice, again male, full and throaty with a hint of reverb coloring his words. <*I step aside as a kid rushes past, late for the school bell*> "Now brothers and sisters some people will tell you that the size of the sin is what matters." A priest is addressing a congregation, I haven't heard this character before. <*Along the street, I turn into a twitten, with high fences on either side*>. Voices heard in the background, calling out their affirmations and halleluiahs. <*A bramble catches my jacket*> This is a church. <*I pick it off*> I am listening to a preacher, speaking to a black congregation about the nature of sin. <*The main road is up ahead*> The pastor is confident, proud, his audience small, the church humble and functional. <*I reach the curb and pause*> "Are you going to be able to tell him you never lined the Devil's pockets?" <*The traffic is heavy this morning*> The scene ends. <*Cars are backed up. Shall I go now?*> A new voice. Male. I recognize it but can't attach a name to it. "You know what he was talking to me about, right?" <*Over to the central reservation*> "Curtis Randolph, do you take me for a fool?" A woman replies. <*A car stops. The driver, a woman smiles at me. I wonder why she stopped for me? People don't usually do that when I'm on my own*> I've lost track of the dialogue. Two characters are outside the church arguing about the meaning of the preacher's sermon. <*I set off up the hill to home*> The reverend approaches. <*One of my neighbors is walking down the street towards me*> "Say I wonder if I could speak to you for a moment." <*I don't want to talk to her, not now, not when I'm listening*> That's the preacher cutting in again. The EQ on his voice makes it clear that they are outside, in front of the church. <*I need to avoid eye contact*> Curtis Randolph doesn't seem happy with the priest, but his parishioners are around them, walking by, offering praise. <*We approach each other*> There is tension between the pastor and the gangster. <*I smile and nod and move on*> I've lost the thread again. The pastor is now asking Curtis for money . . . <*I'm not sure why*>.

A familiar walk home from dropping my son at the school gates is overlaid with the meetings and machinations of K. C. Wayland's *Bronzeville*. A bifurcated experience that splices the real-life sensory input of walking through contemporary southeast England suburbia with an audio imagining of a 1930s American city. The two intertwine, interrupt, and overlay. Neither of them are complex experiences; the dramatic scene is simple, the walk familiar, but they are not comfortable partners. For Wayland audio drama exists at the "in-between point between movies and books" (Wayland 2017), a linear sensory experience that plays out in the listener's mind. As I listen to his work I create the sets; I cast the actors, dress them in costume, and block their movements; I arrange the lights and set the perspective. He tries to give signals, he "takes things slowly," to give me time to assemble the mise-en-scene but without a narrator or storyteller there is still a lot for me to do as I attempt to cross roads and avoid social contact.

Audio drama works with the imagination, as Douglas explains: "When information comes solely through our auditory system, our mental imaging systems have freewheeling authority to generate whatever visual they want" (2004: 28). The action of the drama takes place inside the listener's head, inside their mind's eye a "private and unique creation of each person who hears it" (Crissell 1994: 153–4). This is an experience that is intimate and powerful, recreating the listener as participant in a way a television viewer cannot (Hendy 2000: 118). There is something of the dreamlike in this experience, the hallucinatory qualities that are forced upon the listener. This is a "mise-en-sense" as Verma has it, a scene built that "obeys the logic of contingency and expectation, of hint and hallucination" (Verma 2017a: 15). Audio and mental experiences of this intensity are not a part of the large proportion of *radio* listening. Radio, having been pushed out of the living room and into the kitchen and the car, has remediated itself as a "secondary medium." It has become reliant on a steady patter of music and chat that is part of the fabric of listeners' lives. Music "does not refer to anything in the way that speech does, and so does not require us to use [our imagination]: it therefore makes ideal background listening" (Crissell 1994: 14). Although radio audiences can shift their modes of listening during the day between informational listening (unimaginative fact gathering), dimensional (imaginative and image building), and associational (relating to our lived experience) (Douglas 2004: 27), radio itself has been reduced to a form of sonic wallpaper that "burbles on" in the background, until your attention is drawn to it (Mortimer 2016; Hall 2016).

Earbud listening offers something more: the opportunity to access the listeners' imagination and attention very deeply, and with it a fourth mode of deep or immersive listening. This is what Brendan Baker, producer and sound designer on *Love + Radio* expects of his perfect listener, someone who is not distracted or multitasking but is still, "eyes closed" and making the podcast "the primary thing that they are focusing on" (2016). He assumes that his listeners are wearing headphones and his role is to create "immersive soundscapes" for them. This is a form of close listening where the outside world is shut out and the phenomenological work of experiencing and responding to the aural content is the listener's only concern. This is the ideal way that a full-cast audio drama should be consumed, something, as Wayland notes, akin to reading a book. Feature maker Alan Hall hoped that podcasting would offer a space where immersive listening would be possible, allowing for montaged, layered, and immersive works to be appreciated (2016). That was the early promise of podcasting but as drama producer Jeremy Mortimer notes: "Most people are listening on headphones, so they are excluding the rest of the world, unless they are driving" (2016). According to Edison Research, 22 percent of the audience are driving, along with another 27 percent who are at work, walking, or on public transport (Edison 2017). The podcast has joined the repertoire of media used for urban personal listening. The Walkman, the personal CD player, the iPod, the smartphone—a sequence of technologies that are used to recreate public space as private space, a reorientating and respatializing of experience in solipsistic and aesthetic terms (Bull 2004). Headphones allow the listener to move through the world while simultaneously retreating from it (Groening quoted in Nyre 2015), avoiding people and problems, and passing neighbors. Bull describes the use of personal audio as being a means of augmenting personal space and time by creating "a form of accompanied solitude for its users in which they feel empowered, in control and self-sufficient as they travel through the spaces of the city" (2005: 355).

Immersive listening is not centripetal; it does not "pull you into the world" as Douglas suggests (2004: 30) or add to lived experience, rather it replaces it with another. Audio drama requires that the listener shut out the real world and overlay it with a constructed reality. Attempting to experience both at once, the real and the imagined, places the listener in two phenomenological states simultaneously, unable to fully commit to either. Nyre carried out a study with test subjects detailing how they experience audio content when they were traveling around London. They were asked to listen to BBC Radio Four's *In Our Time*, which required them to engage with "lots of uncommon or unknown words, references, and trying to envision the historical progression across the millennia. This is difficult intellectual work" (Nyre 2015: 294). Respondents described how they would "lose the thread of the podcast" and would have to back-scan. One respondent said of the program that it was something that she would listen to at home while cooking and maybe "not crossing a road or where a platform is or [seeking] what time a train is. These are new things, whereas chopping carrots and celery is something you know how to do already, so it's automatic" (Laura quoted in Nyre 2015: 295). While it may be asserted that this study is flawed, because many of the programs used as part of the research are either lectures or were originally, as is the case with *In Our Time*, made for radio, it does highlight issues that producers confront when creating work for a potentially mobile audience. Information must be packaged such that the listener can be led through the programming by hosts and presenters who take them "by the hand" (Hall 2016) and lead them through an experience saying, "Hey listen, come here, listen to this, and then explain it . . . [In podcasting] there is a lot of help, and there is a lot of signposting, and there is a lot of recapitulation, and there is a lot of catching up with where we were left, and clarifying of points" (Hall 2016).

A presenter can lead the audience through a complex narrative but sonically a podcast cannot be complex. The use of found footage, the avoidance of non-diegetic sound, the featuring of familiar formats, and the reliance upon dialogue are all ways of stripping down the audio experience for the listener. *Welcome to Night Vale* is reliant upon a presenter, a storyteller who avoids description and conjures up a cast of monstrosities that are already formed in the audience's subconscious. *The Truth* relies on set up and dialogue for drama that is played out often between familiar people in familiar places undergoing unfamiliar interactions. In fantastical works there are methods and means by which phenomenological work is bypassed; the two speakers in "They're Made out of Meat" do not have bodies, no meat, so there is nothing for us to imagine. *Homecoming* has scenes in hospital cafeterias, in the street, even in the cabin of a big wheel (conjuring images of *The Third Man*), but there is no action. No physicality. Not between people that we must block out and map in our minds. The drama occurs in the words that are shared between people, not in their movements. *We're Alive*, despite its ballistic action and high body count, functions as a podcast drama because it is set in a world built around a familiar narrative frame and populated by clear-cut characters. Recorded crisply and perfectly by actors standing inches away from the largest of large-diaphragm microphones, there is no ambiguity in the soundscape, nothing will be missed by listeners whether they be in cars, on buses or sat in front of hi-fi speakers. They are not being required to engage in listening as a potentially divertive phenomenological experience.

What podcasting does allow the dramaturgist is the freedom to work with an audience who can choose when and where to listen. They can control their sonic environment. If the phone rings, a nappy needs changing, or the boss enters their office, they need only take a temporarily break from the narrative, the pause button can be pushed, and the story resumed at a more convenient moment. This allows for complex plotting and intricate storytelling. This combination of deeply intricately stories told in a simple manner is best exemplified by the podcast series of Paul Bae and Terry Miles, who work together as Pacific Northwest Stories.

Paul Bae and Terry Miles—*The Black Tapes, Tanis,* and *Rabbits*

[Dann (interviewer):] Talking about your process, how long does it take to create
    an episode and how many people are involved? What is your production team?
[Bae:] (laughing) Oh yeah right.
[Miles:] Hmmmm.
[Bae:] Tell him about your "team" Terry.
[Miles:] Huh!
[Dann:] You record it yourself?
[Miles:] Yes.
[Dann:] Do you edit it yourself?
[Miles:] Yes.
[Dann:] You do the music?
[Miles:] Yes.
[Dann:] You act in it?
[Miles:] Well . . . yes. The production is pretty much me . . . there is a helper. It's
    much better this way, this way I don't have to wait on anyone. I can edit it at
    1am in my pyjamas!

—Bae and Miles (2017)

Together Terry Miles and Paul Bae write and produce the serialized horror podcast *The Black Tapes*, which is part of their network Pacific Northwest Stories. Miles also writes and produces the PNS shows *Tanis*, a "fictional documentary" detailing the search for a lost city, and *Rabbits*, an investigation into an alternate reality game that is played out for real. Since the release of the first episode of *The Black Tapes* in May 2015 Miles has written and self-produced eighty-eight episodes, or approximately forty-four hours, of audio drama across these three series. He describes a production process that is by necessity lean and stripped back to allow for this rapid turnover of content. Actors are recorded either in his home studio ("left over" from his days as a musician) or on location, without the use of extensive crews or production schedules. Post-production, sound design, and music scoring are all completed alone, allowing the freedom to work in his "pyjamas," while weighing him with the burden of the project's success. As he notes: "It's getting too much you know? I need to sleep more so the production schedules are starting to expand, with success comes a lot less sleep, and a lot more stress" (Bae and Miles 2017). The shows produced by Pacific Northwest have been garnering huge audiences: those eighty-eight episodes have been downloaded more than fifty million times in total (Bae and Miles 2017).

The three series use the same formula; each features an investigation into a world of conspiracy and horror. Each show is presented as audio vérité, with Pacific Northwest portrayed as a real-world podcast network from which the producers and presenters of various projects cross over, meet up, and collaborate. The success of these series is predicated by the format that Bae and Miles have developed, one that allows them to turn over episodes quickly and cheaply, and presents the material in a stripped out form suited to podcasting. Listening to *The Black Tapes* is a familiar experience; we know the voice, the tone, and the style. Sarah Koenig's self-reflective, doubt-filled process is reconstructed vividly by the piece. *The Black Tapes* borrows phrases from *Serial*, both linguistic (the term "full disclosure" is used as a verbal motif throughout the work) and musical (in the repetition of piano notes that build and hold tension). Miles and Bae developed the project before they knew about *Serial*, the release of which served as an accelerant to their process. They were convinced that the format, of an investigative reporter uncovering supernatural horrors, would be used elsewhere: "We were rushing against the clock because we thought 'why isn't anybody doing what we're doing.' I would wake up at night, and call Paul and be like 'Seriously Paul we gotta hurry.' And he'd be like 'yeah, okay' and we'd talk each other off the ledge and just get to work" (Bae and Miles 2017).

The first episode of *The Black Tapes* was released in May 2015, and it took just six weeks and six episodes for its audience to begin to grow rapidly (Bae and Miles 2017). The series was promoted not through a marketing strategy or a coordinated social media campaign, but by word of mouth, assisted by key influencers, including the Nerdist website and Joseph Fink and Jeffrey Cranor of *Welcome to Night Vale.* The show benefited from the timing of its release and from Bae and Miles's understanding of how to produce work rapidly and efficiently. Both had previous experience working in the media—Bae as a comedian and Miles as an independent filmmaker. They saw podcasting as a means of realizing their ideas cheaply and immediately, and had the skills, resources, and contacts to launch their project without the necessity of sourcing investment funding or production fees. The show was cast from friends and actors with whom they had previously worked, using a point system to pay cast members. Neither had created audio drama previously, and, in common with many podcast drama producers, do not appear to have a great affinity with the form. Miles discusses having listened to the *Mystery Theatre* radio shows as a child, and Bae to having heard radio drama on Canada's CBC network as he grew up. Their influences are drawn from cinema, TV, genre literature, video, and role-playing games. These interests gel with those of their audience: the educated, tech-aware, twenty-five-to forty-year-olds who are core to podcast listening.

In the same way that *Welcome to Night Vale* employs characters and imagery drawn from the broad sweep of 150 years of the American Gothic, so *The Black Tapes* taps into its audience's collective memory with scenes from the canon of the last twenty-five years of screen horror. The series features recordings of psychic experiments gone awry, ghostly shapes flickering across baby monitors and figures plunging to their death in the background of tourist videos. These are images that are part of the audience's cultural memory, imprinted by films such as *Paranormal Activity, The Blair Witch Project,* and the Japanese J-horror series *Ringu* and *Ju-on.* The characters often experience events second hand, via screens. Just as Richard Hughes in *Comedy of Danger* reduced his character's sensory awareness to the same level as the audience, so equanimity is created between Bae and Miles's protagonist and their listeners. For most of the first two seasons host Alex Reagan experiences the horror second hand, being told stories or watching recordings of events as they are played back to her. *The Black Tapes* works as a podcast because the phenomenological load it puts on its listener is lightened. The settings are simple (studios, cafés, hotel rooms), descriptions are paired down, and the situations are drawn from a pool of imagery that lies dormant within its audience's imagination.

The artifice that Pacific Northwest is an actual company and that all this could be real provides conceptual scaffolding to frame the show's presentational format while heightening the visceral nature of the horror, making the suspension of disbelief easier because everything feels so "real." This is H. G. Wells's *The War of the Worlds* played out for a post-digital audience who have grown up on the mimetic myths of creepypasta and Slenderman; where everything posted online could be true is most probably false and the dividing line between the two is effectively invisible. *The Black Tapes* and particularly *Tanis* draw on the well of conspiracy and mythology that is available at the end of a Google search, and implicit in the experience is that the audience check sources and enquire into the veracity of what they have been listening to. Pacific Northwest Stories produce podcasting fashioned as a transmedia experience, one that is intended to appeal to the outer reaches of forensic fandom (Jenkins 2006). While Bae and Miles do not engage with their audiences directly, at least not with regard to issues concerning the plotting of their various series, the community of Pacific Northwest Stories fandom is active and highly engaged. Fan art is swapped, wikis are built, theories constructed and shared while Bae and Miles stand to one side, sometimes observing, never participating, allowing each individual's "headcanon," their version of what the story means, to stand and maintain its own validity.

The Black Tapes can be accused of exhibiting the limitations of the podcast drama format. It is the epitome of the "light paranoid suspense serials that reminisce television shows like *The X-Files*" that Verdana (2017a: 4) cites as an example of how restricted drama producers' creative ambitions have become. It is these same qualities of lean production, of calling on a familiar pool of imagery, of lacking respect or awareness for the history of audio drama, and of the simplicity of the sonic experience that explain its success. These are the limits of what podcast drama is; it is the nature of the form and the key to its popularity.

The freedom of forgetting

There exists a sense and a desire that podcast drama may be about to "blow up" (Wayland 2017), in terms of its profile and its cultural status. It may yet have its "*Serial* moment," with a single project bursting through and capturing mainstream attention. Interviewees spoke in these terms with a confidence born of the palpable growth of the form over a period of the past three years. Current works may be simply providing what audio drama producer Fred Greenhalgh describes as "training wheels" for the audience before they are ready for "the real thing" (Greenhalgh 2017). The expectation that the form will become sophisticated may be misplaced, as realistic as standing at an EDM (Electronic Dance Music) gig and hoping that the music will evolve into something resembling Handel, if only it were given time. Individual producers may change and diversify, but the movement itself is born of an audience and a relationship to that audience. Production costs are high, and without external funding, there needs to be some guarantee of an audience, the necessity of their being a return on investment in terms of either fiscal or labor input inhibits the form.

What podcast drama has gained is a coherent and definable identity, one that is not slaved to other media or apologetic for its sensory deficiencies. After seventy years of the flame of audio drama being kept alive in the hallowed studios of the BBC Radio Drama Department, that flame has spread and is growing, in sometimes surprising, sometimes ugly, and sometimes wonderful ways. The form has its limits. It appears to be locked into a world of conspiracy and paranormal, of found footage and covert recording. It is being created without a sense of the history of the audio drama, and of the potential of the form. When Eli Horowitz discussed his podcast drama in terms that described it as a "new" medium he was at once dooming himself to repeat the mistakes of the past, and freeing himself from it. The necessity of being "original" is a burden; it can stifle decision-making. The lack of a coherent history of audio drama, and particularly radio drama, may in fact be a great strength. In his essay "delete" Viktor Mayer-Schönberger made an appeal for the right of society to forget, to erase the digital past, and to move on unimpeded by reminders and expectations of what has gone before (2009). When a group of friends pick up guitars and decide to form a band in their garage, they must compete against the noise of the entire history of rock music playing out at the end of a simple Google search. Audio drama's history is less immediately apparent, collating it is the work of academics, because so much of it has been lost, or buried, or simply was never recorded. This allows podcast drama producers to simply write a script, set up a microphone, and record a show without having to raise themselves onto the shoulders of the giants of the past. As Wayland says:

> It's an art movement that's basically like an art renaissance. We're figuring out what we're doing at the same time as growing; there's some growing pains but I definitely know and feel that it's going in the right direction. It's just a little unpredictable right now because as everything grows, like a tree, it can go in a good direction or a bad direction. You have to just let it go. (2017)

A Utopian Moment: *Podium.me*, Diversity, and Youth Podcasting

As we increasingly inhabit "media saturated" spaces of intimacy, so we increasingly desire to make the public spaces passed through mimic our desires, thus, ironically, furthering the absence of meaning attributed to those spaces. This is the dialectic of iPod culture.

—Michael Bull (2007)

On my train ride up from Brighton to London to interview Camilla Byk, one of the founders of the young person's podcasting initiative *Podium.me*, four loud, jovial, and drinking men in their early twenties sat opposite me and started swapping stories about their girlfriends. They wanted to include me in their world and conversation and went so far as to offer me a can of cider. I smiled, politely declined, and put on my earphones, preferring to travel to London in my own space rather than with them. When I told Byk about this scene at the start of her interview she laughed and said that if she had been in my place she would have pulled out the weekly *Podium.me* story brief and pressed the young men to get their phones out and do some interviewing (2016).

In early August 2011, the police shooting death of twenty-nine-year-old Mark Duggan in Tottenham, North London, was followed by a wave of protests involving thousands of people that escalated into riots, looting, a mass deployment of the police, and a further five deaths. Before the culmination of violence, the London Riots, as they would come to be known, spread across Hackney, Brixton, Walthamstow, Peckham, Enfield, Battersea, Clapham, Croydon, Ealing, Barking, Woolwich, Lewisham, and East Ham. Byk, a former television and radio producer and area resident, remembered the smashed-up shops and burned buildings at the end of her road, the community's "broom army" (Rowley 2014) that swept up in the wake, and her own conversations with disillusioned young people she encountered during the cleanup. But her most troubling memory of those days was the demonization of young people, particularly minority young people, that she saw as a defining feature of the broadcast media coverage in the immediate aftermath. These portrayals did not at all resonate with her own experience of watching neighborhood teens clearing up the broken glass (Byk 2015).

Over the following weeks and months her conversations with another area resident, Annabel Merrett, repeatedly turned to the problematic coverage of these events and to the general lack of a well-defined media space for young people to tell their own stories from their own perspectives. In less than a year Byk and Merrett had launched *Podium.me*, a platform which offered short podcasts every week on music, sports, culture, and politics; these were produced by, and featured the voices of, those under twenty (it later expanded its age range to under twenty-five and expanded its content to include short dramas). Participants discovered *Podium.me* and got involved through talks at schools and universities given by current or previous journalists or staff, through careers workshops, through suggestion made by BBC editors and staff at other production companies after unsuccessful internship applications, through social media networks, and through simply stumbling across its content online. They were attracted to it for opportunities to express themselves and contribute to debates, to improve their journalism and media skills, to expand their professional/social networks, and, occasionally, simply to add a credentialing line to their resumes. Administratively, *Podium.me* was organized as a charity funded with grants and eventually also with the help of commissions for other broadcasters. At any given time there were roughly fifty active contributors working with two paid part-time staff; Byk herself volunteered roughly five hours per day to project (2015).[1]

Podium.me is uniquely relevant to this book's analysis because it was born into the moment when podcasting was crystalizing into a specific and distinctive medium. The particular and more mature forms, formats, shapes, and relationships of podcasting were built into *Podium.me* from its inception— it could never have been anything other than a podcast. Byk's early research into

---

[1] *Podium.me* can also be seen as distinctive among similar podcast projects (as well as the other podcasts discussed in this book) in that it was born out of the happenings in a specific geographical place. Even as it expanded internationally, it maintained a strong sense of its grounding in a particular physical location: "The Pod," an office/studio in a small room in Byk's house. This tethering to a real hub lent it an idiosyncratic sense of material community that is alien to many podcasting production projects—an important marker for Byk.

the medium was inspiring: she found that (as remains the case today) the vast majority of podcasts were not produced by radio professionals yet they offered a platform to reach potentially millions on what she then perceived as a much more even playing field.

Drawing on interviews with Byk as well as an extensive qualitative survey of a diverse group of recent young *Podium.me* journalists,[2] this chapter offers some insight into:

1. the relationship between podcast listening and podcast making;
2. the utopian potential of a production-centered, collaborative project somewhat at odds with conventional media approaches to branding and garnering "likes" and "listens";
3. how the social value of making podcasts is enabled by young people's use of smartphones; this offers an advancement on/challenge to the social formations that have been observed around earlier mobile audio technology and allows us to frame podcasting itself as a form of social media;
4. how young podcasters navigate the vocational currents of a neoliberal media market; and
5. how Millennials, and the Gen X facilitators who support them and the critics who often write about them, have different perspectives on podcasting diversity, minority representation and access in media, and the narcissism and self-promotion often associated with social media.

As diversifying mainstream media representations was an aim for *Podium.me*, and because our survey participants reference the BBC far more than any other media outlet,[3] it makes sense to begin with a thumbnail sketch of the Corporation's diversity policy (at the time of this writing). The government's parliamentary report "A BBC for the Future" (2016) is particularly noteworthy as issues of diversity are framed as problems to be resolved rather than opportunities to be explored. It institutes 2020 targets for representational diversity: 15 percent of leading roles going to BAME actors and 50 percent going to women actors. It offers similar targets for staffing of senior positions, wants to ensure "that

---

[2] Participants we interviewed described their nationality as British, American, Irish, Pakistani, Hong Konger, Turkish, Canadian, and German. They described themselves ethnically as White European, Black British, African, British, Scottish, Bangladeshi, South Asian, Turkish, Argentinian, and Irish. Twenty participants took part in individual hour-long interviews over the phone or video call; five were given a follow-up interview or provided further information via email. The survey was conducted in 2016.

[3] A full three-quarters of them mentioned the BBC as a point of comparison.

independent producers have diversity in their thinking from the very start of the creative process," and describes initiatives to make focus groups more diverse. While an advance on previous parliamentary papers, in this document "diversity" remains something of an abstract concept; youth representation or access do not figure in its targets and there is no mention of intersectionality in its discussion of minorities.

Podium.me's diversity project began by developing relationships first with schools, universities, and other media outlets in London, then in Britain, and eventually in other countries. Through this liaising, Byk built a network of roughly 350 young journalists and producers who receive a weekly email brief requesting material for podcasts in the production pipeline, soliciting pitches for other stories, and often highlighting the work of one particular *Podium.me* journalist. Byk described *Podium.me* as constantly looking to expand its network of young producers and repeatedly emphasized the low barrier to editorial participation (especially relative to institutions like the BBC). She prided herself on responding to every pitch received and figuring out a way to involve young people at whatever stage of media development. Also, she emphasized that technical barriers to participation were virtually nonexistent. *Podium.me* was second only to the LBC in London in using mobile phones for interviews and production (2015). The fact that "every young person had the means within their pockets to record themselves and upload something to a drop box" is also the feature of *Podium.me* which highlights one of podcasting's broadest implications for debates around portable media: For Byk the mobile phone is a *recording device* before it is a *listening device*. As we will see in detail later in this chapter, this flips the script on the long-running historical focus on portable media devices as sites of consumption, of colonization by the culture industry, and of (often unsatisfying) attempts to articulate identity through curating pre-existing media products.

Podium.me and the podcasting form

While expressing attachment to and appreciation of the BBC's old-school journalistic institutional structures that ensure rigorous standards, Byk describes *Podium.me* as born, to some extent, out of the Corporation's failings into the "the general playground of the internet where anything goes" (2016). She conceives of *Podium.me*'s relationship to its audience in a very un-radio-like way as well: Beyond its loose youth media foundation, the project was not overly fixated on a consistent brand identity in terms of content or a style which would imprint its work and reach. Podcasts were produced under one of the larger *Podium.me* content headings but were often particular enough to allow them to be promoted to more specific—not necessarily "youth"—audiences (e.g., a story about Italians living outside Italy was promoted through the Italian Institute of London). The objective quality of *Podium.me*'s podcasts is also incredibly varied: A podcast about a young woman's personal account of breast reduction surgery was complex enough and edited well enough that it might have sounded at home on professional public service radio. Another, called "Wolf-whistling: Compliment or Crime," was an easy-to-produce-and-consume extended voxpop with a montage at the end encouraging listeners to "have your say" by getting involved.

While this approach to podcasting—diverse outputs of varying production values which can then be niche marketed—might seem random and unsuited to commercial or professional podcast undertakings, it has helped *Podium.me* avoid what Blum-Ross identified as a problem in many youth media projects facilitated by adult professionals. Blum-Ross sees these youth media endeavors as often trapped between two contradictory impulses or desires: an impulse to equip young people to critique and challenge existing media power structures through their own creative expression on the one hand, and what she describes as a vocational or professionalizing impulse designed to equip young people to enter a media workforce (2015: 315–17) on the other. Byk's conception of the internet as a "playground" means, to some extent, that *Podium.me* can tick both boxes. Interestingly, in recent years, *Podium.me* has pivoted slightly back toward radio which helps fund what Byk calls the more "maverick" work of its podcast-only output.

Podium.me's intentions

Who invented the rules of journalism? They are based on a premise that we trust the person who's speaking because they work for a particular organization that has certain guidelines and structures in place. That, at some point, was invented by somebody. There will be new rules. Society will impose new rules . . . . What we are doing is providing this independent space for people to do what the media isn't doing.

—Camilla Byk (2015)

Any contemporary discussion of youth media and diversity must be couched in caveats (Das 2010), not least of which is remembering that for Millennials convenient demographic subcategories are very fluid and slippery and that media use within them is tremendously varied. This often means that it is easier for media projects with a diversity agenda to describe themselves in terms of opposition. Byk, for example, can express resistance to conventional ideas of "youth content" and even more so to "youth culture" finding them often overly didactic and patronizing, or, worse, chiefly used to delineate and target groups of consumers. In a space where young people are already organically producing their own media and forming media communities with little or no adult support descriptors like these feel artificial for Byk. She sees *Podium.me*, in some ways, as simply tapping into an energy that already exists online then collecting it, channeling it, and extending it (2015). Further, Byk's focus on the creative work of young people and the collaborative production environment of *Podium.me* invites us to shift our thinking around the relationship of media to identity formation; it moves our attention from a curating of media products for personal consumption to an identity construction with creative media making and exchange at its core.

"Diversity" on *Podium.me* then is best described as an opportunity, a practice, or an activity much more than it is a list of targets or categories, or a branding device. There is no finely crafted diversity policy beyond growing *Podium.me* into geographic areas where it does not already have journalists. In the end, it appears less about explicitly changing media representations than it is about creating opportunities for different faces to make and distribute media. While an impulse to change representation is heard in their podcasts, it happens largely in casting young people as voices of authority. In their episode "20 and Undecided" about the British EU referendum in June of 2016, for example, a political science undergraduate is called upon to weigh-in on the pros and cons. The most significant contribution here is not primarily to the referendum debate but to the interviewee's sense of herself as an expert and to the producer's sense of herself as a journalist.

While there are potentially thousands of *Podium.me* podcast listeners online and potentially millions of listeners to *Podium.me* material heard on Radio One, Byk refuses to define success in terms of listener numbers:

> The [participatory] ethos behind *Podium.me*, and the fact that the producers of the content are as important as the listeners . . . that tends to get us round this very difficult concept of "are you successful?" . . . . I won't be swayed by figures. (2015)

The goal of *Podium.me* is more ambitious and more ephemeral than statistics. She is not interested in producing "click bait" (2016), but rather in opening opportunities for young people's self-expression. This ethos is tremendously attractive to the young journalists who seek out *Podium.me*. When we asked those who responded to our survey to list reasons for their involvement, self-expression, often to the point of compulsion, was the most consistent answer. But very interestingly, for many of the more considered and accomplished young producers we interviewed, this self-expression happens within a network of listening relationships. For Abe, for example, listening to podcasts and making podcasts occupy a similar creative and expressive space within identity formation:

> So there's a recurring theme across podcasts of discovering one's self through listening. That's one of the reasons I make them, to offer an alternative perspective on different ideas. I'm a strong believer of expressing opinion and I think people should understand things whether [these things challenge] them or not.

Here, what Lacey has described as "listening out" (2013), the politically engaged openness to hearing material that is potentially personally unsettling or destabilizing, seems rolled into Abe's creative generative media practice. The personal perspectives of others are processed into his own personal perspective which he then reshapes into a broadly progressive social position.[4]

Many of our other respondents also described an approach to podcasting in which listening and making practices were similarly integrated. This prompts us to consider podcasting itself, at least for these young producers, as part of social media—as itself a social medium. This suggestion is supported by a comparison to other data from other surveys. Next to the respondents of Edison Research's cumulative annual survey of podcast listening habits ("The Infinite Dial"),[5] our respondents showed a much greater use of social media in general and higher levels of integration of their podcasting experiences into

---

[4] This will prove a useful note when we take up criticisms of youth media and narcissism later in the chapter. The integrated practice on display here, and the often intimate material it produces, is only possible if, in Byk's words, there is a "safe space" in which the specter of hyper-critical listeners, or even listeners in general, does not loom too large in the imagination. Indeed part of her role seems to be thinking to some extent about listeners (imagining listeners) in ways that model more complex considerations around risk, exploitation, exhibitionism, and voyeurism for her young producers: she is prepared to kill story ideas and cites features about teen suicide and eating disorders as examples of things she stopped (2015) for what we might call "pastoral" reasons.

[5] Edison's respondents were a representative sample of the US population twelve and older. Edison Research's annual reports "Infinite Dial" and "Share of Ear" are arguably the most comprehensive analyses of podcast listening practices (and other related audio practices) produced in the United States each year. See also Webster (2016).

social media: 100 percent of our respondents described themselves as frequent users of social media whereas the number was 60 percent for Edison's podcast consumers; a further 42 percent of our respondents said they had listened to a podcasts that had been brought to their attention via their social media accounts—these were largely personal recommendations from friends rather than generic retweets that originated from media production companies. Many young *Podium.me* producers reported acutely listening to each other's podcasts which led them to discover different areas of news coverage, and which in turn then led them to produce podcasts on subjects new to them. This means that the podcasts themselves on *Podium.me* can often be heard in conversation with each other. The listening practices of these young producers leads specifically into relationships (imagined and material) with others; their production practices are then founded on an awareness of and a willingness to enter into similar relationships. It is the nature and the quality of these relationships that mark *Podium.me* as a success rather than any number of listeners.

When our young producer respondents describe what they like to listen to beyond *Podium.me*, the notion of some kind of relationship comes to the fore. While audible "care," "effort," and craftsmanship were notable features of the podcasts they liked, these were eclipsed in the responses by words like "story," "genuine," and "authenticity." And even the appeal of finely crafted compositions which use sound well is often appreciated in terms of story and personal connection. Our respondent Tania was a case in point. She said, "I love a clever piece of sound that draws me in, but [when] you get to know the personality of the speaker it almost feels like a friend going on an adventure."

Particularly in light of the ties between personal connections and narrative appeal discussed in Chapters 3, 4, and 8, it is interesting to note how often our respondents here described podcasting relationships happening in the context of good stories. The language that they use to talk about podcast narratives resonates very strongly with the language of Ira Glass; this is unsurprising given that most of them list highly narrative American podcasts as their favorites. Our respondent James put it very clearly, "I want there to be a beaten path to follow." Others, aware of descriptions of American-style podcasts as being too "hand holding" or even patronizing (ideas discussed at length in Chapter 4), were unconvinced by those criticisms and said they preferred this aspect of many American-produced podcasts to those produced elsewhere.[6]

---

[6] Interestingly, only two of our respondents self-identified as American.

Many of the appealing podcast characteristics mentioned here by our respondents that might involve relationships might be listed under the heading of "human element" because they all reference strong emotional connections of some kind. Again, these characteristics were often labeled "American" by those surveyed. Monica was a case in point:

> It's a type of journalism that seems to be much bigger in America than it is here . . . . [T]he journalist insert themselves into the story, so it's usually like personality journalism, it's a story they partake in, that's usually the kind I like.

Monica was not alone in describing this affinity; numerous others (often discussing *Serial*) said this approach appealed because it was more "honest," and hence more believable. Very interestingly these are also characteristics they use to describe the ethos and listening appeal of *Podium.me* podcasts. Gloria, for example, said that it was very pleasing to hear her interviewees respond with, "I have no idea." "It's honest," she reiterated.

Diversity in the practical and theoretical landscape of podcasting

The first time you're told that people of a different colour, or a different religion, or a different gender or sexual orientation, live in a different world than you, that's going to get you to start asking questions. And those questions are going to lead you to answers that are going to give you empathy to people that aren't like you and give you an understanding of the world you live in. And that's ultimately going to make it better, I'd like to think.

—James (survey respondent)

The problem of an insufficiently diverse media is not new, nor are the solutions. The typical institutional response (at least in Britain) has been to establish a policy that usually involves specific targets. But this approach, given that the majority of our media (especially the media consumed by young people) is now distributed in a space with less institutional control, few borders, and even fewer gatekeepers, seems less useful—particularly for podcasting. Even when operating with older media structures in mind this approach has been shown to have limited use. Ayobami Ojebode's comparative analysis of approaches to diversity at the BBC and Nigeria's DBS led him to conclude that "diversity is not better achieved by official policies and targets, than without them" (2009: 216). Ojebode described a series of well-articulated measures at the BBC, including docking bonuses for senior staff who failed to meet workforce diversity targets. His research suggests that the BBC does not do a better job of maintaining either diversity of access or "diversity consciousness" than does the DBS. He attributes this to deep-seated cultural factors which widely imprint socialization long before broadcasting policy: the simple fact of growing up in a culture that is overtly collective and inescapably multiethnic and multilingual generates "a constant awareness of the other and their interests" (222), while fear of embarrassment and alienating social partners invites balanced representations.

The attachment to diversity policy (and even to the notion of "diversity" itself) then might appear as a very logocentric and Western response to a very Western dilemma, one that Ojebode locates much more broadly within the explicit problems of neoliberalism:

> The study of diversity has not been diverse. Deliberative and radical democrats alike have narrowed their theorizing and counter-theorizing to the predominantly literate western societies with a fast-dwindling sense of community. In such societies, even interpersonal relationships are firmly guided by law and policy, and individualism and privacy are indeed deified. (226–7)

What Ojebode describes then is a more experiential diversity that resonates with the *Podium.me* project. Broadly speaking, our respondents seem to exhibit what Ojebode would call a more Nigerian appreciation of "difference," while *Podium. me* itself engages with diversity via socialization rather than explicit policy. It can do this because of its relatively small scale and its self-funding nature.

Some larger, more institutional, podcasting organizations appear to be wrestling with policy/quota approaches to diversity in an effort either to integrate them or evolve beyond them. During a diversity panel discussion at the 2016 Podcast Movement conference in Chicago, Carrie Hoffman, CEO of PRX, spoke at length about their "Pod Quest" and "Talent Quest" initiatives as PRX's attempts to diversify the medium. Nick Quah, the panel chair and publisher of the weekly industry newsletter *Hot Pod*, cut immediately to the nub of the policy problem for the larger media world, for podcasting more specifically, and for himself personally with the admission, "I have no idea what we mean when we use the word 'diversity.'" He observed that when speaking of representation "diversity" seemed too often cast through the lens of race and gender, while excluding geographic and socioeconomic categories. Beyond this, representation was in fact a secondary issue[7] for the all-minority panel as compared to the much harder-to-quantify issues of influence, decision-making power, and pay equality. Quah's summation resonated with label-resistant Millennials as he suggested that perhaps we have reached a stage where the notion of "diversity" (like the notion of "youth culture") has become merely another commodity to be traded, arguing instead for a more "fluid" approach around all discourses of diversity. Somewhat amorphous and slippery, this closing did serve to underscore that while much thought (most of it unsatisfying) has been given to diversity as an institutional issue, much less energy has been given to describing real diversity experiences of both users and makers (especially young ones) in the smaller corners of the podcast ecosphere.

The difference in thinking about the diversity policies of institutions and the diversity experiences of producers and listeners is the difference between two questions: "How can media be made more diverse?" and "How do people currently express and understand diversity in their media-saturated world?" Sarita Malik's research offers an extremely cogent analysis of the first of those questions: she studies how conceptions of multiculturalism and diversity have evolved in tandem with prevailing political constructions and market forces, and have been pulled between the poles of minority integration into mainstream programming versus niche programming to serve (rather ghettoized) minority audiences (2008). When applied to *Podium.me*, Malik's work invites us to consider the relative and parallel merits of "belonging" and "difference." Byk's initial conception was largely to provide a "safe space" (what might have been uncharitably called a "ghetto") for youth voices. This space evolved quickly and rhisomatically with a full 58 percent of our interviewees reporting that they have done their own podcasts outside of the safety of the *Podium.me* umbrella.

Put another way, Quah's thinking, *Podium.me*'s practice, and the evolving realities of podcasting all help us bracket, at least for the moment, concerns about *representational* diversity in mainstream media outlets/board rooms/editorial meetings/schedules. Instead, particularly through *Podium.me*, we are invited to consider an *experiential* diversity. Conceiving of diversity in this way means seeing it as a nexus of making, listening, sharing, social interaction, and group and individual identity formation around a podcast. This is a conceptual evolution still very much in process and vestiges of older approaches to diversity are still

---

[7] Shannon Cason, host of the *Homemade Stories* podcast released by WBEZ, repeatedly emphasized that he only ever coincidentally speaks of race on his podcast and that he is much more concerned with both access and narrative quality.

present, even in the minds of our respondents. Indeed one of our ethnic-minority respondents acknowledged that he "might be naïve" when he says that in his experience of podcasting (participating in a podcasting scene and making and listening to podcasts) he has not felt any discrimination. He and others seem more interested in experiencing and contributing to "difference" than they do in tallying exclusion, inclusion, or misrepresentation.

This refocusing of diversity thinking in terms of experience is a consistent theme among those we interviewed; most of them (minority and nonminority alike) used personal language to describe diversity rather than using abstract terms. Abe, for example, said one of his most memorable podcast listening experiences came from another *Podium.me* producer and was about her gender reassignment procedure. It was significant for him not because he felt he shared a fluid gender identity with her, but because he felt it conveyed to him something authentic about herself and because they were both involved in the *Podium.me* project of youth expression. The act of expression for him was a moment of real human contact and invited a moment of deep understanding. In the shared act of personal podcast storytelling, difference is neither erased nor does it become a barrier to interpersonal connection.

Many of our interviewees spoke of the value of actively seeking out cultural difference; Simon, for example, mentioned his recent discovery of the podcast *2 Dope Queens* in those terms:

> It's like the experience of two black women living in Manhattan. That is as far removed from my experience of living in a rural area of England as a white bloke as it's possible to be.

These listening practices, because they happen on what our respondents perceived as the relatively level playing field of the podcast space, do not seem tainted by any sense of threat or insecurity. Podcasting was very distinct in this regard in the minds of our respondents in comparison to other media. While 60 percent of them thought that the "media industry" as a whole was not "sufficiently diverse," only 11 percent felt that way about the podcast ecosphere. The fact that they felt the podcast space was more diverse—and that they felt an ownership of that space—is interesting in light of the fact that relatively few of them described liking podcasts because they felt some sort of straightforward demographic kinship with the hosts. When they think of diversity they described the appeal of difference (as Simon does above). It may be that our respondents do not need simplistic demographic connections for identity formation through podcasts. Alternatively, they may feel identifications, or recognize elements of themselves, across a wider range of (or more loosely defined) demographic categories.[8]

For our respondents, it is clear that conventional rubrics of diversity have themselves been reshuffled with several of them seeing "diversity of thought" as more important than any other kind of diversity. What is also clear is that there is a sense among them that they are in a position to create for themselves their own podcast diversity experiences rather than having to petition for changes from institutions. "Diversity," as it has been historically framed, seemed for most of them a problem of another generation. Whether valid, utopian, or uncritical, this thinking is in keeping with several old truisms about the internet's democratizing potential and low participation barriers—ideas that also mark much writing about podcasting. It should be noted however that very few of our survey respondents were even attempting, at this stage in their careers, to live more autonomous lives funded by their media work. Perhaps when this becomes more important their engagement with diversity will come to more closely resemble those on the Podcast Movement diversity panel and questions will arise about why equality in opportunity does not coincide with equality of pay. Alternatively, they may continue in the creative, collaborative vein of *Podium.me*—which is the vein shared by the majority of podcast makers—and hold podcasting as a means to shape and express identity, participate in communities, or meet other psychological, personal, or professional needs as opposed to seeing podcasting alone or media work in general as a means to survive financially.

Narcissism and related concerns

Many young people who put themselves out on the internet are keen to have as many followers as possible, to generate as much interest for their personal brand. Podium.me is very very different from that. It is a community of people

---

[8] Kimberlé Crenshaw's (1989) pioneering work on "intersectionality" might offer a useful template here. She introduced the term to better describe the compound discrimination faced by black women—members of more than one subordinated grouping. We might invert this idea and use it to describe the plural identifications, or simply more commonly human identifications, that many of our respondents describe.

who are working together on projects. It's not about the self; it's about the group.

. . .

The only way to get people to listen to your podcast in any volume is to use social media.

—Camilla Byk (2015)

At this stage the ".me" context of *Podium.me* requires some unpacking. Byk was keenly aware of both the need to tap the self-promotional currents of social media and the threats those currents might pose to her larger collaborative ethos and her producers' pursuits of difference and experiential diversity. This problem was perhaps best summed up by Malikhao and Servaes when they argued that as "globalization within media systems" increases "individualism in society" increases in tandem (2011: 66). This individualism, they then suggest, specifically correlates to narcissism and an "inflated view of self." Their conclusion, that narcissism is a likely by-product of an over-emphasis on self-expression in contemporary (American) culture (69), does, at least on the surface, seem to be an obstacle for *Podium.me*'s more progressive intentions.

Theirs resonates with quite a common theme in scholarship. Narcissism and addiction are arguably the two most popular critical lenses through which to view social media. In their meta-analytical review of narcissism and social media (conducted in 2016), McCain and Campbell refer to more than sixty major research studies into this connection (2018). Andreassen et al. (2017), in one of the largest studies of its kind, looked at data from more than 23,000 people in an effort to discover connections between social media, narcissism, and self-esteem. Generating a working definition of narcissism on social media from preceding studies, they describe it as "a relatively broad behavioral trait domain, expressed by, among others, self-centered grandiosity, arrogance, manipulativeness, and similar features"; this, they suggest, manifests itself in seeking visual rewards, such as likes, follows, or downloads. They found that kinds of social media addiction associated with narcissism were more prevalent among young people, students, women, people with less education, and people with a lower income (288). Indeed some of the young journalists we interviewed, when asked about who they thought listened to their podcasts, said that they themselves were the audience and discussed their listening in terms of ripples made in their social media spheres. This would seem a rather textbook and literal case of narcissism. Others cited friends of friends listening on Facebook and described the pleasure of receiving feedback comments.

The dilemma for *Podium.me*'s young contributors who fall into at least one of these studies' vulnerable categories might be summed up as follows: On the one hand, middle-aged, (likely) middle-class facilitators are encouraging them to express themselves as a remedy for a disaffection that they might feel, while on the other hand, other middle-aged, (likely) middle-class academics are describing them as narcissistic for participating in many of these same self-expressive activities.

In fact McCain and Campbell's study (one of the largest and most nuanced) does begin to suggest some problems (along generational lines) with associating narcissism too simplistically with social media. Using the clinical distinction between the more problematic grandiose narcissism (extrovert, high self-esteem) and vulnerable narcissism (introvert, low self-esteem) their study found the link between grandiose narcissism and social media use was significantly more prevalent in Gen X respondents than it was in Millennial respondents (2018: 308–11). This observation opens the way for a less anxious reading of our own respondents' perceptions and use of social media[9] with reference to narcissism: While some were circumspect about the self-promotional requirements of using social media to draw listeners, none of them expressed any moral or existential qualms about it. In fact, the idea of narcissism associated with social media and the judgment implied in the label "narcissist" was not something that they engaged with or concerned them. (Indeed a number of our respondents were quite clear that self-expression was only meaningful within a context of broader social or political engagement.) While a lack of focus on narcissism per se should not necessarily suggest an immunity to the condition, it does help us suggest (especially when coupled with the McCain-Campbell study) that the emphasis on narcissism's connection to social media might have more to do with Gen X social scientists and journalists projecting their own neuroses than it does with anything essential to Millennials.

The closest our respondents (and Byk as well) came to identifying narcissism as a potential problem was around the issue of personal branding. It is safe to say that the majority of our respondents recognized personal branding as

---

[9] Only 21 percent of our survey respondents could be described as enthusiastically marketing their podcasts on social media. Another 21 percent did no social media marketing at all, while 58 percent could be described as engaging in minimal social media promotion.

something of a necessity of active participation in a wider media world beyond their own relatively small circles, even if they were not currently developing their own brands (and even though Byk was at times critical of the practice). For them, personal branding seems less tethered to narcissism. In the *Podium. me* installment "How to Look at Boobs" we actually hear the idea of personal branding being negotiated: The piece begins with the *Podium.me* audio signature that foregrounds "our stories" and "our voices" after which the reporter, in quite a personal tone, uses mostly vox pop material to reflect on unwanted or objectifying gazes. Then we hear the most significant interviewee as utterly unapologetic about showing off her breasts. She asserts that she is constructing "my own sexuality in my own branded way." What she does with her breasts is an expression of her brand and this particular act of self-expression is represented as "empowering." What can seem troubling here to a more mature (Gen X) listener (particularly one familiar with the cultural/critical theory of movements like the Frankfurt School) is not that the interviewee might be sex-positive or comfortable in articulating an identity through her body, but that she so casually associates it with the act of "branding." With this move, it might rightly be feared, her body, or, by extension, her self, could be subsumed in exploitation or commodification.

The reason why the potential problems of narcissism and auto-commodification through personal branding do not create much anxiety for these young producers (and by extension the peers they interview) might lie in the way they frame their own work in making podcasts. Typically they did not think of their podcasting work as an expression of their own egos (as an auteur might); instead they most often described it as existing in recognition of, acknowledgment of, or relationship with another. Our interviewee Marci provides a clear example of this:

> It's also the thing of providing a service for other people—you're providing entertainment, you're doing something to make another person's day a little bit better when they commute to work or they come home and they're just chilling out . . . and it feels good that I've contributed to that a little bit I think.

Similarly, Tania finds her fulfillment when the podcasting circuit begins to inform her that her listeners took some pleasure in her work:

> The most rewarding thing for me is knowing that you've given someone something that they've enjoyed . . . I made one about silence, it was all about our

relationship with technology, and I had people saying I'd opened their eyes. It's that feedback that makes you want to create more.

Whether or not the stated aims of these producers or their responses to feedback belie some unconscious neurosis is beside the point. Their impressions here offer an explanation as to why critiques of personal branding or concerns of narcissism do not, and likely will not, land with this generation of podcast makers.

Beyond the pleasure in social relationships in *Podium.me* podcast distribution and consumption (evident in the responses from Marci and Tania above), Byk sees even more value in the social relations that form through the act of podcast making:

> I think the interview in itself is the reward personally. The interaction between two people who've taken the time to listen, and record a conversation is massive .... And that's what a lot of our journalists' feedback is. They say "I really enjoyed doing that interview." To me, job done, whether you broadcast it or not. (2016)

This emphasis on the value of interaction and exchange is central to her thinking about most aspects of podcasting. For example (returning briefly to listening for a moment), when asked to speculate on the future of the medium, she describes scenes reminiscent of early popular radio, with people around a speaker in a communal listening experience, often in public places (2015). Very interestingly for a podcasting pioneer, she is quite explicitly against headphone or earbud listening in public which she describes as "quite unsafe." While it might be physically unsafe for an individual listener on a busy street, there is a sense in Byk's responses that it might be unsafe for a conception of the Public as well. Her thinking here, as well as her emphasis on the social value of the act of interviewing and her reminder that the cell phone is a recording device as much as it is a listening device, all mark a challenge to (or an advancement on) much recent thinking which sees the social impact of portable audio devices in terms of privatization. Her vision for podcasting runs counter to sociological analyses in the recent history of listening as typified in Bull's rigorously individual iPod user:

> It is a hyper-post-Fordist culture in which subjects construct what they imagine to be their own individualised schedules of daily life—their own daily soundtrack of media messages, there own soundscape as they move through shopping centres, their own work-out soundtrack as they modulate the movements of their bodies in the gym. With its enveloping acoustics iPod users move through

space in their auditory bubble, on the street, in their automobiles, on public transport . . . . Their chosen music enables them to focus on their feelings, desires, and auditory memories. (2007: 3)

Described here is a thorough privatization of otherwise public spaces through the personalized curation of soundtracks. This curation of largely mass-produced music was seen by Bull as a means of grounding identity against an anonymity of urban spaces.[10] Yet in the podcasting world of young people (particularly in the case of *Podium.me* and its emphasis on self-expression) in which making and listening are overlapping activities, podcasting offers a more active means of creating an identity using the same digital tools. Seen from this perspective, identity formation need not be chiefly limited to the curation of other people's sounds. If iPod listeners are "enveloped in what they imagine to be their own reality," and "their own private mobile auditory world" (4), then the podcast producers of *Podium.me* might be seen as *making* their own homespun media realities.

The evolution from the iPod to the smartphone is a movement from imagining your own reality through curating your own playlist to making your own reality (or at least gesturing toward it) in the composition, writing, and production of your own podcast. And crucially, that reality is made in and firmly integrated into social media networks. The work of *Podium.me* producers explicitly contributes to a sense of community (around the podcasts and beyond) that is demonstrably different from one that might be created through curating (and even sharing) a playlist. The practice and the relationships are qualitatively different and, it seems plausible to argue, the attachments to them are qualitatively different as well. We can further argue that the act of composing and sharing a podcast, which often includes collecting voices and opinions different from your own, participates differently in the discourses of identity and community: a playlist is most often a statement of what "I" like and what "I" desire at a given moment—it is a less ambiguous statement of identity; a podcast exists as a contribution to a community and may be made for a host of reasons beyond the aesthetic, the personal, or the tribal.[11]

---

[10] Bull borrows from Adorno to help frame iPod culture as instantiating "mediated we-ness" (2007: 80). The consumption of mass-produced music is an antidote for the lack of social connectivity in modern culture—a technologically mediated form of experience becomes an ersatz substitute for direct experience.

[11] It is also interesting to note that while Bull situates iPod listening within, and as a response to, alienating and depersonalized urban spaces, "The Pod" (the administrative base for *Podium.me*) is located in a real and tangible domestic space (a spare room in Byk's house) that is a welcoming, rather than alienating, meeting place for *Podium.me* producers. *Podium.me*'s audio is grounded in a real space of material interactions.

Flipping the script on a Frankfurt School critique: Recording before listening

As Bull suggested in the lines that headed this chapter, there was an unavoidable and circular trap in iPod listening. The problem, concisely stated, is that through iPod use the collective remedy offered by music for the alienation of modern society becomes a privatized psychological remedy. A craving for a safe and solitary sanctuary from modernity comes hand in hand with greater social isolation. Bull describes one of his respondents as walling off real-world acoustic interaction behind his headphones; this practice grows addiction-like—the more he listens alone the more he is driven to find comfort from his loneliness behind his headphones (53). This is an analysis built on the work of Horkheimer and Adorno who saw popular music creating "an illusion of immediacy in a totally mediated world, of proximity between strangers, the warmth of those who come to feel a chill of unmitigated struggle of all against all" (1973: 46). Bull's critical contribution to the history of audio is one of many compelling and incisive analyses of digital culture with roots in the Frankfurt School which include: the deconstruction of the recycled and unrealistic promotional rhetoric around social media in particular and the internet in general;[12] the observation that a cultural focus on increased media production opportunities for individuals can limit possibilities for material social change; the analysis of how social media platforms monetize friendship;[13] and the argument that "appification" functions primarily to depoliticize listening and commodify listeners.[14] While keenly aware of the power of this body of work, I contend that a project like *Podium.me* helps us shift our technological focus and find a way out of this thicket of disempowering problems. And it does so by inviting us to conceive of smartphones (the Millennial's and the Gen Zer's mobile audio devices) as devices for podcast *production* at least as much as devices for podcast consumption.

Further, *Podium.me* offers to this history an integrated case study of recording, making, and distribution within the context social media. As recent years have seen efforts to push cultural and social history from the visual into the sonic (Hendy 2014), so the analysis of *Podium.me* invites a focus on the high-quality microphone of the smartphone (which is, arguably, the most essential feature of our phones).

---

[12] See, for example, Spinelli (1996a).
[13] See, for example, Lenhart (2015).
[14] See, for example, Morris and Patterson (2015).

A focus on the microphone flips the script on what Bull saw as the "private and mobile auditory worship"(2007: 2) facilitated by the deaf iPod. This is the dynamic that played out on my train ride up to interview Byk and her response to it: I used a mobile audio device to privatize while she would have used it to socialize.[15]

In the analysis of iPod listening, a self is driven to assuage fears and meet needs in ways which seem only to heighten those fears and needs. Instead, the analysis of *Podium.me* draws attention to the microphone and helps us paint a picture of podcasting's contribution to new identity formations beyond the modernist notions of self (and, by extension, "diversity") of previous critics. Rather than merely fulfilling a basic need, *Podium.me* might be seen as engaging with an aspiration for social communion or extending social experience. This social potential of podcasting is elaborated through the smartphone microphone. The microphone which enables the interview, spontaneous or planned, addresses that poignant Frankfurt School "chill" not with more privatization, but with socialization, collectivity, and interactivity. In the hands of the *Podium.me* journalists the mobile audio device is not a tool for withdrawing from social spaces and other people, but a means of interacting with them.[16] The smartphone—on which it is as easy to record as it is to listen to audio—invites others to be literally *present* with *Podium.me*'s young journalist.[17]

None of this is meant to undo, or even challenge, Bull's observation of cultural privatization through the iPod. Rather, it is intended to reframe the tension between the desires for isolation (individuality) and for connectivity (socialization). It is possible to imagine an evolution: previously, a use and a version of mobile audio technology had privatized urban spaces; now a new use and version of this same technology can be seen as opening opportunities for socialization and addressing the desire for interconnected and communal experiences. This happens in *Podium.me* first through the interviews that

---

[15] While certainly the listening function of smartphones will remain more used than the production function, the reminder that its production function exists as seen in the real-world practice of projects like *Podium.me* offers a remedy to the malaise of Frankfurt School critiques worth considering. For a practical guide to this production function of mobile devices in the broader world of journalism, see Burum and Quinn (2015).

[16] Nearly all of *Podium.me*'s online instructional and recruitment webpages, videos, and blogs discussed or demonstrated recording on your phone or tablet rather than other, more expensive and exclusionary audio gear.

[17] It is worth noting that *Podium.me*'s first large commission for BBC Radio One was a documentary about the positive social potential of smartphones which examined an array of projects and innovations initiated by young people, from an app to help blind people travel the world to a campaign to end slave labor at shoe companies. Documentaries like these are part of a larger *Podium.me* agenda to alter perceptions of young people and the technologies and behaviors often associated with them.

the smartphone's microphone makes possible and then through every stage of the production and distribution processes. The device can and is used to socialize spaces it was used to privatize ten years earlier. In this way, and in spite of Frankfurt School critiques, *Podium.me* might then be seen as offering an alternative to the neoliberal currents of privatization, isolation, and narcissism that swirl around so much thinking about contemporary online culture.

Podium.me's impact on its participants and the larger media ecology

We're really enthusiastic about the production, not the promotion . . . . For us the work that we do with young people is actually about the work we do with young people. If someone wants to listen then that's like an added benefit.
—Camilla Byk (2016)

It is important to note that much of Byk's work extends beyond opportunities for identity construction and a sense of participation in a shared youth project. *Podium.me* would be less viable for Byk if it did not include a significant vocational element. Networking events and attention paid to the future careers of young journalists help enable *Podium.me*'s conception of diversity to move beyond one, relatively small, podcast series into a larger media world.[18] This is also an important draw for most young participants (who tended to frame their *Podium.me* work in roughly equal terms of idealism and ambition). Eighty-five percent of them described the opportunities for professional networking as a "very important" reason to get involved. They felt these opportunities were generally quite effective with 37 percent reporting that, subsequently, they went on to secure some paying media work as a direct result of contacts made through *Podium.me* (60 percent reported getting unpaid work). Concrete practical skills were the skills most often mentioned by our interviewees in discussing what they got out of the experience with *Podium.me*. Among these, interviewing techniques topped the list, followed by story structuring, editing, using audio equipment, scheduling and working to deadlines, and experimenting with different styles of audio production. More generic personal skills were also

---

[18] *Podium.me* seems to succeed in the notoriously difficult task of marrying a self-expression/diversity agenda with a vocational agenda in single youth media project. For a more detailed discussion of this tension in other projects, see the previously cited Blum-Ross (2015).

mentioned: the ability to feel more confident, a recognition of the importance of social media and the ability to ask for help.

At the level of craft and composition, participants mentioned an understanding of media structures and narrative concepts as a benefit of their involvement in *Podium. me*. They described: an awareness of podcasting as an audio media distinct from radio, a respect for how much effort is involved in producing substantial media projects, a new understanding of storytelling as a powerful means of engaging with an audience, a caution around predicting what stories will go viral or even be popular, and a respect for an audience's interests and attention span when conceiving of media projects. Finally, and consistently, our respondents mentioned (often with some surprise) that they discovered that good, nonexploitative media organizations do exist and that there are people (chiefly Byk) generous enough with their time to create genuine opportunities for would-be journalists and producers. This aspect was brought into sharp relief by disappointing, unsatisfactory, or exploitative unpaid experiences they had had as interns or work-study students with other media outfits. Almost all of our interviewees had a sense of the problems presented by the "internship economy" (many with first-hand experience), but few of them had figured out a systematic or productive approach to the dilemma. While some of our interviewees believed that corporate internships were simply necessary for a first job in media, 55 percent said that the internship economy was a genuine obstacle to securing paying media work.[19]

Numerous unlucky experiences dotted our survey. Sofia's series of expensive unpaid internships had left her quite disillusioned:

It's free work and the organizations take it all out of you. I graduated in 2015 and I've done so much work experience that you can't fit it onto a CV, and it's all unpaid . . . . I've been to London twice, lived there on my own expenses, I've been to [a northern city], lived there on my own expenses to do work experience and I've got nothing back from it. Personally it has put me off journalism, it has put me off media so I am looking into further work fields.

Despite nearly two years of (unpaid) internships she was still being told when being rejected for paying media jobs that she did not have enough experience. She felt that this situation was likely to continue.

---

[19] The anxiety that several of our respondents mentioned around unpaid internships outside of *Podium. me* also makes it harder to maintain the accusations of narcissism discussed earlier. In the context of trying to get attention at the companies that hosted them for internships some mentioned an unease at "shoving" their work or ideas on people and "forcing it down people's throats" in order to be given responsibilities greater than making coffee. The internship economy, they felt, was forcing them into fierce self-promotion, a self-promotion that might easily be perceived as narcissism by a casual observer.

Kate, who had similar experiences, came to feel a de facto classism around contemporary media careers as a result of her internship experience:

> It was a really great opportunity but if you weren't really rich and couldn't afford to live in London with your parents paying for you then you were screwed. I had to leave halfway through. They had a list of 400 people to replace me. They were like, "We want to keep you on and pay you but we can't and there's loads of people waiting so it was really nice to have you here, bye." So I ended up being a receptionist at [a car dealership].

Similarly, the interviewee Alex opted out of the internship economy altogether because, he says, "I value myself higher than unpaid." But as of the date of his contribution to our research he had not found a paid media position within a company despite months of trying.

Perhaps unsurprisingly, our respondents who had what might be called the greatest vocational "success" combined very active independent media producer profiles (often a profile framed in terms of "alternative," "progressive," or "diversity") with seeking work for established companies; interestingly, most of these successes happened outside Britain. Former *Podium.me* journalist Chang is perhaps the most impressive example. A Hong Konger undergraduate student studying media in the UK, when Chang returned home his experiences with *Podium.me* informed his development of a podcast with some like-minded friends. That podcast, as he described it, was a dissident political series that used humor and parody to criticize, poke fun at, and otherwise antagonize the relatively new Chinese government of Hong Kong. One recent installment covered the opening of an Mass Transit Railway (MTR) station—a giant transport corporation with international reach and UK assets and projects, is pilloried for its appalling use of English (the de facto legal language of Hong Kong) on station billboards.

More pointedly, their episode about a Remembrance Day celebration in Hong Kong exposes the Chinese government's attempts to rewrite the history of the Commonwealth government and pre-communist China. Of this installment, Chang said:

> Our agenda was to make our audience think about historical facts and make them feel good about Hong Kong, and probably remind them that the regime, which is currently in power, doesn't respect our own history. We didn't make acute criticisms; we just laid out facts.

At the point of our last follow-up correspondence Chang was working part-time as a journalist for RTHK, the public service broadcaster in Hong Kong, while one of his collaborators was working for a progressive Hong Kong MP. Now somewhat more cautious about their positions, they are considering concealing more of their barbs in parody. One podcast endeavor that they were planning to take up was a "Make Hong Kong Great Again" campaign that would gently suggest that aspects of Hong Kong life were better under the Commonwealth and how progress might be made under the current Chinese government.

While Chang has evolved as a journalist since *Podium.me*, ideas about diversity and media that he might have absorbed during his time with *Podium. me* have also evolved: his thinking is fluid, his disruptive media projects are situational, and he is not explicitly concerned with issues like integration, inclusion, representation, or even access. He inhabits an online environment that provides him all the unfettered access he feels he needs. Through podcasting Chang is able to express dissent (youthful or otherwise) away from the constraints of more official broadcasting. But throughout his development his commitment to critique and the value of media intervention have remained constant, even as he considers less telegraphed punches. This critical awareness, this ability to identify structural and ideological problems in whatever media environment one finds oneself, might become more important for *Podium.me* as it continues to grow into an increasingly international venture in a world where young people in vastly different locations face vastly different problems with their own versions of mainstream media.

7

Blood Culture: Gaming the Podcast System

It's Saturday night and I'm out with my family, taking a break from work-ing on Blood Culture. *After two years writing, directing and producing the series, it was launched this weekend. We're in a pub, my eight-year-old son is playing bar billiards for the first time. This is a family moment, but then my phone buzzes. A text from Phil, one of my co-writers. "We're at number 1. We've beaten the Archers!" I leave the family, and rush out into the night air. I'm checking my phone, calling up data. It's as I hoped. Number one in the Arts chart and into the top 40 of the podcast chart proper. The red square of* Blood Culture's *logo is sandwiched between those of* Radiolab *and* The Adam Buxton Show. *I stare at it. It looks incongruous there, but I had planned this. I'd found out enough about the way Apple runs its charts to know that this would happen. Inside Monty takes his first shot on a pool table . . . but I miss the moment.*

Blood Culture was a ten-part audio drama series—a "hyperkinetic" techno-thriller that was told through podcast, radio broadcast, film, blog, social media, web, and SMS text game. It was launched in April 2017, and was the product of a team of forty writers, designers, actors, coders, producers, and publicists, who were funded by the biomedical charity The Wellcome Trust. In the six months after its release it topped the iTunes podcast chart, gained over 150,000 listeners and won multiple radio and audio industry awards. This chapter will detail the development of the project, the processes by which it was produced, and the way the audience responded to it. It is presented not as a blueprint for the production of podcasting as a transmedia form, or as a guide of how to produce audio drama, but as an analysis of the development, creation, and distribution of a podcast as part of a digital media experience. The intention is that this serves as a piece of grounded research located in the very real, pragmatic, and tangential decisions that are taken in the creation of practical work. The mechanisms of media production are not clean and do not occur in isolation, but are the results of methodologies that are untidy, subject to mediation, and contingent. This is a study that will include discussion of the considerations that shape the form of a media product, qualitative research into how an audience relates to that product, and an analysis of a piece of transmedia experience design. It is also a description of how I worked with a team to create a show that topped the Apple Podcast charts, and how those charts, which are currently a vital part of the podcasting infrastructure, can be "gamed," or even directly manipulated.

Blood Culture follows the adventures of two women, A'isha Cowan and Livi Thwaite, as they attempt to expose the corruption that lies at the heart of MetaCorp, a dystopian multinational tech giant. Employees of the corporation are being tested, monitored, and pushed to extremes by a culture of overwork and high expectation. Interns are dying, and the company is doing nothing about it, cloaking their activities behind a cult that has built up around Richard Dreyer, Meta's charismatic CEO. A'isha and Livi follow a trail of evidence through underground labs, frozen storage centers, data hubs, and out into the rolling hills of the English countryside. They fight and hide, they break into buildings and uncover hidden truths that challenge not just the company, but conceptions of who they are. *Blood Culture* was pitched to the Wellcome Trust as a biomedical whodunit, a techno-thriller that required its audience to engage with details of science to understand the show's central mystery. This scientific awareness was at the foundation of the project, it was present not only in the story but in the after-show discussions and through the layers of transmedia. The audience engaged with these issues not directly, there was no teaching, but through the beats of the narrative. *Blood Culture* was ostensibly not about blood, stem cells, or hematological research, it was about two women fighting against an exploitative and uncaring corporation; it was about action, dynamism, risk, and human frailty.

Development

The Wellcome Trust granted the project £40,000 in response to a funding bid that was submitted to its "People Awards" public engagement scheme. A grant proposal of this nature possesses a status somewhere between a promise of performance and an aspirational wish list. We asserted that we could garner an audience of a particular size and of a particular identity. Our claim was that the series would "introduce a diverse and digitally native Millennial audience to debates and research related to the commodification of blood and blood products." This statement was the key driver in the development of the project.

Traditional broadcast media is produced with an acute awareness of who the audience are, and how they are likely to be engaging with the text. Radio broadcasts are scheduled to appeal to very particular audience demographics, the needs and likely responses of whom have been predetermined through research and testing (Hendy 2001; Dann 2015). When writing and producing a radio drama for the UK's BBC Radio Four there is an awareness of who the audience are likely to be. They are identified as being aged 45+, of the social class ABC1, and predominantly female (BBC 1999). Despite this, there is little information fed through to writers and presenters after a show's transmission about how the audience responded, and in what numbers they listened. The podcast producer has an understanding of their audience in terms of broad data sets. Podcast services provide statistics that detail how many people have listened to a show, where they listened from, and when they listened, but there is no direct data on *who* listened. There is broad-based demographic research released from Edison about the podcast industry, and there is anecdotal information, for instance, that tells us that *Welcome to Night Vale* is popular with Millennial audiences (Cranor 2015), and that *Serial* was listened to by car drivers (Rosin 2016). There is no specific data currently available that details the demography of a show's audience, particularly if it is an independently produced project, and being released outside a podcast network.

The arts radio station, Resonance 104.4 FM, oversaw the production of the project, and later broadcast it across London. Since its launch in 2002 Resonance has built a reputation for its open, free flowing, and experimental programming (Trilling 2007). It is a station the prides itself on spontaneity, that is willfully diverse and delights in wrong footing its audience,[1] the demographic identity of whom have never been clearly identified. The station offers a space where experimentation can occur, creativity is expressed, ideas trialed, and limits pushed without fear of failure or of confusing and losing the audience. This provides tremendous artistic freedom for those working with and for the station, and also the terror of the blank page for those involved. Boundaries are fluid

---

[1] I had previously worked with the station on a voluntary basis as a nonexecutive board member and for three years as head of commissioning, a role that entailed sorting through hundreds of unsolicited program ideas and finding programming slots for those that gained my attention and fitted with the stations open remit.

at Resonance, and station guidelines and rules applied pragmatically. A phone call to the station's CEO, Ed Baxter, about what duration he felt the program episodes should be gained the gnomic response: "They should be as long as they need to be, Lance."

This degree of freedom positioned me, as creative lead and series producer, as the most significant stakeholder in terms of the tone and content of the work. It was my place to decide how we would reach our target "Millennial and digitally native" audience. I had an extensive understanding of the form we were working in and its creative possibilities. I am an experienced audio drama and radio producer, having worked in New York theatre and won awards for my radio work. Five years previously I had produced *The Flickerman*, a cross-media audio project that gained a following with a similar audience to that which we hopped for *Blood Culture*. I was also a forty-something white male academic (with a writing team of a similar age[2]) who had made a promise that he could produce work that would appeal to a diverse audience that was at least twenty years younger than himself. Creating work with the sole intent of fulfilling the promises made in a bid document would have effectively destroyed any sense of freedom and spontaneity for the project. I decided that our creative process had to fulfill a simple criteria, one that I had learned when devising plays with the avant-garde New York theatre company The Wooster Group.[3] We would create work that resonated for us, in that moment, and had to assume that there would be other people who would also be moved and entertained by it. When developing *Blood Culture*, when breaking the episodes in the writers' room and working with Dr. Cristina Lo Celso, our biomedical consultant, and when building the various elements of the online experience, we had to ensure that the work was punchy, dynamic, and most importantly that it excited us. The hope being that the themes that the story addresses, of the commodification

---

[2] The production team for the project was assembled on an ad hoc basis over a period of twelve months and represents the activation of what Starkay et al. term a "latent network" (2000). Old contacts were called up, friends sourced, and collaborators drawn in from previous projects. Recruitment choices are made on a basis of who is known, who is dependable, and who answers their phone first. This can lead to a degree of heterogeneity.

[3] In 2000, after several years of working with and for the BBC, I joined The Wooster Group, an avant-garde touring theatre company based in New York. Following their performances, they would have question and answer sessions with the audience, in which the company would attempt to give the most obtuse answers possible to the audience's perfectly reasonable questions about their work. One night they were asked, "Why do you make the work that you make? Who do you make it for?" Their answer was disarmingly simple, and yet a revelation to someone who had spent the better part of a decade working with the BBC: "We make work for ourselves, we try to entertain and challenge each other and we just kind of hope that there are enough people out there like us who'll also enjoy what we do."

of the body, of the exploitation of interns, and the oppressive behavior of tech companies, would resonate not only with us, but more importantly with our target audience.

The audio elements of the series were developed to be broadcast on radio as five episodes, each of an hour in length. These were recut, and scheduled as ten podcasts of thirty-minute duration, which was close to the twenty-two minutes that is quoted by several web sources as being the average time listeners spend with a podcast (Bridge Ratings 2017). Each episode would address a specific theme, raising a possible cause of the deaths at Meta, such as blood doping, the testing of synthetic blood, or blood farming. This format, a biomedical version of the "monster of the week,"[4] was augmented with metanarrative strands that evolved over the series, and that climaxed at the last episode. The original conception of the project was that it be a fictional reversioning of *Serial*, using the motif of a self-reflexive reporter whom, through questioning and dogged investigation, would unpick the tangled web of the story's mystery. This was part of the original bid, submitted in late 2014 at the peak of *Serial*'s success. It took twelve months for the proposal to be written, accepted, and for the preliminary research to be completed, and during that time shows such as *Limetown* and *The Black Tapes* had gained success using this format. The launch of *Blood Culture* was in April 2017, by which time these storytelling tropes would have been a cliché, and this approach was abandoned in the spring of 2016 to avoid any sense that the work was derivative.

The writing team reconceived the series as a full-cast production with A'isha, the show's protagonist providing narration.[5] Unlike other podcast dramas (including *Homecoming, Bright Sessions, Tanis,* and *Rabbits*) there would be no explanation or context for why the audio existed, no microphones placed in characters' hands or devices that could capture sound featured in the script. We wrote the narration such that it would be delivered in short bursts, punching in-between action in real time and cutting through dialogue to provide subtextual comment and insight. The language was stripped bare, adjectives expunged, and description avoided. The audience were allowed freedom to conceive and create the characters and the environments for themselves. Physical traits and appearances were merely suggested with specifics only occasionally being given; for instance, the grebo-punk Livi was described as having "flowing blonde dreadlocks" and "heavy boots" in the opening scenes of the series, but after that

---

[4] "Monster of the week" is a term use for a form of media storytelling where a different antagonist is encountered, challenged, and defeated in each episode of a series.
[5] This team consisted of myself, David Wigram, and Phil Connolly.

there are no more details of her appearance. The audience are left to respond to the actor's performance, the dialogue, and the setting to create their own mental images; allowing them a personalized "headcanon," or version of the production, which is respected and not usurped by contradictory information appearing in later episodes.

This narrator-led format did not present the opportunity to directly engage the audience, to break the fourth wall, and acknowledge their presence in a personal and intimate manner. A forum was needed within the production that would allow us to address the audience outside the remit of the drama. This would allow us to create bonds with the listeners, and to discuss issues and ideas contained in the narrative. To fulfill this need, the show was bookended with roundtable discussions featuring the cast, crew, and consultants. Hosted by series writer David Wigram these sessions were informal and unscripted, produced with the intention of providing a sense of human context and personality for the series, to allow the audience over time to build a relationship, not just to the characters, but also to us as producers and creators.

Production

The recording of the actors and the Foley took place in studios over three weeks in October 2016. When audio drama recordings are set up, there is a balance to be considered between issues of the sound quality, the freedom that actors are permitted, and how the audience are likely to be listening. The room can be rigged so that it functions like a set or sound stage, with microphones mounted on booms and following actors who can roam and move, physically inhabiting the work and dynamically responding to one another. This technique, which is similar to that used by John Dryden in his work for the BBC and Panoply (Dryden 2017), benefits close headphone listening and captures a raw natural sound, both in terms of acoustics and performance. Another approach, and one which is employed by K. C. Wayland (*We're Alive*) involves close-miking the cast using a large diaphragm microphone (Wayland 2017).[6] Actors deliver their lines from fixed points, wearing headphones, ensuring that the audio quality is

---

[6] This technique is used by Dirk Maggs for projects where timescales and budgets are "tight." Maggs sets out the studio and adapts his techniques dependent on the project's story, audience, and finances (Maggs 2018).

uninterrupted and consistent in both level and location. Movements, effects, and body Foley are then added as part of post-production. This technique is favored by some American producers (Greenhalgh 2017) because the recordings have a higher quality that is redolent of dialogue that has been recorded for cinema. It is suited to listening in cars, with the crisp-treated voice recordings cutting over the low frequency drone of engine noise.

Blood Culture used an amalgamation of these techniques. Simon James, the project's lead sound designer, configured the studio space using dividers to create the acoustic environment of each scene. Furniture was drawn in where needed, simple props placed, and then a stereo pair of microphones was used to capture actors as they moved through the action. This gave a controlled sound for the production, while allowing the cast to experience at least some dynamism in their performance. Location recording of actors was attempted, with the results being at once deeply satisfying, because of the quality of the voice and the integration of unplanned sonic artifacts that lent a sense of authenticity (birdsong, distant air traffic, passers-by) and also deeply frustrating and time consuming for exactly the same reason.

When postproducing and mixing audio work decisions are made about the manner in which the audience will be listening, with a tendency being to master the audio for the "worst-case" scenario. A drama broadcast on radio has to be balanced in such a fashion that it can be appreciated in a car, on a mono kitchen radio, in an echoing bathroom, or over high-quality stereo speakers. Panning must be limited, and music used sparingly and mixed far below the level of the voice, even in the more ambitious productions sound design must be stripped out and simplified. We assumed that *Blood Culture* listeners would be using earbuds, and, when mastering, regularly switched from studio monitors to headphones to recreate their experience. This allowed the production of a more intricate soundscape, but it also required more precise editing and balancing of sonic elements (such close listening highlights even the smallest glitches and errors in the audio). Through a combination of creative obsessiveness and willing self-exploitation the sound design team (consisting of Simon James, Marley Cole, and myself) spent several weeks working on each episode. This created a sound world that was multilayered and immersive. James describes, in a postshow discussion, an experience that is almost fractal in its nature: His process involved digging deeper and deeper into the soundscape, creating every swish of a cloth, every creak of a shoe, and every rattle of a cup until he had to stop himself (or be stopped by his producer). The results of this work rewarded deep listening, the kind described by *Love + Radio* producer Brendan Baker, where the audience surrender themselves to the experience: headphones locked to ears, eyes shut, distractions removed (Baker 2016). This meant that we were guilty of producing work not for the worse-case scenario, but for the best, for the idealized and perfect listener who is not out walking their dog, or doing the cooking or driving the car, but is giving us all their undivided attention.

> Hi, I'm just a listener, or want to be one. I tried listening to the show while driving home on the freeway, and for whatever reason, I just could not make out what people were saying. I don't think it's just a question of accent, the many voices and sound backgrounds make the performance that much more interesting. But I do wish there was some way to bring out the voices a bit better. I ended up turning off the podcast, and leaving it to "late night walk" listening where I hope I will be able to understand it that much better.
>
> (Anonymous Direct Message to @bloodcultural, May 10, 2017)

Experience design

When designing a project that involves multiple media sources and interaction points it must be assumed that the audience respond in varying degrees of intensity and across tiers of engagement (Shirky 2008). *Blood Culture* is primarily a podcast drama, with the audio element comprising its central text. Most of its audience would be listeners who experience the work only when it is broadcast on radio, or they have downloaded it as part of their diet of digital audio entertainment. There would be a small grouping of audience members who would be inclined to extend their involvement with the text through discursive relationships with other listeners, or with the producers of the text itself. These followers, Fiske's enunciative fans, are important because they will spread the project through digital and interpersonal recommendation, becoming a component of the marketing strategy. A third group, a very small minority, will be actively engaged with the project, its story, and its extended storyworld. They will initiate discussions, create blogs, produce fan art, support crowdfunding campaigns, and actively search out any content related to the text. These are Jenkins's forensic fans, Shirky's power users, or Fiske's textual producers. Members of this group are essential for bringing vitality and life to works of interactive media, but because they are such a small proportion of the base audience they cannot be made to be the focus of the media production. Work cannot be produced for these fans alone; each cohort must be accounted for and catered to when designing a functioning and fully rounded media experience.

I had encountered this hierarchy of engagement when designing and producing the audio drama and web media work *The Flickerman*. The project's audience were directly encouraged to search out pictures online, watch films, follow action on maps, and interact with characters through social media. Between 2008 and 2011 *The Flickerman* gained approximately two million listeners[7] through radio broadcast and via podcast download; of this number approximately 10,000 visited the project's core website, 5,000 searched for pictures online, 1,000 watched films on Vimeo, 500 friended characters on social media, 50 engaged actively with them, 10 were deeply involved in attempting to crack the many mysteries of the series, and 2 people managed to find out where I lived (in the hope that I would tell them what the series was about). This fall off in the numbers of people engaging is typical for interactive works, the rapidity of the drop will vary dependent on the design and nature of the piece. This is the long tail or the power-law ratio of engagement, an inevitable component of the distribution of digital works.

The design of a digital media experience requires a delicate balance. Each element must be a satisfying and rewarding experience in and of itself; it must augment the core text and allow the audience to feel that they are gaining through their increased engagement. When the producers of *Serial* included information and documents as part of the web-component of the first season, they provided a means by which the audience could feel that they were actively involved in the investigation of the case. They recreated the passive listener as coinvestigator, and responded to their fans' evidence and input as the series progressed. *Serial's* second season packaged each audio episode with a selection maps, army pamphlets, training videos, and new reports that were intended to augment the central text. These materials could be found readily elsewhere online, and they simply provided context or color. They did not make the audience feel that they were part of something, that they were contributing to a world that was beyond their everyday experience. Fan contributions are spontaneous, and they are born of a personal urge to respond to a text through a productive act. Effective transmedia is designed to create the impression that the audience member is doing something that personally involves them in a unique manner.

---

[7]   This figure is an estimate based on combined audience listening figures of ABC (National) Australia, VPRO (Holland), CBC (Canada), Resonance 104.4 FM (UK), KPDA and WFMU (United States), and a range of small community stations that broadcast the series.

Blood Culture was a closed room mystery; it was puzzle that the audience were encouraged to solve. Supplementary media material had to be designed in such a way that key elements of the plot or evidence were not hidden from the less engaged members of the audience. Fundamentally, the story had to make sense to everyone, no matter whether they were an ardent fan, or just listened in to a few episodes on the radio. Another consideration was that these elements could not focus on specific characters. Podcasting is an asynchronous and longitudinal form, and episodes remain online for as long as the creators wish. A year after *Blood Culture* was released people are still encountering the story for the first time, and each of them is engaging with the series on a schedule of listening personal to them. These new listeners will not want to interact with a blog or social media account that gives away the ending, or that tells them who lived and who died, they do not want to know "whodunit." In response to these issues, the focus of the project's digital experience was placed on the broader storyworld, as manifested by the faceless and oppressive corporate behemoth, Meta. This fictional tech company provided an opportunity to create an experience that would hint at the mysteries of the main plot, without revealing them. Meta's outputs on its social media and websites were constructed from the technobabble and management double speak of twenty-first-century corporate life:

> At Meta we embrace flexible working, which is why we are so happy to see so many of our employees here on Sunday. Well done guys!

> We're trialling beanbags on Level 4 of Meta, designed to smooth your creation flow and expand your informal headroom for brainthink.
>
> (Tweets from @metaselected.co.uk, May 2017)

The company's online presence satirized the self-aggrandizing language of Google, the oppressive employee practices of Amazon, and the cult of personality of Jobs's Apple. It was a representation of the attempts by knowledge companies to reposition the act and place of work as being one of play. This is a process described by sociologist Andrew Ross as "an insidious hazard of no-collar work that . . . can enlist employees' freest thoughts and impulses in the service of salaried time" (Ross 2004: 19). Workers at Meta are allowed no time or moment that is their own. Richard Dreyer, CEO of the company, tells A'isha in episode one: "Work? We don't work here. It is our life, it is our play. It is our mana and our very being" (2017). These ideas, of the reconfiguring of the workplace as an oppressive playground, resonated with the audience. They recognized the references and the tone of the language. They played along with it, challenging the company, arguing with them and occasionally abusing them on social media:

@metaselected: We have a leader who will bring strength and stability.
@iloveknives: Now where have we heard that load of old BATWANK before?
@metaselected: Your dissent has been noted in the Meta-Logging System.
@iloveknives: As usual, although when have I ever been intimidated?
@metaselected: We have a LONG file on you now.
@iloveknives: Good—I'll use it to hold open a door or something.
@metaselected: We will prevail.
@iloveknives: Yes dear. "pats."
@metaselected: Patting is not permitted. Your pats have been noted on the Meta-Logging System.

(Twitter conversation between @metaselected
and user @iloveknives, May 20, 2017)

Blood Culture's core site (www.blood-culture.com) served as a repository for the show's audio media, a video trailer, and links to www.metabeta.co.uk, the in-world recruiting site for MetaCorp.[8] Here visitors encountered a side scrolling company website loaded with fatuous business aphorisms, company biographies, and an application page for the intern scheme. This faux-recruitment process was trailed heavily in the postshow discussions, and via social media. Listeners were encouraged to apply to join Meta, and win a *Blood Culture* T-shirt if they were accepted. This call to action was the first stage of *Blood Culture*'s tiered transmedia experience; it was the "rabbit hole," a portal for deeper and more intense engagement. After completing an online isometric test, applicants submitted their personal details including their mobile phone number. If they were willing to surrender this information, they were rewarded, moments later, with an SMS text message from the company:

Hi, my name is Justine. I'm here to tell you that you have been chosen to go forward to the next stage of the Meta-recruit programme. This company is a huge family and we're looking forward to having you as a member. If you would like to join us at the next stage—please reply YES.

(Introductory message from *Blood Culture* text game)

If the player responded by texting back "Yes," Justine would take them through the next stage of the application process. This was the beginning of a forty-minute

---

[8]   The Metabeta site and the @metaselected Twitter handle were designed and maintained by Dr. James Morris of City University, London.

interaction, a text conversation with a worker at Meta who would ask them questions and respond openly to their comments. Over time Justine would begin to express her doubts and finally admit that she needed help to break into the company offices. The player was asked to provide distractions as she moved around the building. Eventually Justine would be discovered and, cornered, she would text the player a final plea to tell someone what was happening at Meta.

Justine was a chatbot, a bespoke computer program[9] that was designed to respond to a series of open text comments. SMS text was chosen for this element of the experience because it would draw the player away from their browsers and ask them to interface with a technology that is often reserved for personal communication. The software was coded to predict player responses, and to lead them through a simple branching storyline that always had the same end point. This created the impression that the experience was interactive, that the player was helping guide Justine and effecting the outcome of her adventures, while ensuring that the passage of the story followed a set pathway. Interaction recorded in the software's logging system revealed a diverse range of responses from the players: some were unsure as to whether they were talking to a real person, some played along with the game, others tried to confuse her, break her, or ask her out for a drink.

> 21:26 Justine: I'm in. We've got I guess 5 minutes. Her computer is unlocked. I'll download the data.
> 21:26 Player 87: Shall I call the police?
> 21:26 Justine: I'm so nervous. Let me get on with this.
> 21:28 Player 87: Sorry.
> 21:28 Justine: I'm going through her drawers, there's some pills, hidden away. EPO. What is EPO? Can you look it up? What is she up to?
> 21:29 Player 87: How do I know.
> 21:29 Justine: Well you're online I'm not. Figure it out for me will you please!
> 21:29 Player 87: I'm in the pub!
> 21:34 Justine: We'll deal with that later. Right—this data is taking forever to download . . . come on. Oh no, she's coming back . . ."
> 21:43 Player 87: Are you for real?
>
> (Play log from *Blood Culture* text game, May 8, 2017)

When she was caught, Justine asked that the player to contact Livi, one of the protagonists of the story, and tell her what had happened. They were given her

---

[9] Developed and implemented by Stephen Cooper of the digital agency Millipedia.

phone number, which triggered an answering message from the actor playing Livi, and they were asked to record her a message. This moment provided the player with insight into the very first beat of an audio series. In the opening scene Livi breaks into Meta, and confronts the CEO, Richard Dreyer, about the death of interns at the company. It is never explained to the casual listener how she found this out. The engaged fan who completes the game knows not only where she received this information, but that they gave it to her. This gives them a reward, it is their secret, one that does not disrupt the enjoyment of those with a more casual relationship to the text. *Blood Culture*'s transmedia was set up as a series of hurdles, a ludic experience that was designed not to reward "success," or the correct playing of a game, but the act of participation itself.

We launched *Blood Culture* online in April 2017 with episodes being released across the next ten weeks, after which it was broadcast on Resonance 104.4FM in London, and on Radio Reverb in Brighton. In the six months after its release it is estimated that 175,000 people listened to the series either on radio or online. It was downloaded or streamed 75,000 times by 25,000 people. The trailer for the series was viewed 7,000 times; blood-culture.com received 18,000 visitors and meta-beta.co.uk 2,750. Three hundred twenty people applied for jobs at Meta, Justine sent hundred texts to applicants and fifty-three players reached the end of the game of whom eleven left a message on Livi's phone. No one, thus far, has taken the trouble to work out where I live.

Marketing

To gain a following our audience had to be able to find us, and to be discoverable *Blood Culture* required either press, publicity, reviews, or a prominent position on the most important of podcast aggregators. The absence of the first three meant that we were reliant on being featured in the iTunes store.[10] There were 325,000 individual podcasts on iTunes globally and to be noticed in this "sea of audio" (Shapiro 2016) shows have to be visible in some way on the store's pages or inside the podcasting app (Levine 2017; Wayland 2017; Bae 2017). These can be on the "new and noteworthy" show listings, featured banners, curated lists, and in the charts themselves. *Blood Culture*'s online traffic of

---

[10] Apple does not have a monopoly on the podcast market, other platforms including Spotify, Pocketcast, and Stitcher are having an impact (Blumberg 2017), but in 2016, 80 percent of podcast traffic used its services (Walch 2017).

75,000 downloads and streams over twelve months does not bear comparison to the millions of downloads of leading podcast dramas. *The Black Tapes* has been downloaded thirty million times, *We're Alive* eighty million times, *Welcome to Night Vale* 100 million times. Despite this, *Blood Culture* reached number one in the Apple Podcast Arts chart three days after launch and remained in the top ten for several weeks. The show also entered the top forty of the UK's main podcast chart, positioning it many places above *We're Alive, The Black Tapes*, and *Welcome to Night Vale*. This anomaly is a product of the algorithms used by Apple to calculate chart positions, which I had sufficient understanding of to slightly "game" their systems, and thus successfully promote the show.

Apple is not forthcoming with information about how they decide which shows to feature or how their charts are calculated. This has left the field open for conjecture and rumor circulated among a plethora of self-described online "podcasting gurus," "social media experts," and "radio futurologists." Rob Walch, as VP for Public Relations for the podcasting service provider Libsyn, has a close working relationship with Apple and was able to provide insight into their methodologies. He asserts that there is some curation of content carried out by the Apple podcast team. Shows are selected to be included in the curated lists or featured on the front page. The "new and noteworthy" category is constructed from shows released in the past eight weeks and is based on a mixture of user reviews, ratings, and subscriber numbers combined some editorial oversight. The chart itself is not based on the number of downloads a show receives in each period, but on the number of new subscribers it has. According to Walch (2017), Apple calculates its charts several times each day using the follow formula:

1. the number of new subscribers on the day of chart multiplied by 4;
2. plus the number of new subscribers on the previous day multiplied by 3;
3. plus the number of new subscribers two days ago multiplied by 2;
4. plus the number of new subscribers three days ago;
5. plus the number of new subscribers four days ago;
6. plus the number of new subscribers five days ago;
7. plus the number of new subscribers six days ago;
8. divide the total number by 13.

To give context to this formula the first month's downloaded activity for *Blood Culture* is detailed here:

> April 21 to April 28—1,039 subscribers (2,200 downloads)
> April 29 to May 5—385 subscribers (1,774 downloads)

May 6 to May 12—384 subscribers (1,992 downloads)

May 13 to May 19—432 subscribers (2,311 downloads)

(The number of new subscribers has been assumed to equal the number of downloads for the first episode of the series).

Blood Culture was able to gain 500 subscribers on its first day of release, which positioned it next to *The Adam Buxton* Show podcast in the UK iTunes chart. It was only able to maintain this position for a day, the next day 339 people subscribed, and the show began to slowly move back down the chart. By comparison Buxton's show held its position, meaning that presumably it gains 500 new listeners every day, or 3,500 a week, or 175,000 a year. *Blood Culture* had a higher rate of downloads later in the month, but fewer subscribers, thus it did not have such a high chart position. Later in 2017 the project was featured on an episode *of Radio Drama Revival,* an audio drama review show that is part of the Wondery network. In the week that followed there was a considerable boost in the number of downloads, but not in its chart position. The show's audience figure for this period were as follows:

September 16 to September 24—391 subscribers (3,351 downloads)

There was a peak in downloaded activity, but not in the numbers of new subscribers. This was because new listeners had access to the entire series, and were downloading all ten episodes as a single "binge listen" package.

This method of calculating position means that the charts are, as Berry notes, "a poor external indicator of success, as popularity is measured by attention rather than consumption" (2016a: 663). It also creates dynamism and movement within the podcast industry (Walch 2017), and allows shows, like *Blood Culture,* to break through and benefit from a small surge in the number of followers. The use of these metrics makes the successful launch for a podcast an essential component of its long-term marketing. If a show does not have an in-built audience because of its association with celebrity, a recognizable franchise or a media network, then other methods are needed to generate a bank of new subscribers.

In the weeks leading to launch we circulated a promo video for *Blood Culture,* a bombastic movie-style trailer that was cut by Phil Connolly. This was then forwarded to Twitter users who were followers of similar shows and were self-identified fans of audio drama.[11] This process of direct marketing was labor

---

[11] This process involved social media manager Lizzie Parkinson and I filtering lists of shows Twitter followers and picking out those who featured terms such as "podcast addict," "true crime junky," or "audio drama lover" in their personal profile.

intensive and did not have a high response rate (approximately 10 percent). It was the digital equivalent of standing outside a nightclub or gig venue handing out band flyers: we knew that we were targeting the right audience, we could engage with them and speak with them directly, but a lot of our communication was ignored or simply discarded. Hundreds of tweets were sent during this period, and this was sufficient to build up a body of interest among audio drama fans. These potential subscribers could then be added to the pools of personal contacts the production team were able to bring to the project. Agrawal (cited in Davidson and Poor 2015: 294) found that family and friends are important early backers of crowdfunding projects, serving as a positive signal that attracts additional investors. This is also true of launching a podcast, when *Blood Culture* was released we were exploiting whatever social contacts we had:

> Please, please, please, can anyone who has ever known me or been taught by me or been married to me or been drunk with me or fallen out with me or been related to me click this link and then subscribe to my show. Subscribes are worth gold in the iTunes charts and we're number 16 at the moment and we want to get the Archers off number 1!
>
> (Facebook Post Lance Dann, April 20, 2017)

This call out was mirrored on the social media outputs of other members of the production team (though in less extreme terms). Through the combination of our direct marketing efforts, the social media outreach of Resonance 104.4 FM and some coverage in our local press we were able to gain sufficient subscribers for the show to lift it into the charts. I had been able to use my insight to "game" Apple's systems, and give the project enough of a boost to draw attention to it.

There are also more direct ways available to message audience numbers, and falsify success:

> I Will Promote And Market by Get Ranking For Your Podcast
>
> Hello. Are you looking to improve your great podcast?? Do you have a podcast in the USA iTunes store??? I will promote your podcast and get it in the top ranking on the iTunes store. I have 3 packages. You can choose my first package for to check my service for $5. I will show how your podcast will rank up number into the top ten. THANK YOU.
>
> (Gig offer, Fiverr.com, May 2017)

Fiverr.com is a digital platform that offers "freelance services for the digital entrepreneur." A manifestation of the gig economy in one of its purest forms, Fiverr provides a marketplace where small one-off jobs are offered in return for a minimum $5 fee. Categories of work offered include simple IT jobs, translation services, voice-over and jingle recording, business advice, and digital media marketing. It is under this last heading that a shifting coterie of providers offer "podcast marketing services," which guarantee Apple Podcast chart placements, the duration of which is dependent upon a fee of between $5 and $70. I tested these services by approaching three separate service providers and paying them to promote a dormant podcast in June 2017. I sent each service $5, gave them the RSS feed, and told them which country I wanted to see the show chart in. Over the next three days the show rose rapidly up through its category, eventually returning to the top position of its chart for a day. There was little increase in the numbers of downloads for the project during this time, a very slight rise which was the result of the show's appearance at number one, as opposed to the cause of it. After three days my payment had run out, the gig was over, and the show gradually slid back down the chart.

According to Walch these "podcast marketing" services use small groups of computers that are running a piece of software to create subscriptions over a virtual private network.[12] "Click farms" are also used for this work with multiple devices being set up, and an operator being employed to move from one to the other, clicking on each podcast and subscribing to its feed. A podcast can be banned from the iTunes store for using these techniques, and presumably the subscriber's account shut down, but the service itself is not illegal. Click farms have been raided in Thailand and Malaysia but the only charges brought have concerned the legality of workers and their working conditions, not because of the actions that they are carrying out (Deahl 2017). Those offering the services are guarded about their techniques, and deny that they are attempting to directly influence the chart:

> Lance Dann: Do you mind if I ask. How come you were so good at it! Where you doing downloads + reviews + subscriptions?
> Stevensmith: Great!! I hope you'll come back in future. Actually, I have a friend who works for a podcast promotion company and he helped me provide your service. Also, I have some friends, who I asked to subscribe to your podcast and listen to it. Really, I am happy because you are satisfied with my service. Thank you so much!!!
> (Personal online communication via Fiverr website)

---

[12] A virtual private network. A means of disguising the origin of a computer's IPN, and that can also falsify its country of origin.

That the Apple Podcast charts can be influenced with just a few hundred extra subscriptions makes them vulnerable to manipulation. Apple are aware of the issue, they can recognize a show that is buying subscriptions because of the imbalance between the subscription rate and the download rate. According to Walch, Apple may soon begin to act against offenders, until then there is some reassurance in the fact that the techniques are not widespread[13] and have yet to reach epidemic proportions.

Blood Culture's engaged community

Shifts in the technologies of media distribution and production have elevated fandom from the fringes of audience activity to a central role in the development and production of media texts. Studies of fan cultures (Hills 2002; Duffett 2015; Jenkins 2006) have focused on the relationship of the fans *toward* the media product or text. There has been very little research that uses empirical data detailing how audiences are drawn into projects and the triggers that encourage heightened modes of engagement. *Blood Culture* presented an opportunity to not only gather such data, but also to do so with benefit of insight provided by producers of the text.

The design of the project's web media experience expedited the process by which the fans, or power users, may be identified. They were taken to be those who were willing to drill down through the online experience, complete the SMS text game, and leave their personal contacts. This allowed a piece of qualitative research to be initiated that would involve interviewing these fans about their relationships to the text, to the form, and to each other. All of those contacted agreed to participate and were interviewed by Dr. Alastair Goode, a consumer psychologist, via either Skype or by phone. Interviews lasted between forty-five and ninety minutes and each subject was asked the same set of questions with the intention of gathering a set of indicative findings about the behavior and identity of this group.

Ten interviews were carried out in summer of 2017. In terms of gender, respondents were split with five who identified as male and five as female. There was also a fifty-fifty split in geographic location, five being based in the United

---

[13] I learned about Fiverr.com from a tech expert, not a podcaster, and no one that I have spoken inside the industry, other than Rob Walch, has known how to manipulate the charts in this fashion.

Kingdom and five in the United States. Eight of the group were Millennials, using Howe and Strauss's definition of having been born after 1982, meaning that they were between eighteen and thirty-five years of age. The remaining two respondents were aged thirty-five to forty-four. This demographic information coincides with data detailing *Blood Culture*'s following on Twitter. In July 2017 the @bloodcultural account was followed by 539 people of whom 73 percent were in the 18- to 34-year-old age group. All of those interviewed used Twitter as well at least one other social media platform several times a day.

The respondents were all active followers of podcasting, and their listening covered a range of high-profile shows from the United States including: *S-Town, Serial, Reply All,* and *Heavyweight.* They identified as being fans of audio drama, this being one of their main topics of conversation and interaction online. Their listening in this field was specialist and included well-known shows such as *Rabbits, The Black Tapes, Tanis,* and *Homecoming* alongside more niche productions including *Sword and Scale, Spines, Maple, Tunnels,* and *The Scottish Podcast.* That these are all genre works, with a focus on horror and thrillers is indicative of audience tastes and the production focus of podcast drama (as discussed in Chapter 5). What is noteworthy is that this group had a very positive association with UK media productions, with several listing the TV series *Dr. Who* and *Sherlock* as part of their media diet. There was a halo effect associated with the BBC, a recognition that professionally produced audio was released by the Corporation and that *Blood Culture* benefited with this group because it was a British production.

Five of the interviewees discovered the series through recommendations of other social media users who were circulating the show's video trailer. Four respondents were sent direct contacts from the @bloodcultural account, and a single person discovered the project having been sent to the meta-beta.co.uk site by a friend. The high-production values of the trailer were commented on. It made the project worthy of attention and indicated that this was a "professional" entry into what is mostly an "amateur" creative milieu.

A striking commonality within the group interviewed was how and when they chose to listen to podcasts, which tended to be in the workplace. This was an educated group, with degree-level qualifications who were engaged in white-collar jobs. Their day-to-day work tended to be repetitive, and was described as being "mundane" or "dull." Kelly, a thirty-year-old American insurance worker, described her job as being "boring" and that "we are not supposed to listen to anything, but I put my hair down and put earbuds in, so I don't get caught. We talk about podcasts between us at work." Among the respondents there were those who were filing reports, tending fish at a research lab, or managing data for admin departments. They were carrying out tasks that were neither physically or cerebrally taxing. Their jobs allowed them to listen for long periods of time without distraction. Podcasts filled a space in their diet of media consumption that opened up when they were at work. Emily, a twenty-year-old American college student, described how she would listen at work on a daily basis: "when you work at a desk you have to have something in your ears and I listen to music and fiction podcasts." Audio provided the perfect form to allow them to both carry out their job and engage with a narrative, to be taken away from what they were doing or simply feel that they had some "company." They also listened to a lot of material, up to seven hours a day, because of the nature of their work and the long hours that needed "filling." The popularity of the show with people in these working situations could also be explained by its subject matter. A satire of the culture of twenty-first-century corporate workplaces is likely to be appealing to those who work in those environments.

The show was also listened to in bed, in the bath, or at the gym, but only one person mentioned listening when they were out in public spaces. *Blood Culture* was designed to be an immersive experience, listening to it required that the listener prioritize the aural over other senses and to actively engage in the mental process of mapping out action, creating characters and building sets.[14] Those who were listening at work, in spaces that were familiar to them, where they carried out tasks that they had learned by rote, had the "spare" capacity to undertake this form of mental activity. The show was both sonically and phenomenologically too layered for these activities to be an "easy" listen when in public, or as noted earlier, when driving a car.

These were fans of audio drama in general, of which *Blood Culture* was a "well-produced," "well-acted," "atmospheric," and "exciting" example. Their relationship to the narrative was relaxed, this was a story that they wanted simply for entertainment, something to help them fill their time. The biomedical content that was embedded in the plot was treated as little more than a narrative device, something that they had to only pay enough attention to help understand the story. It was only later, when they listened to the postshow discussion, that they came to the realization that it was based on actual case studies and research.

---

[14] A discussion of the nature of this phenomenological process and its influence upon the form of podcast drama can be found in Chapter 5, "Don't Look Back: The New Possibilities of Podcast Drama."

Louis, a forty-four-year-old English pub landlord, describes how he "took some information on through the drama but it's not until you hear the doctor speaking afterwards that you can see how it actually works." Joel, a Scottish café worker, said of the project that because "it's a drama you think it is made up, it was the after-show stuff that made you realize it was real." Nine of the ten interviewees listened to the postshow talks, and it was here that any learning associated with the project occurred. Two respondents reported incidents where they surprised themselves, and their friends, with their detailed knowledge of the causes and effects of sickle cell thalassemia. A'isha, the show's protagonist, suffers from this condition, and it is something that is discussed several times by Dr. Lo Celso in the postshow sessions. Louis, the landlord quoted above, told of how he provided a long and detailed answer to a pub quiz about sickle cells to the "amazement" of his customers. The postshow talks were key to the project's public engagement and to the learning and retention of information and concepts. The show's drama and action drew the audience in, gave them context for what was being discussed, and gave them a reason to listen. For ten to fifteen minutes a digitally native (and predominantly Millennial) audience listened to a leading expert (Dr. Lo Celso) in the field of stem cell research and hematology discuss her work. From the point of view of public engagement those moments were the peak of the entire project, and the promise of the original funding bid was fulfilled.

The interviewees admired the transmedia elements of the story, and recognized that there was something unique about them. They described how they enjoyed feeling that they were "in control of the characters" and that it "was a thrill" to "extend" the experience in this way. They played the online game because it was unusual, and they were intrigued to find what the experience might offer, because they wanted to "dig deeper" into the storyworld, or because they wanted to see how the chatbot worked and were trying to make her "fall down" or break. Their relationship to the material was relaxed. They were not avidly seeking out these materials, desperate to extend their relationship to the core text. Sarah, a drama teacher from the UK, described how she was "intrigued about the characters" and explored the game "because it was there, and I was on holiday, on the sofa and there was nothing on the telly." These were not necessarily hyperactive, forensic fans, eagerly digging in all the media that was presented to them. The series was too new to have built up those relationships and that kind of following. Rather, they were inquisitive, open minded, and willing to play along, suspending their disbelief and entering the world of the story. From a creative point of view there is a lesson here. Whether you are producing a drama, designing interactive media, or writing a book, your audience never pay quite as much attention as you imagine they will.

The subjects related to audio drama not just as fans of a genre, but as members of a community. They made judgments about the aesthetic and technical qualities of other shows, they were aware of their deficiencies, but they still listened to them. Many podcast dramas could be classified as UGC or fan productions. They are produced without budgets, recorded on location or in bedrooms, and performed by groups of friends or amateur actors. A sense of criticality toward these works was suspended, and instead they were encouraging and supportive of their peers' efforts. The production values of *Blood Culture* were often commented upon and the project possessed a different status to those works produced from within the audio drama community. Some interviewees did not make a distinction between being in communication with myself and celebrity media producers, such as Stephen Moffat, the internationally renowned show runner of the BBC TV series *Dr Who*. When we ran out of T-shirts to send as prizes, signed production scripts were offered in their place, and these were received with a disorientating degree of enthusiasm:

> I am SO EXCITED and honored to receive a production draft from @ bloodcultural. I still absolutely LOVE it! It holds a very special place in my swag collection! Thank you all SO MUCH again for both this and the show!!
>
> (Twitter message to @bloodcultural, September 2017)

This is a community that identifies itself through its media tastes and forms connections based on communal interests. Kaitlin, a lab worker from the United States, describes how she does not "talk about podcasts to a lot of people in real life, online I've found this space where I can get together with people and we have a shared interest." As discussed in Chapter 3 social media transforms the solitary activity of listening to a podcast into a social one. It allows audiences to share and discuss shows that they experience individually, and realize the imagined community of listeners who previously would have been unknowable to one another. Among the audio drama fans these links are made manifest through the active recommending and sharing of new podcasts, the circulation of reviews, the quoting of favorite lines, responses to episodes, and games such as "Audio Drama Bingo," where a grid of sixteen logos is loaded online and players cross off those shows that they are following. The community has a hashtag, #audiodramasunday, where each week favorite or seasonally relevant shows are promoted, retweeted, and shared by the community.

Social collateral and standing in this group is gained through knowledge of up-and-coming projects, which shows are being released and are deemed to be worthy of attention. Two of the interview subjects ran review sites that allowed them to position themselves as tastemakers or opinion formers within the field. Others were more socially orientated mavens, with hundreds, and in one case thousands of web media connections, that they took pleasure in introducing to, and connecting with, one another:

> Oh man—you two should get to know one another if you don't already. There's an intriguing cross-pollination :D
>
> (Tweet: @radiodrama responding to @lancedann and @kangakanga, October 30, 2017)

The interviewees had found commonality through an interest and love for audio drama. Sarah, from the UK, expresses this bond: "I'm a massive fan . . . and it's great when you find someone else who has listened to it. Really it's about finding your tribe." Drama serves as a starting point from which discussions of other issues evolve and develop. They share their doubts, support one another over mental health issues, praise each other's achievements and joke and rant about global politics and political figures. They have found identity through an entertainment form, in the same manner previous generations used music genres and scenes to differentiate themselves and to recognize kindred spirits. They appreciated *Blood Culture*, they were excited by it, engaged with it deeply and learned something from the series, but they were not fans of *Blood Culture*. Not specifically. It was part of their daily audio media consumption, they enjoyed the show, recommended it to each other online, and then the next day went to work and listened to something else.

Conclusion

I'm slouched in my seat at the Audio Production Awards ceremony in London. I'm sat between Martin, the co-author of this book, and Phil, one of the writers of Blood Culture. *There are a lot of people here, it's a swanky event, a lot of suits and ties and power handshakes. I've been nominated for the Best Drama Producer category, and I'm sulking like a teenager. I'm not going to win, I never win these things, I'm always invited but they always go to work that is a little more sensible, and a little less noisy. I hunker down as a woman reads the nominees' names out. I'm sealing myself off from the moment, protecting myself against disappointment. She reads out the winner of the Bronze Award. Nope, not me. Silver Award. Nope, not me again. It won't happen "And the Gold Award goes to—," and she says my name and she says Blood Culture and my ears ring and my head swings. People are clapping, I'm on my feet. I look a mess. I have no idea what to say. My shirt is untucked. How can this have happened? I get on stage. I didn't prepare for this. I collect the award. This wasn't meant to happen. I walk to the mike, I have to say something. "Well . . . " I begin "This wasn't meant to happen was it?"*

Blood Culture gained a reputation as a niche work followed by a community of audio drama fans. That this group could be considered "Millennial" and "digitally literate" allowed us to fulfill the demographic requirements of our original funding bid. Without a recognized cast, or marketing budget of note, we were not able to spread the project far beyond this group. The series was not featured on iTunes, or entered into their new and noteworthy listings. It did not receive any mainstream press coverage. Timing and circumstances are key to the success of a podcast, a few weeks previously *S-Town* by *This American Life* had been released and been the most rapidly downloaded show in history, journalists had already run their "podcasting" story for the month.

In the hope of extending the profile of the series, particularly in the United States, in the summer of 2017 I began discussions with representatives of two major US podcast networks. They were attracted by the possibility of being able to offer a highly produced, full-cast drama tailored for a younger audience. I entered into negotiations with their executives in Los Angeles and Brooklyn. The first rejected the project because it was "too English" and the second because it was "too experimental." The core audience for a podcast drama was described to me as being "a twenty-something" male who lives in middle America. Our story was of a mixed-race woman from Croydon (South London) who had to take care of her ex-raver Dad who lives in a caravan. Her best friend was an anarcho-punk with a Barnsley (North England) accent and her nemesis a growling Scot. The language, the idioms, and humor of the work were intrinsically British. Its plot and form were unusual—we had written and produced a work that had entertained us. It had amused and excited us when we were in the writers' room, in the recording studio and the editing suite. It did not always hit the most obvious story beats, its music was unsettling, its soundscape dense and aurally challenging. The work was deemed a quirky and unusual piece, and unsuited for mainstream audiences.

In the autumn of 2017 the UK audio and radio industry award season began. *Blood Culture* was nominated for best storytelling at the ARIAS (the UK Radio Academy Awards), Marley Cole won the Bronze Award for Best Sound Designer and I won the Gold Award for Best Drama Producer at the Audio Production Awards (the Audible-backed UK Radio Independent Group awards). In 2018, it was nominated for Podcast/Online Production at the BBC Radio Drama awards and the series won the Silver award in the Fiction category at the British Podcast Awards. These accolades had no long-term impact on our audience figures, but the standing of the project within the industry increased.

Meanwhile the series has continued to quietly gather a growing and dedicated following of listeners who identify themselves as "audio drama fans."

8

The Truth about *Serial*: It's Not Really about a Murder

When they were talking about it, podcasting didn't have a huge audience, and so they thought of it as: "Oh, we'll do this little side project, it'll be kind of fun. We'll do it out of Sarah's basement; it won't be such a big deal; it won't be a tremendously heavy lift. It'll just be a fun thing that we do."

—Dana Chivvis (2016)

Whether apocryphal or not, the stories the producers of *Serial* tell about the beginning of season one are remarkably nonchalant given the phenomenon that it became. I first heard of it in early November of 2014 at an awards event for young journalists at the Reuters News Agency international headquarters in London (one of my students had been shortlisted). While having drinks in one of the lounges of that impressive Canary Wharf building I flitted from one clutch of young people to the next and asked them what new programs they had been listening to and what they recommended. At every stop I made, someone enthused about *Serial*. One of them said, "I can't not listen." Another said, "It's totally compelling and you've just got to find out if he did it. And Sarah is so great in the way she tells the story—I want to do what she does." The next day I downloaded all of the available episodes and binge listened.

This chapter focuses primarily on season one of *Serial*; this is not intended to slight other *Serial* projects, but because season one had a unique and unrepeated cultural impact, and it happened at the convergence of several important technological and social currents that make it an invaluable marker in a history of podcasting. Episodes of season one were released from early October through mid-December of 2014; in them, reporter Sarah Koenig reexamines the 1999 murder of Baltimore high school student Hae Min Lee and the trial and conviction of her ex-boyfriend Adnan Syed. The material details relayed through the series would have seemed at home on most crime documentaries, or even on most dramatized true-crime series produced within the past seventy-five years of audio. But the mechanics of the *Serial*'s production, dissemination, and consumption, and the relationships it engendered with its listeners, were quite unconventional and provided an opportunity for Koenig, as well as listeners, to rethink what journalism (particularly podcast journalism) might become.

The features that distinguish *Serial* as a podcast were often difficult to pin down, even for its producers (who were radio natives).[1] With that in mind, one of the basic goals of this chapter is to try to articulate some of these aspects as more native to podcasting. We will examine:

1. *Serial*'s thorough integration into a much larger, preexisting media ecosphere;[2]
2. variable lengths of the episodes and variable episode release dates which meant something of a liberation from production scheduling issues;[3]
3. *Serial*'s in-depth live production—material was sourced and thoroughly processed while the series was being produced without knowing where it might lead;[4]
4. *Serial*'s thoroughly integrated online participation in which listeners are involved as contributors of substantive source material and in which they can easily participate in the story on consistently deeper levels;
5. formal creative freedom and soft-touch editorial control—while produced by consummate audio narrative professionals, its status "as a podcast" gave it a more authentic and less rigorously vetted feel; and

---

[1] Chivvis (2016) and Carr (2014) cite Koenig's straightforward intention for *Serial* as "making radio." Even Mark Friend, BBC Controller, says when discussing *Serial* being broadcast on Radio Four Extra that he felt it worked well on radio (2016).

[2] By this I mean being part of a larger media constellation or family. Rosin, president of Edison Research, says of *Serial*, "If you were forced to identify a single biggest reason it did as well as it did, it's because the first episode was aired as part of *This American Life*" (2016).

[3] While this liberation obviously meant that listeners choose to listen when it suited them (a common feature of much contemporary media life), Berry notes that *Serial*'s appeal was so strong that it reinvigorated the older media concept of "appointment listening." His survey respondents generally tried to listen to episodes within twenty-four hours of their release. *Serial* listening parties were also organized which points to an older mode of heightened social listening (Berry 2015b: 174–5).

[4] Of particular note here is *Serial*'s use of social media to crowd-source content material. This material seems to have grown organically out of the podcast's online presence and redistribution over social media, rather than being a pre-conceived part of the development of the series. There were no direct appeals to listeners for information to aid the investigation, instead tips came in, largely via email from listeners, without solicitation. While this does not seem to have been a part of the original conception of *Serial*, Chivvis (2016) says it was a tremendous benefit to season one. This technique though was not used in *S-Town* in which all of the episodes were released simultaneously, perhaps because both *Serial* as a brand and podcasting itself had matured to a point where some of the legal/ethical considerations discussed below in this chapter had to be taken more seriously.

6. the way the depth (and occasionally tangential feel) of its detail encouraged and worked with podcast listeners' easy ability to repeat listen to whole episodes and to back-scan denser passages.

Even if these aspects were not immediately obvious to most podcast listeners (and many podcast producers) at the time, there was a broad sense in the popular media that *Serial* represented a different species of thing. By the end of that season *Serial* had become a cultural shorthand which opened doors to discussions about what podcasting was and could become. As Chivvis puts it, "So *Serial* is a podcast; you've heard of *Serial*? So let's talk about podcasting" (2016). Rosin, described a "*Serial* phenomenon": in the year following season one his tracking of the evolution of podcasting numbers witnessed the most significant spike he had then ever recorded in podcast awareness and he called it "the biggest thing ever by a significant margin" (2016). The most important impact he observed of *Serial*, he says, was that it left an enormous appetite among listeners for more high-quality narrative podcasts.

Not surprisingly, the bulk of the coverage of *Serial* season one focused on simple statistics, asking what those statistics meant and why they seemed so striking. Berry, in reminding us that *Serial* did not happen in isolation, provided a very useful picture of its context: The market had been primed by earlier projects like *99% Invisible* that experimented with some of the formal tropes of *Serial*. He also, in a view shared by Rosin, cites Ira Glass's appearance on NBC's *The Tonight Show with Jimmy Fallon* as being a key factor in spurring downloads for the series. That appearance also featured a video of Glass's elderly neighbor explaining how to access *Serial* via an app on a smartphone (Berry 2015b: 174). This, and other relatively high-profile promotion and coverage, meant that within four weeks *Serial* had four million downloads per episode; it took Glass's *This American Life* four years to reach the same milestone (Quirk 2015).

After the euphoria over *Serial*'s numbers began to subside, most of the critical energy (especially in the more popular media) approached the podcast in terms of race and ethnicity. Because this analysis has been taken up powerfully elsewhere, it does not feature prominently in this chapter; but a summary of it is helpful to a full understanding of *Serial*'s context and its purported subjects. Not surprisingly, this thread most often flags up what it sees as an absence of a discourse around race in *Serial* or an unwillingness to deal with it in a meaningful way. Race is, at best, a subtext in *Serial*, something that Koenig does not or cannot speak about well. All race, according to Kang (2014), for example, is flattened out into a conventional white/other dichotomy, in which Koenig appears as a "cultural tourist," a white journalist telling a deracinated yet somehow vaguely ethnic story. Evidence to support this reading is not terribly difficult to find. In episode two, for example, Koenig does seem to assume a uniformity of immigrant experience (05:21) among Korean-American and Pakistani-American cultures. From this vantage point, moments like these do stick out. And as Kang, and to some extent Chaudry (the original proponent of *Serial*'s reopening of the case) (2016), convincingly suggest, the influence of Adnan's religion and ethnicity on his arrest and conviction do seem to get whitewashed in Koenig's efforts to create "relatable" characters for an imagined white audience.[5] This critique has remained present (and valid) since season one; but to be fair, it is also a critique leveled not just at *Serial* but at much of public broadcasting in the United States (Kumanyika 2015). Mengiste is also noteworthy here; writing about the *Serial* team's 2017 production *S-Town*, she argues that this reluctance to engage with a racial dimension "removes a history of blackness." She says that the producers "made an assumption that rings false, that frankly, rings white: that it is possible to move through this land and simply tuck race into a corner until it's convenient" (2017).

The fact that *Serial* is primarily an audio experience makes this a problem easier to slip into, both for producers and listeners. We do not have, for example, any proper visuals of Adnan's majority black jury. While critics of the (lack of) portrayal of race in *Serial* have been extremely useful in suggesting that the podcast is more about Koenig than it is about Syed (Pakistani American), Lee (Korean American), or Jay Wilds (African American), they seem to desire a more conventional approach to both race and audio documentary that, I argue, is consciously not a part of *Serial*'s larger project. *Serial*'s producers certainly might have, and even *could have*, chosen to tell a story more centered on issues of race. They might have, for example, taken up a generational thread mentioned in episode two (11:10) to investigate rigid understandings of race and religion in the minds of both parents and detectives, and compared them with the more fluid approach of the younger, multiethnic generation. While not making an excuse, it does seem relevant to note that *Serial*'s producers did not intend to intervene in or even make a contribution to a national discourse on race; they frame their project in the more plain journalistic language of portraying "a moment"

---

[5] This is a strong argument until episode seven in which the racial bias of the State's case becomes central to the story.

(Chivvis 2016). This chapter, however, asserts that *Serial* is not exclusively—or even primarily—*about* events that happened in Baltimore in 1999.

While a murder, an investigation, a trial, a prisoner, and even racism command instant attention in season one, the "truth" about *Serial* is that there is another story being told. This is a much more complex story with much broader social implications and much deeper significance for media culture: it is the story of Koenig struggling to negotiate a new set of rules for podcast journalism; it is a story of how journalism is being influenced by certain emergent podcasting aesthetics and ethics, and a story about how journalism was then being done and how it should be done.

The success of *Serial*

The overwhelming majority of popular writing about *Serial* has been about its numbers. Apart from those already mentioned, *Serial* was the fastest podcast to ever reach five million downloads or streams (Davies 2014) and 28,000 people discussed *Serial* on Reddit (Roberts 2014). While numbers like these are deployed to *signify* something impressive, when probed more deeply it becomes difficult to generate much of anything meaningful from them. Chivvis thought at the time that the listening data for radio programs was likely to be more accurate and useful than it was for podcasts; and Seth Lind, *Serial's* Director of Operations, noted that advertisers were concerned about conflating "downloads" with "listens."[6] At the time of this writing he informed me that the combined episodes of *Serial* had been downloaded 234.9 million times (Lind 2016). Media coverage of the (numbers-based) *Serial* phenomenon generally focuses on Glass's promotion and also the technological timing of *Serial's* release. Not long before its launch a dedicated "Podcasts" app appeared preloaded on the iPhone's OS (Chivvis 2016). But download numbers by themselves tell relatively little about a podcast's engagement with an audience. This, in conjunction with

---

[6]   Hence, using number like these as an indication of success (then as now) needed to be done with caution. Critics both pre- and post-*Serial* have noted that podcast download numbers cannot be converted with much confidence directly into "listeners" or even "listens" (O'Baoill 2009 and Davies 2014). I, for example, have downloaded every episode of *Serial* twice (once on two separate devices) and have listened to most installments three, four, or five times, while others download and never listen. Davies was critical of Apple, the company he saw as best positioned to help create a more meaningful understanding of podcast numbers, for being unwilling to collate data or being possessive with its information. In June of 2017 this particular situation was slated to improve (Kafka 2017).

the fact that simple podcast data collection via apps and platforms had been slow to mature (Rosin 2016), prompted the use of surveys to better describe impact. One such survey, conducted by the McKinney Ad Agency in conjunction with *Serial*, corroborated Chivvis's suggestion that *Serial* might be seen as a gateway into podcasting: 23 percent of responders said *Serial* was the first podcast they had ever listened to and 89 percent of those reported then moving on to listen to other podcasts (McKinney 2015).

This follow-through on podcasting post-*Serial* indicates (and Rosin agrees) that it was not simply a cocktail of new technology and cunning promotion that made *Serial* what it became. The skill of its narrative construction was an essential factor in its successful engagement. These narrative techniques (along with most of *Serial*'s staff) came from *This American Life*. Glass's contributions to Abel's handbook *Out on the Wire* (2015) detail many of these and the principles that ground them which include: having something at stake (for the listener or a character), telling a larger story while using smaller anecdotes to support it, and offering moments of reflection and moments of genuine emotion. The style produced, cutely described as "an approachable, grad-school-Columbo aesthetic of unpolished, 'hold up a sec—let me, like, try and wrap my head around this' narration" (Weiner 2014), has evolved over Glass's three decades of radio and audio work, but he locates its origin in his introduction to Roland Barthes while studying semiotics as an undergraduate (Schulz 2017). Without delving too deeply into *S/Z*, two of Barthes's codes for analyzing meaning and engagement around a text seem particularly relevant to *Serial* and once we know these codes have informed the thinking of the producers it is quite easy to hear them in the structuring of the episodes: first, the *hermeneutic code* (or *enigma code*) offers a puzzle or a mystery, something to be solved or resolved by the listener. In *Serial* this involved devices like withholding a piece of information, inviting consideration of its opposite, and then finally revealing it.[7] Second, the *cultural code* navigates through larger bodies of knowledge contested outside a text. In *Serial* this involves primarily testing the limits and values of existent principles of journalism. These codes become more useful later in this chapter.

While principles borrowed from *This American Life* are clearly a point of departure for *Serial*, a large part of its success came from reinventing those

---

[7] Interestingly Chivvis, in reflecting on why there was less buzz around season two, notes that it lacked a "who-done-it feel." She also confirms that *Serial* was built with many structural techniques borrowed from *This American Life*. For a more detailed treatment of *Serial*'s narrative structure, see McMurtry's analysis of *Serial*'s "plotting-for-effect" (2016: 312).

principles for the podcast form. Chivvis said: "The freedom that being a podcast versus a radio show affords us is no small thing, and it's useful in the way that we are able to tell the story, and the way we are able to report the story." Specifically, she cited a "freedom just to let the story dictate how long it's going to be, instead of just trying to . . . make it fit a formula" (2016). They could, when they needed to, pause their episode release schedule in order to do more reporting or to investigate new directions. And, as is most often mentioned in writing about podcasting, each episode's length is determined by editors' judgments about the content material rather than a standardized clock. The other, more abstract, freedom mentioned by Chivvis in this context might be best described as the *license to try* found at that moment of podcasting: "We're sort of our own bosses," she said, to indicate the then lower level of institutional oversight compared with her radio experience. Koenig too says she was very aware of the latitude they had: "I didn't even know what it should be, and it was extremely freeing. I was like, it's a podcast! Who cares? Try it! What does it matter? Nobody listens to podcasts!" (quoted in Larson 2015). Looking forward, she added, "That openness is what I hope we can keep."

Serial in the wider context of journalism

Schudson, in writing about the evolving idea of "objectivity" in American journalism, raises a very useful question: What happens when norms that have existed simply as a set of prevalent practices become articulated as a set of self-conscious, prescriptive rules (2001: 151)? Our study takes up the logical next question: What happens when a journalistic practice can no longer be contained by those prescriptive rules? Throughout season one of *Serial* we see Koenig wrestling with those rules more passionately than any other issue. For example, she says implicitly and explicitly throughout the series that she wants simply to tell a story. She invokes objectivity, balance, and detachment in an almost ritualized way to maintain a conventional position of authority as a journalist, as distinct from the millions of other voices on the internet. But as she performs these rituals she will eventually and subtly call them into question. While she and the producers of *Serial* are consummate audio professionals who often surround themselves with signifiers of professional competence, there is, comparatively speaking, a homespun quality to much of *Serial's* narrative that grants it license to explore. While she often underscores her commitments to objectivity, in the end she will ultimately loosen her grip on them. And while the ideal of journalistic detachment is repeatedly invoked in the early episodes of the series, it is eclipsed in the final episode.

None of this is necessarily new to journalism. In fact, *Serial* is best seen not as an abandonment of immortal principles, but as a wave on a historic tide in American journalism that ebbs and flows between the ideas of impartiality and advocacy, of detachment and connection,[8] a wave pushed by the specific characteristics of podcasting. My contention is not that *Serial* is without precedent, rather my contention is that *Serial*, like *Radiolab*, is emblematic of a transition from a radio-centric conception of audio making to a podcast-centric conception of audio making.

What I hear as a productive tension on *Serial* between the established journalistic ethics of impartiality and the potential of more intimate podcasting modes of storytelling has been noted by other scholars; and nearly all of them prefer to sit on the journalism side of the fence. For example, Goldstein argues that the trope of withholding information which journalists already know to be true for the sake of a dramatic arch measured in weekly episodes is not conventionally ethical; it could have meant a murderer remained free to roam the streets. Others, like Wasserman (referenced in Goldstein 2014), do not see a conceptual tension being creatively explored but a minefield being wandered into. He highlights *Serial*'s particular problem of "reverb" happening in a story that is being told concurrently with its research and development. He argues that many of the people that the producers interview are listening to the podcast from week to week, thus the interview material they provide will necessarily be influenced by what they have been hearing[9] and the biases they have developed from listening (Goldstein 2014); the material they offer then must be seen as tainted. For example, listener-sources seem eager to weigh-in on whether or not there was a phone booth in the lobby of the Best Buy (the appliances store that features in the series) only after it is revealed as a crucial bit of evidence in Syed's case. Wasserman also notes that defamation is a

---

[8] Perhaps the last time we witnessed such a clear example of a shift in this current (an example dealing with similar subject matter and with arguably an even higher degree of cultural buzz) was Truman Capote's classic of New Journalism, *In Cold Blood* (1966). Interestingly, the advent and popularization of podcasting has happened in conjunction with a renaissance in the more emotive, personal, and invested forms of New Journalism. For evidence of this trend see Boynton (2005) and Hart (2012).

[9] Listen to, for example, episode nine (04:49) and episode eleven (01:48). These interviews often result from a listener's email.

related problem when distributing a podcast while it is still in production: if you publicly offer a plausible, or even possible, critique or an explanation for an incriminating piece of evidence or for an alibi, and that suggestion turns out (in the course of your further research) to be speculation or even false, the wronged party might have a legitimate legal claim. Wasserman would clearly sacrifice dramatic impact for a maintenance of existing ethical standards.

But podcasters should bear in mind that these rules are not fixed. Schudson is again useful in reminding us that even the framework of "analytical fairness" was not a secure part of a journalistic code until journalists developed deeper ties to their own professional community and their audiences than to their publishers' political agendas. And, similarly, a self-conscious adherence to objectivity was born out of desire to upgrade the position of journalist from laborer to professional (161–66). Historically, the codes of journalism are often rewritten. Noble and well-reasoned as the defenses of journalistic principles that *Serial* prompted are, they did not then and cannot now take into account the nature of the podcasting environment into which *Serial* was born and which has spawned hundreds of similar project since: it is a space largely without the editorial gatekeepers and institutional structures of radio but with far more opportunities for different kinds of sourcing and engagement.

Interestingly though, and perhaps because *Serial*'s producers were primarily radio producers, they began with a clear commitment to a relatively universal "set of journalistic ethical standards" (Chivvis 2016). And when they encounter a new media situation around which established journalistic codes of practice do not quite fit, they offer their audience an honest "transparency" about what they are doing.[10] At one level, expressed attachment to ethical standards might seem anachronistic, a commitment to an abstract ideal that *Serial* itself was outgrowing. More broadly though, contemporary professional journalists often publicly aspire to principles they consider worthy but acknowledge as impossible in less visible places (Hearns-Branaman 2014: 29); what is unique about *Serial* is that the wrestling with this aspiration is not confined to interviews conducted with academics. It is audible, and even explicit at times, *in the episodes*. I argue that *Serial* makes this gap, this wound, between current journalistic ideals and

---

[10] This is not to say that all of *Serial*'s ethical contretemps were calculated renegotiations of new standards for podcasting. Oversights happened and mistakes were made; for example, courtroom audio that was not legally broadcastable was included in season one ("Adnan Syed's Setback" 2016). However, the uncertain status of podcasting in 2014 might account for slips like this.

the current journalistic reality a primary theme, the focal point of what the podcast in really *about*.

Before moving on to a discussion of how we actually *hear Serial* deal with this wound, we should pay attention to that idea of "transparency" for a moment, how it can be seen as a substitute for objectivity, and the anxiety that can cause. Historically speaking, while transparency was not included by the American Society of Newspaper Editors in its original 1922–23 Canons of Journalism (Schudson 2001: 162), an idea with perhaps some similarities ("Be Accountable") was written into the historic code for the Society of Professional Journalists (Ward 2015: 52). For practicing reporters today, this means making your audience aware of your frame, aware of the interpretive assumptions you are likely to make in your reporting because you are the person you are and you have lived the life you have. This disclosure serves, at least it is often hoped, as an inoculation against the charge of "bias."

As an attachment to objectivity as a principle had receded in recent years, the notion of transparency tended to fill its space. This trend, which happened in conjunction with the ascendance of digital media, has been met with some concern. Ward, in "The Magical Concept of Transparency," writes that transparency has become a "god" in "the pantheon of journalism ethics" and that it should not be confused with either responsibility or accountability, which should take precedence (Ward 2015: 45). Interestingly, his concern that transparent mechanisms are not "causally sufficient to ensure good governance in institutions" (Ward 2015: 49) focuses not on the audiences or subjects of journalism, but on the cultural standing of news organizations. Further, Ward suggests that transparency might even be at odds with the goal of safeguarding that standing of, and maintaining public trust in, those institutions. He cites National Public Radio (the larger institutional backdrop for *Serial*) as restricting how transparent their journalist are about their personal political views everywhere because their professional actions must always be seen to be "impartial."[11] But in the podcast space that *Serial* entered into, again a space, broadly speaking, with fewer institutional supports and structures—and seemingly with less need to protect a staid and reliable brand image—it remains unclear how relevant fundamentals like objectivity and impartiality really were or are. The fact that *Serial* is quite rigorously transparent suggests, perhaps, the advent of a new set of ethical criteria for podcast journalism.

---

[11] "Never say in public or on other media what you would not say as an impartial journalist on NPR programs" (quoted in Ward 2005: 53–4). Also see Fincham (2014: 179).

None of this is meant to suggest that *Serial* simply abandoned old rules and practices for new ones. The producers did not. But this context does help make the case that the central tension in *Serial* happens around the negotiation of new journalistic values more native to podcasting. Koenig is transparent, and when she openly considers her own inevitable partiality we hear her anxiety about how far she has strayed from the security of Ward's and Wasserman's once unimpeachable rules of journalism, an anxiety compounded by the fact that she narrates this wandering away from tradition *within the actual content of the programs.*

It is tempting to hear in season two of *Serial,* and in *Serial's* 2017 spin-off *S-Town,* a backing away from an exploration of this tension between new media production practices and traditional journalistic methods and less wrestling with espoused principles of journalism. *S-Town,* after all, was wholly developed and produced in advance of its same-day release as a completed podcast series, a move that could not make use of crowd sourcing and side-steps issues of defamation due to incomplete research. Similarly season two of *Serial* did not (certainly not with the dynamism of season one at any rate) interrogate journalistic codes in a new way. But rather than diminish the critical importance of season one, I think this move only highlights its significance. An emotional, high-profile, and in-depth engagement with journalism's shifting ethics and its evolving podcast form—especially in the same setting and context—cannot make the same impact twice.

Starting to unpick *Serial's* secrets with the help of close analytical listenings

While the *Serial* producers were professional journalists, and while they still often found it appealing to cling to a process firmly rooted in a radio tradition, our close listenings to the episodes reveal a straining toward new ways of conceiving of audio. Clearly there is evidence that the producers aspire to adhere to established journalistic principles, yet at the same time—in external interviews and in the episodes themselves—they mull over the limitations, the shortcomings, and even the impossibility of those principles. For nearly every hunch or opinion or "feeling" (certainly in the earlier episodes) there is at least one restatement of a journalistic standard to try to pull back in equal measure. For example, here are two very simple instances of Koenig straining at journalistic conventions: In episode two, at 26:47, Koenig offers her personal assessment of the prosecution's case: "At this point I'm just going to say flat out that I don't buy the motive for this murder, at least not how the State explained it. I just don't see it." Also in episode two, at 27:14, Koenig shares her personal assessment of Syed: "I don't think he was some empty shell of a kid who'd betrayed his family and his religion and was now left with nothing and conjured up a murderous rage for a girl who broke his heart." These are pulled into tension with countervailing, professionalizing measures. Note these examples: In episode three, at 21:09, Koenig uses language that signals her practice as that of a classical reporter and that foregrounds her commitment to objectivity: "Again, I can only go by the reports and files." In episode four, at 03:40, Koenig signals to us that she is alert to the potential problem of defamation; she is a professional reporter, not a gossip: "So far, I only have guesses that I can't responsibly say out loud." In episode four, at 32:30, and in episode five, at 03:14, she describes the logistics of professional reporting. And in episode five, at 28:21, she reminds us of her correct ethical positioning by telling us she got special permission to include potentially embarrassing material.

This practice of actively aspiring to a set of fixed principles while suggesting that achieving them fully remains impossible is relatively common in journalism and is described as "fetishistic disavowal" by Hearns-Branaman who borrows the term from Žižek. Simply put, actively admitting the limitations of an ideology makes it easier to maintain that ideology; applied to journalism, it is "the ability and necessity to actively critique one's profession as long as one keeps on working" (2014: 21). When we hear Koenig wrestling to sublimate her own values and her own impressions, her own explicitly human feelings (as Chivvis says, "we are not robots" (2016)), our trust in her increases. At the end of the series when she cannot sublimate her own values (and wrestles with this failure for all to hear in the podcast rather than hiding it away in an interview or a blog), it is almost as if a new moral norm is being proposed: We, as journalists, endeavor to be impartial but we cannot. We, as journalists, are human and we should be open to what that makes possible.

Whether this is a rejection of fetishistic disavowal or simply the next stage of it—we accept the value of impartiality but we openly acknowledge its limits in the face of other, greater, human concerns of empathy and engagement— bears further probing through *Serial*. Traditionally the practice unfolds like this: Journalists should strive for objectivity and impartiality in their work. Outside their work they should note that these goals are unrealizable but they strive to achieve them nonetheless. Through this self-talk cognitive dissonance can be returned to equilibrium and the status quo can be maintained. But *Serial* does not fit this pattern. It represents not a fetishistic disavowal in the service of maintaining an old set of principles,[12] but an ideological shift, a change in how audio journalism *should be* and a change in norms. When we listen very closely to *Serial*, we hear in the end that journalism *should not aspire* to impartiality in quite blatant, clear, and obvious ways. It should instead aspire to recognizing human connections, to be, in short, human. *Serial* marks a transition from ritualistic professionalizing norms, norms that served to distinguish sturdy, old-fashioned journalists from mere bloggers and the subjects of documentaries from their listeners. That *Serial* was so hugely popular while framing itself as journalism suggests that such distinctions are no longer wanted or necessary. This supports the case that season one was really about moving into a new understanding of journalism, a podcast understanding of journalism that has outgrown the need for the psychological security blanket of fetishistic disavowal in favor of the security of narrative. In this shift of priorities instigated through podcasting, as the grip on a robotic journalistic professionalism is loosened, the grip on a universal appeal of human stories tightens.[13]

The development of podcasting has paralleled a development of this tension in the larger sphere of journalism. The award-winning Mexican journalist Alma Guillermoprieto brings this contested terrain into sharp focus: "Stories," she says, "are the opposite of hard news, the opposite of easy anecdote." And as a journalist she is rigorously committed to "story" before "news" because news merely feeds "the strangely comforting sensation that the world spins too fast to really think about it" (in Kramer and Call 2007: 155–56). In positioning story against decontextualized anecdotes and simplistic facts, and casting story as a route to something that she describes as a "truth," she offers a useful template for thinking about the work of *Serial*. Koenig's detailed narrative reflections on both Syed's case and her own interventions into it, as well as interviews "that are built on conversations, not sound bites" (Carr 2014), certainly slow down the world for our careful examination. To the consternation of some critics (referenced

---

12 Hearns-Branaman writes, "Professionalism is held as the ultimate achievement for journalists to reach, yet at the same time it is a desire that can never be fulfilled, a fact that the journalists can and should articulate as long *as they still behave as if the ideal can be reached*" [italics in original] (2014: 30). *Serial* deviates in that, certainly in the final episode, Koenig *does not behave* as if the ideal can, or even *should*, be reached.

13 Literary, journalism, and media critics have, for decades, offered storytelling as a universal human characteristic, Jacqui Banaszynski's "Stories Matter" being a particularly poignant example (in Kramer and Call 2007: 3–6). See also Harrington (1997).

throughout this chapter), Koenig's storytelling offers us a point of connection to the world—and particular human beings in it—while a stream of unrelatable facts would run the risk of cutting us off from that same world and those same people. Koenig's narrative journalistic approach, and later the actions Koenig models for us, invite a particularly intense human engagement.

While Guillermoprieto's suggestion is compelling, and while it clearly resonates with Koenig's approach, a regular criticism of setting off on story's road to a truth is that it inevitably involves a manipulation of an audience (McHugh 2016: 73). With such a caveat in mind, manipulations do seem to crop up at many points: At 37:51 in episode five, Koenig, in an effort to maintain dramatic uncertainty and tension, opts to give prosecution witness Wilds the benefit of the doubt when she notes his timeline seemed confused or implausible. At 02:48 of episode six, Koenig lays out the prosecution's case against Syed only after she and her audience have developed a connection with him. Also, in an effort to cultivate tension and uncertainty at 23:16 in episode six, Syed is presented as shrewd, intelligent, and perhaps even calculating when making a point that suggests his innocence, to which Koenig replies (in-studio voice-over) "Maybe, maybe not." And at 13:49 and 29:28 in episode seven, Koenig narrates her balancing act steadfastly on the fence again to maintain dramatic tension and to model the cognitive process she hopes from her audience. In most of these examples there seems a conscious effort to get the audience to believe something that she knows is going to be undone in next minutes or at least suspects will be undone in the next episode. But given that (certainly based on numbers) this would seem a manipulation in which listeners are happy to collude, perhaps it makes more sense to read these moments as evidence of journalistic *construction* instead of manipulation. After all the listeners' "payoff" (the thrill of a good story) for their collusion in this manipulation is a common trait of many good journalistic features in a variety of formats (Kramer and Call 2007: 28).

It is also important to note that Koenig is extremely open and self-conscious about her practice of narrative construction. Episode one alone is peppered with her references to story composition (01:12, 01:26, 09:05, 12:36, 41:38, and 44:37 in addition to other implied references) to be savored by alert and complicit listeners. She is also aware, in the content of the episodes, that other journalistic approaches can tax listener attention—put another way, they can be boring (episode five, 33:44). These moments where Koenig's constructions are foregrounded are part of that larger tension in *Serial* between old journalistic tropes and podcast ones, but they also serve as evidence that Koenig seems to have assumed, relatively early on in *Serial*, that her cognoscenti listeners will prefer self-conscious "story" constructs to unconsciously imperfect "news."

Like other dramatic devices *Serial* borrowed, its creation of "characters" has drawn a great deal of critical attention.[14] McMurtry, for example, suggests that everyone involved in *Serial* ultimately becomes a dramatic character, including Koenig (2016: 313). Uniquely, she argues that Koenig is cast in a rather clichéd role as one-half of an unrequited or doomed romantic relationship. Support for this reading can be found throughout the series, but nowhere more poignantly than when Koenig reflects on the possibility that she might have been duped by a charming psychopath at several points in episode eleven. But what if the story is viewed less as an impossible soap-opera romance and more an existential crisis for professional journalism, or even a pioneer story for podcast journalism? After all, the hard-boiled hack is as much an archetypal character as the charming psychopath. In this version of the story, Koenig, playing a white, middle-class journalist, wrestles with the issues of white middle-class journalism in which she is a stakeholder, not a "tourist."

Curiously, those NPR rules restricting the expression of personal views both on air and online (Fincham 2014: 179) seem to work quite well in this framing of the reporter as a character. Those guidelines would ask that Koenig create a professional persona, a "character," that is manifestly *not her* but who follows her around everywhere and speaks for her. But this ultimately becomes *Serial*'s point of critique: Over the course of season one, we witness the breakdown of this character creation and the healing of this split between objective reporter and real person as Koenig emerges in the final episode as simply a human narrator. This, however, is a slow and tense realization marked by small fits and starts and swings between the poles of empathetic participant and impartial newsperson as she struggles to find an integrated identity.

The tension between these poles is perhaps no more striking than in episode one when she uses the word "idiotic" to characterize her own thinking not once, but twice (20:19). While describing the physical changes that she noticed in Syed from his teenage photos to the thirty-two-year-old in front of her in prison, she pauses on his "giant brown eyes, like a dairy cow." Objective distance lapses in a moment of real-world impression and she wonders whether someone with eyes like that could have strangled his girlfriend. The official reporter in Koenig

---

[14] See Goldstein (2014). But for a more positive exploration of the journalistic opportunities opened up by allowing the reporter to become a character, see Brown's "First Person Singular: Sometimes, It Is About You" (in Kramer and Call 2007: 82).

intervenes immediately and labels that line of thinking "idiotic"; it is partial, subjective, and unprofessional. But the fact that she over-emphasizes "idiotic" by repeating it sets something up in the future: by episode twelve this professional overconfidence has cracked and when the evidence (such as it is) lets her down, these impressions, intuitive as they might be, appear less absurd. In these moments of self-doubt (and even self-ridicule) Koenig reveals something authentic about her work on and thinking about *Serial* itself, and while the podcast may indeed be about her, it becomes harder to hear her as a character in a drama.

In these moments of crisis, reflection, and intense questioning the human narrator of Koenig bonds with her listeners. As Larson (2015) has noted, intimacy is *Serial*'s strong suit; but as Koenig is bonding with us, we are also bonding with other subjects, particularly Syed. Of the techniques on *Serial* that invite this human bond, two stand out. First, there is a lingering on what Barthes calls the "grain of the voice" in more poetic contexts (1992). Best described as the nonverbal communicative elements of speech, the grain grounds the speaking in a material body (a real human person) through sighs, slurps, coughs, audible scowls or smiles on the voice, mouth sounds, the inhalation of breath, and so forth. These moments were left in the final cut of the *Serial* episodes more generously than they would have been in conventional, professional radio documentaries. But beyond that, Koenig pauses on them and unpacks them for her listeners to make sure their nonverbal meaning is driven home. A clear example of this comes in episode one at 48:42 where an interviewee sighs on the phone: Koenig first tells us that it was a sigh and then says she shares some of the exasperation and confusion that justice might have miscarried in Syed's case contained in that sigh. Shortly after, speaking to Syed, he comments on the "elation" he hears in her voice and apologizes for not being able to share it. Through conversations like these between them, and through Koenig's reflections that feel like conversations with us, the podcast pitches itself into the register of emotional intelligence, rather than the realm of conventional and impartial fact. And through a meditation on these instigating speech sounds, Koenig bonds with Syed and we bond with both of them.[15]

---

[15] While not part of the discussion of "grain," the general intimacy of the interview conversations in *Serial* is very prominent and was already a part of the history of journalism (perhaps most prevalently in print). Walt Harrington, writing in *Intimate Journalism*, discusses the importance of gathering interior monologue material from subjects for facts, but also for the meaning those facts have for subjects. He proposes: "This kind of journalism is simply closer to human truth than what most journalists do. You will feel that closeness when you accomplish it. And once felt, you'll want to feel it again and again" (1997: xlvi).

The second technique for cultivating this intimacy has already been touched on: consistent and open honesty and transparency. At several points Koenig tells us what she has excluded or discounted behind the scenes and why. Beyond that, in efforts of ethical transparency and full disclosure, she tells us when she is paying for interviewees' time (e.g., in episode eight at 12:05). In the credits for episode one Koenig even thanks her in-laws for hosting her on her many trips to Baltimore. This functions as much more than a gracious "thank you" unnecessary in a conventional radio documentary—it includes us as listeners in an intimate domestic, familial relationship. These moments sometimes have the tone of secrets revealed and over the course of the series they steadily build trust.

The intimacy with her subjects is not one-sided and extends to the prosecution's star witness Jay Wilds as well. After her first encounter with him she calls him "very sweet" and says: "He's right there. He's a person. He's saying it and he sounds like he really means it" (episode eight, 22:24). Wilds too is presented as human and beyond functioning as simply a narrative prop to maintain a dramatic "who-done-it" tension, moments like these contribute to a general sense of intimacy in the series and trust in Koenig.[16]

Serial's listeners

Serial's direct address to listeners also, and obviously, contributes to its sense of intimacy. We do not just hear Koenig speaking in the first person—the "you," Koenig's direct appeal to the listener, is a key feature of every episode.[17] Tuning in carefully to the way that "you" is deployed also gives some clues as to how

---

[16] Perhaps expectedly, *Serial's* level of intimacy with its subjects and Koenig's attachment to them have drawn fire from critics within prestigious schools of journalism (as noted earlier). Perhaps less expectedly, many of the Britons who contributed interviews to this book found *Serial's* level of closeness and attachment rather cloying. Differences in national podcast styles, as well as cultural differences in podcast tastes, certainly merit further investigation.

[17] While direct address to listeners had, obviously, existed on radio for years prior to *Serial*, it was far less prevalent in general radio use than it appeared on podcasts. A close analytical listening to the BBC Radio Four documentary *Exonerated* (2017), a program which uses some of the same interviewing devices found on *Serial* and deals with similar material, aspires to a similar kind of intimacy which it never quite achieves. The fact that the program does not contain a single use of the word "you" is arguably a factor in this shortcoming. Typically, when BBC radio documentaries include the word "you" it is used rhetorically or as an abstract stand-in that might easily be replaced by the word "one" (as in "when *you* think" vs. "when *one* thinks"). In effect, this use can exclude or alienate rather than foster any kind of connection. This shortcoming in *Exonerated* might also be attributed to the lack of any significant reflection or interior narration or grappling with personal judgments by the presenter John Toal in spite of the fact that the material offers those opportunities.

Serial (unconsciously or intentionally) conceives of its audience. In episode one, at 01:44, for example, Koenig's use of the word "you" very quickly slides into interviewing random teenagers for anecdotal evidence about the unreliability of the memories of young people. This, obviously, has implications for the case and her investigation, but it also, cunningly or accidentally, reveals an imagined typical multicultural Millennial listener for the podcast.

Beyond this more straightforward listener identification, techniques like these invite a mental participation by potentially all listeners. Koenig's "You are going to hear . . ." at 09:05 in episode one situates the audience within the rhetorical frame of her investigation. Combined with all the other intimacies and undertones, this invokes for listeners a thrilling sense of complicity in an important project and a shared responsibility for its implications. There are repeated and explicit overtures to this kind of participation: At 05:49 in episode four, for example, when Koenig says, "If you want to figure out this case with me, now is the time to start paying close attention," listeners are clearly framed as coinvestigators.[18] Similarly, when she reflects on her own thought process at 39:49 in episode six, she models a kind investigative thinking that a listener is tacitly invited to adopt. This sense of involvement, investment, collusion, and even complicity on the part of listeners is heightened by the fact that Koenig often empathizes with them and expresses "care" for them as she does at 13:24 of episode one when she alerts them to potentially upsetting tape coming up soon.

These moments of modeling responses (which I have mentioned in other sections) bear special attention as we think about *Serial*'s relationship with its listeners. They are often more about trying to anticipate listener responses than they are about guiding them. Chivvis described producers standing in for listeners throughout virtually every stage of an episode's development: when listening to Koenig reading potential script material she repeatedly asked, "What am I feeling? Am I feeling bored here, am I feeling confused? You know, am I feeling like that was all important information but I don't know what to make of it?" She concluded by saying: "We are just . . . responding to it as listeners ourselves" (2016). When this process of anticipation flags up a potential moment of confusion in the minds of listeners, Koenig often takes that moment as an opportunity to further empathize with those listeners. For example, at 03:32 in episode two, Koenig describes the racially charged and stereotypical language in

---

[18] Critic Josie Duffy also noted this collaborative thread in *Serial* season one. She says the series made *her* feel like Nancy Drew (cited in McMurtry 2016: 317).

the prosecution's case as "spin." Then she says: "And the trouble with spin is that you can't totally disregard it. Because swirling around somewhere inside, some tendril of it is true." Here she seems caught in the same dilemma as her audience and responds to it with the same equivocation as she imagines they would.

"Truth" in a human journalism

It is tempting to see in the period of *Serial*'s release and the years that followed it (the beginning of podcasting's second wave) a particularly deep political discord and entrenchment in both the United States and the United Kingdom. In a time of media bubbles and "alternative facts" the idea of "truth" often seemed to haunt journalism like a resentful ghost. But the dilemma of what to make of this wispy phantasm has occupied the minds of journalism critics at least as long as we have been talking about postmodernism. Clark, in his 2001 essay "The Line Between Fact and Fiction," offers a familiar exasperation when grappling with the knowledge that witnesses' memories have been shown to be unreliable. In a description that might have been applied to *Radiolab*'s approach a year or two later, he wonders aloud what this means for hopes for a journalistic truth:

> The postmodernist might think all this irrelevant, arguing that there are no facts, only points of view, only takes on reality influenced by our personal histories, our cultures, our race and gender, our social class. The best journalists can do in such a world is offer multiple frames through which events and issues can be seen. *Report the Truth?* they ask. *Whose truth?*

In the end the best he can offer is a plea that the reporter minimize subjective selections and impressions, and a blanket injunction against "invention": "*Do not add. Do not deceive*" (italics in original, 165–6). While *Serial* itself as journalistic practice seemed to have moved well beyond the anxiety around this dilemma, most readings of *Serial* that address these topics at all simply revisited the problems of a "personal" truth (McMurtry 2016: 307) and did little to get us beyond this tiresome postmodern stalemate.

To approach a more nuanced conception of truth on *Serial* requires us again to slow down our thinking to the pace of close analytical listening. This method, I contend, leads us to a truth that is neither objectively external to Koenig nor utterly a creation of her own personal history and perception. This is an understanding of truth *as a process*, a truth that is a synthesis between material and events as they exist in the world, and the perspective of the journalist that curates them into potential meaning. That process is then offered to an audience, familiar with the idea of framing, who can then digest it in their own slow and detailed way enabled by the mechanics of podcast listening (we can listen to each episode as many times as we like, pausing to linger over and consider passages when we like). It is a truth that, in terms of honest and unembarrassed engagement, can then continue on Reddit and in fancasts. It is the *working out* that matters, not the results.

Glass sees this "working out" as the real drive behind storytelling in general (Schulz 2017). It emphasizes an *effort to understand* something and even, at a deeper level, an *effort to heal*[19] something rather than simply a desire to tell a tale. In listening to *Serial*, this effort is felt in two places (as we noted earlier): First, and most obviously, there is the effort to heal the wound of the unresolved issues around Lee's murder and Syed's imprisonment, that, pursued and investigated and deliberated upon, might just lead to a firm closure (what we read via Barthes and Glass as the enigma code). Second, and with much broader implications, there is the effort to heal a wound in journalism, a wound actually widening in a podcast era of declining institutional authority, influence, and trust (what we read via Barthes and Glass as the cultural code).

While neither of these threads is tied up neatly at the end of the season, more progress seems to have been made around the status of podcast journalism. Having worked through the twelve episodes, Koenig appears, in the end, neither an antiquated journalist implacably attached to an untenable concept of objectivity, nor a postmodern one for which there is nothing but the play of competing perspectives. She seems to have integrated both positions and moved on from them both: she adheres to and presents established facts as established facts but also is open about presenting and highlighting her own perceptions, impressions, and even gut responses. While this thread does not have a conventional and reassuring resolution, it does have a conclusion: Koenig has evolved and settled with confidence in what might be called a *new human journalism*.

Rather than eschewing, denying, or apologizing for attachments, human connections become central to Koenig's work on *Serial*. Moments highlighting the growth of these connections eventually appear as antidotes to the more conventional and "impartial" moments of the series. For example, at 40:03

---

[19] Glass sees this aspect of narrative first expressed in Freud's work (Schulz 2017).

in episode six, at the end of a particularly fact-laden installment, Koenig tells us that none of the material she had read about the case was as interesting or compelling as the person of Syed. She was literally "hooked" on him.

Moments like these do not pass without comment by Koenig, more often than not she thoroughly interrogates them. Calling Koenig's approach a new human journalism does not imply always deferring to empathy,[20] it is to describe a journalism that includes discussions of how these human bonds are forming and what effect they have on both the investigation and the way the story of *Serial* is processed. Shortly after her "hooked" moment, Koenig examines with Syed his flash of hostility when she suggested that he did not seem capable of this kind of murder (42:00). Syed replies that he wants to be exonerated not because people think he is a nice guy, or because of empathy, but because of the evidence alone. In this moment Syed is much more the orthodox journalist than Koenig; in effect, *he* is trying to push *her* back onto the terrain of conventional journalism and away from the human connection that has become central to her practice and to the podcast. This happens again in episode eleven, at 37:35, when Syed's letter to Koenig pushes back against precisely Koenig's humanizing overtures. He desperately does not want to be seen as manipulative and wants facts rather than feelings to release him from prison. But *Serial* is not really about him. It is much more about a tension that he and Koenig create around the idea of attachment, a tension that, ironically, only serves to increase the attachment levels of listeners because it is inescapably authentic and rare.

So rather than just offering a picture of the human relations in the life of a convict, *Serial* takes the formation of those relations as its subject matter. We hear this most poignantly perhaps in episode nine, at 24:33, in a list of bonds that Syed has felt and the kindnesses that came his way throughout his ordeal. And as Koenig begins to wind down the series in episode eleven, at 32:49, empathy appears for her as the best way of suturing closed the wound of the questions around the murder case and trial:

> I don't think Adnan is a psychopath. I just don't. I think he has empathy, I think he has real feelings, because I have heard and seen him demonstrate empathy and emotion, towards me and towards other people. He is able to imagine how someone else feels.

---

[20] Although for Glass having empathy in the mix is essential: "It's honestly not worth making a story if you're not going to have strong feelings about it, if it's not going to create empathy" (in Schulz 2017).

But, she hastens to remind herself and us, empathy should not be taken as conclusive proof of innocence. Even as she experiments with empathy as a principle of her new human journalism she interrogates it and tests its viability.

The final episode

A close analytical listening to the final episode brings together the main conceptual threads of this chapter: the tension between a classical journalistic ethics of impartiality and detachment versus a new human journalistic acceptance of attachment and impression; the tension between fact and truth (or the tension between objective expression and narrative); the inclusion of subjects and audience in the construction of journalistic narratives; and the viability of fetishistic disavowal as a way for journalists to avoid cognitive dissonance in the face of impossible principles. This analysis helps us articulate a podcast consciousness for journalism more relaxed about its own humanity.

Episode twelve makes an important case study for another reason: after brief forays in earlier episodes, in this episode Syed and his story slip completely into the cultural-coded narrative about the state of journalism (where they remain) and away from the enigma-coded narrative of the murder investigation. At 02:27 Syed is integrated into the meta-story about the whole of the podcast when he observes: "So you don't really have, if you don't mind me asking, so you don't really have no ending?" Koenig immediately reassures us that she does have an ending, but this reassurance is just a tease. And as the episode unfolds, in its latter minutes a sense evolves that Koenig does not, in fact, have an ending to that first, surface-level (enigma-coded) narrative of the investigation. Instead, focus returns to the rubrics of classical journalism. We hear this clearly at 35:42 when Koenig says: "Ninety-nine percent of what we speculate I cannot report, because, well, we can't back it up. It's speculation." With this we are drawn back into the tension about journalism which continues to unwind until Syed suggests *to her* that *he knows* how she should finish the story: by not taking sides. "In a sense, you leave it up to the audience to determine" (50:03). Fantastically, we hear Syed taking up an advisory position as both a seasoned conventional journalist and an authoritative storyteller, and he becomes more real and familiar to us as a virtual cohost of this podcast.

But Koenig cannot take this advice. She takes sides. First, as Syed originally preferred, she takes sides in the role of objective and impartial journalist: With supreme detachment she describes only evidence (which is questionable) and the lack of evidence; the State's case against Syed, she says matter-of-factly, was circumstantial: "What do we know, not what do we think we know? . . . . All we're left with is, Jay knew where the car was. That's it. And that all by itself, that's not a story . . . . It's not enough, to me, to send anyone to prison for life" (50:03). Then, casting herself as juror, Koenig votes to acquit simply because there was not enough evidence. Finally, with utter discipline and respect for the rules of law, Koenig-the-juror says she would acquit even if she *felt* he was really guilty (51:40).

Then she puts aside her roles as impartial juror and detached journalist. She says, instead, that she is a human being, and that if you asked her as human being, while she cannot swear to his innocence, most of the time, for big reasons and for small ones, she does not think he murdered Lee. These are her last words on the investigation:

> I used to think that when Adnan's friends told me, "I can't say for sure if he's innocent. But the guy I knew, there's no way he could have done this," I used to think that was a cop out, a way to avoid asking yourself uncomfortable, disloyal, disheartening questions. But I think I'm there now too. And not for lack of asking myself those hard questions, but because as much as I want to be sure, I'm not. (52:24)

While clinical uncertainty remains in her mind, Koenig's rigorous journalistic process, coupled with an acknowledgment of her own humanity, insists that she give Syed the benefit of the doubt. Her uncertainty can never be dispensed with in any conventional way, but it does come to a conclusion through human charity of thought rather than a desire to err on the side of someone needing to be punished for a horrific crime. At the end of our close listening to the series we have really learned more about Koenig than we have about Syed, and she is pointing the way to a new human podcast journalism in which she finds truth in a process rather than an outcome.

While the enigma-coded story of the investigation is finished (if unresolved), this cultural-coded story of journalism remains open. In time-honored narrative fashion Koenig takes us back to the beginning when "certainty seemed so attainable" (52:47). We hear pangs of nostalgia in her voice when she alludes to a traditional practice of journalism: "Just tell me the facts ma'am, because we didn't have them fifteen years ago, and we still don't have them now." Simple facts and her straightforward pursuit of them have proven insufficient, have let her (and us) down. They do not tell a story, nor do they lead to any familiar and satisfying resolution, neither for Syed in particular nor for podcast journalism more broadly. But we are left with a sense, however twitching, nascent, and incomplete, that Koenig has figured out how things should be in both cases.

The work we see her doing here is so much more than fetishistic disavowal. It is, in fact, an awareness that fetishistic disavowal can only ever take journalists so far. The real delight of *Serial* is in hearing Koenig groping after a new phase of journalism for podcasting, an approach that synthesizes old modes in order to move forward. It seems important to emphasize that this method *does not* leave us in some facile, post-fact, post-truth, postmodern place. Koenig *does not* reject objectivity or impartiality. They remain very much a part of her practice; she does not even, in a gesture of fetishistic disavowal, suggest that they are abstractly impossible. She has instead left us with a more integrated practice that might even be described as impartially human.

9

The Lucky Strike: Success, Value, and Independence in the Golden Age of Podcasting

It is the Winter of 2015, and I'm part of a team producing a spoken word podcast called The Odditorium *(billed as "a portal to the fringes of culture"). After* Serial's *viral success podcasting feels ripe with potential. We launched strongly, making it into the top ten of the iTunes Arts chart, were listed by* The Guardian *as one of "50 podcasts you must listen to in 2016," there is an Odditorium book due to be released, our first season has been downloaded over 100,000 times and . . . we have yet to earn a single penny from the show. We've been invited to meet an advertising company, they want* The Odditorium *to produce branded content in support of a hipster gin company. The meeting is bizarre, it's like a bad version of* Mad Men *where everyone is poorly dressed and tries to speak at the same time. We pitch our idea. They ask us about our audience figures. We reply. Then they ask us how much five episodes of bespoke gin-related podcasting would cost. We tell them, using BBC rates. £50,000. Eyebrows are raised on their side of the table. Cheeks are blown out. To justify those rates, we'd need to clear 350,000 downloads per episode. We're nowhere near that. This isn't going to work. Should we cut a deal for less? The advertising creatives aren't giving anything away. We're playing a dysfunctional and very middle-class game of poker. We hold. They turn down the bid . . . and, after that, my part in the project is over. The Odditorium was fun to produce, we were independent and did what we liked, but, ultimately, we were working for free.*

The Golden Age of Podcasting was born of the synergy between two events that occurred seventeen days apart in the fall of 2014. Apple baked a podcast app into the new release of its iOS 8 iPhone operating system and *This American Life* released the first episode of *Serial*. From this point the profile of the medium surged, audiences grew exponentially, and its commercial potential became abundantly apparent. Through this period the dominant narrative was of the plucky independent podcast, recorded as a passion project in a home studio, going "viral," and gaining huge audiences. This is the story of Aaron Mahnke's *Lore* that has gone from a spare-room production to being advertised on billboards in Times Square; of hip-hop artist Scroobius Pip's *Distraction Pieces* that draws hundreds of thousands to a shambolic mix of celebrity interviews, social invective, and drunken chatter; and of the producers of *My Dad Wrote a Porno* who have taken their comedic chatcast from the kitchen table to sell out shows at the Sydney Opera House.

These tales stand in contrast to the expansion of the form into mass-market medium. They speak of podcasting as a manifestation of the open internet, of it being a media form without gatekeepers, where "grassroots Podcasters" can still "compete on a level playing field with big business" (Berry 2006: 159), a beacon of what Benkler termed "the digital sublime" (2006). Benkler's utopian view of independent media production holds that digital technologies are egalitarian and that divides between producers and audiences will inevitably breakdown as part of what Leadbeater and Miller term the Pro-am revolution (2004). While podcast producers are able to work independently and with freedom, they must also manage to thrive in a space that has few controls, offers them little protection, and few assurances about their future. If they work outside of a network they benefit from great liberty, but there are no commissioners to oversee and nurture the development of their work, no unions to protect their rights, and minimal funding to offset commercial pressures. This is an environment in which each year thousands of shows are conceived and birthed, and exist for a few hopeful episodes, before they, like *The Odditorium*, are abandoned. Podcasting may be framed as a brutal realization of long-tail economics, of what Andrew Ross describes as a "digital jackpot economy" (2009), where success is survival, and it takes a lot of good fortune to survive.

This chapter will ask what lessons might be learned from the podcasters who have thrived during the "Golden Age," detailing the stories and techniques of the producers and presenters in an attempt to find commonalities in their narratives. It will discuss the challenges that they, and all podcasters, must face in order to survive the fervid waters of podcasting's shark tank. It will offer an analysis of the protections and benefits offered by podcast networks, arguing that producers may gather under the umbrella of support offered by an organization such as Radiotopia or Panoply, or may be offered financial support by a commercially driven company such as Gimlet Media. In doing so they are off-setting a loss of the risks of independent work against a loss the freedom that working independently offers. The commonalities in the stories noted here should not be taken primarily as lessons on "how to become a successful podcaster"; instead, they are more lessons on why podcasting itself has become successful.

Lessons of the golden age

(1) Use your freedom: *Richard Herring's Leicester Square Theatre Podcast*

The success of UK comedian Richard Herring's comedy podcast cannot be directly associated with benefits of the "Golden Age." He did not enter the podcast industry as an unknown. He had had a twenty-year career in television and radio when in 2009 he was part of a team that released the sketch show *As It Occurs to Me*. His story is noteworthy because it serves as a model of how an independent podcast producer can exploit the freedoms offered by the form.

As It Occurs to Me and his later longer running series, *Richard Herring's Leicester Square Theatre Podcast* (referred to by Herring as the barely pronounceable *RHLSTP*) were born out of a sense of frustration with the processes involved in creating work for conventional broadcast networks. He began working in podcasting having gone through "a wilderness period" during which time he was feeling "undervalued" and low because "things weren't happening as quickly as they had done five-years previously" (Herring 2016). Podcasting offered him a platform to create work on his own terms and to his own tastes.

He worked on the shows independently, outside of mainstream media companies, and with minimal crew and technical resources. This lightweight approach allowed him to try out ideas, to evolve techniques and approaches in a fluid and iterative manner that would not have been possible when working within the sclerotic systems of broadcast commissioning. He describes *RHLSTP*, as being "long, very rude, and very private." Each episode features an interview with a comedian or celebrity that can last over an hour, providing a platform for extended conversation and for Herring's humor to have full range and take unpredictable turns. This allows him to play with time, with audience discomfort, and with their expectations. "On television" he observes, "you have to cut the boring bits that create the tension, that create the laugh" (2016). On *RHLSTP* humor is allowed space to build across minutes that would have to be cut on television or radio; he has liberty to "dig himself into a hole" by saying things that not only make his guest and audience uncomfortable, but himself as well. This is a long-form comedy that can digress and take unexpected turns that surprise even the comedian. His interviews range freely from profanity to profundity. Extended soliloquies about masturbation sit alongside revealing and insightful discussion about mental health and loneliness. It was on *RHLSTP* that the British writer and presenter Stephen Fry talked, for the first time in public, about his attempted suicide. Herring ascribes Fry's openness to the format of the show, to the time Fry was given, and to the intimacy of the relationship between himself, his guest, and their audience.

Herring's podcast productions are funded through a combination of ticket sales from the recording sessions, a limited amount of crowdfunding, some advertising, and, more holistically, a discernable increase in his profile as a live performer. He is now able to sell out theatre venues across the UK, and notes that most of his audiences are listeners to his podcasts. He no longer has to secure funding by justifying his work to program commissioners or channel controllers. This allows him creative control over his product and a more direct relationship with his audience. It is his choice whether he risks offending or even boring them; and it is their choice as to whether they download his podcasts or carry on listening. He can produce a show such as *Me vs Me*, in which he commentates on a snooker tournament that he plays against himself. *Me vs Me's* comedy lies in its absurdity, and in the pointlessness of the act of both making and listening to the show, Herring refers to it as a "waste of time" (2016). He recognizes that most of his followers will not listen to *Me vs Me*, which draws 5,000 listeners compared to the audience of 150,000 per episode for *RHLSTP* (Herring 2016). This does not matter because by releasing *Me vs Me* he has not lost 145,000 listeners for *RHLSP*, but rather he has served a core audience with a niche and highly targeted experience.

When Herring describes his show as being "very private" he is signaling the complete creative control he has over the podcast. It is his personal space, one that the audience is invited in to engage with, on his terms.[1] Podcasters have chosen to bring their show into being. They own it, they control it. They can decide on the subject matter, the tone, the language. It is their space. There is

---

[1] Red Scott, host of the *Game of Thrones* chatcast *Boars, Gore and Swords,* mirrors this attitude when he asserts the podcast space as being one that is and extension of his personal and that he owns: "Listen, what happens in my own home is none of the government's business, and therefore what two friends record, edit and put out as a podcast should not impose [on their privacy] in any negative way" (Red Scott in "Boars, Gore and Swords S06E06" 2016).

a contract between the podcaster and the listener, an understanding of what they are likely to encounter once they download and press play. This is a direct relationship, unmediated by a commissioner or program controller.

In broadcasting, radio station airtime is a commodity. It is something that must be divided up and portioned out with near scientific precision, after which sections are sold off for advertising to the highest bidder. To "waste" airtime is to waste money. These are the economics of scarcity that demark traditional media consumption, which have been replaced with what Ritzer and Jurgenson term the abundance of prosumer capitalism (2010). Time is not a commodity in the podcast space, at least not program time. It can be played with, extended, experimented with and, in the case of Herring's *Me vs Me,* openly "wasted." What has changed is that audience's personal listening time, their "ear time," is the commodity that is now being competed for. Previously a producer's work was filtered by commissioners and program controls and then distributed by the broadcast network; now it can be distributed freely by producers and is then filtered by the audience. This presents an opportunity to create work outside of industrial and political controls and to create new and illogically hybridized formats. Shows that can be created without the necessity that they be first pitched or that they fit a program manager's schedule. Shows that would, as Herring observes, "never be commissioned" (2016).

(2) You are the audience: Scroobius Pip's *Distraction Pieces*

The format of Scroobius Pip's *Distraction Pieces* is not radical or experimental. Comedians, actors, or other podcasters are interviewed, they are engaged in extended, unmediated, and unguarded discussion. Richard Herring, Joe Rogan, and Adam Buxton all produce shows of a similar nature. It is the tone and the range of subject matter of Pip's podcast that are noteworthy. There is an unpredictability to *Distraction Pieces,* an eclecticism in content that sees the weekly podcast veer between ribald comedy, celebrity gossip, and the unflinching discussion of social issues. There are episodes given over to willfully unstructured discourse, what Pip terms "drunkcasts"—recordings of Pip drinking (to excess) with his friends. These can be followed by shows dedicated to the refugee crisis or the conditions of the homeless. He will spend an hour speaking with a sex worker about the traumas of her life, presenting something that "is not nice to listen to but it's a reality, and it's something that happened. She shouldn't have to censor her conversation on it for everyone else's comfort because it's a reality"

(Pip 2017). There is a gritty honesty to *Distraction Pieces*, an attempt to parcel up the culture and language of the "streets" into a digital audio format. The show's production is not polished (Pip does not listen back to the shows after recording them) and neither is his presentation (he speaks with a discernable stammer which is not cleaned out or mitigated for, but allowed to exist as a distinctive part of his audio identity).[2] He addresses his audience with a voice that is authentic, honest, and unmediated.

Prior to hosting *Distraction Pieces* Pip had a career as a hip-hop artist, a record label manager, and as a DJ. In 2014 he won a Radio Academy Gold Award for the specialist music program *The Beat Down*, a show that was run out of the London music station XFM. He followed up this project with a podcast because of what he believed the form would offer him: "It was 100 percent the freedom, freedom to do anything you want, and for no one to censor it . . . [because] any company you work for, there will be some kind of agenda or path" (Pip 2017). His understanding of the media and experience in marketing work was evidenced in the strategy he adopted with the launch of *Distraction Pieces*. His first guest was the globally recognized comedian Russell Brand. He will use celebrity, including increasingly his own, to draw in an audience, and will then present them with complex material or challenging issues. He can do this because of his ownership of the podcast, and the understanding of who his audience are and how they will respond to his work:

> You can have some weeks where it's such a specific subject it's not going to appeal to everyone but that's what's great about it. That conversation wouldn't happen if it was put in front of a marketing committee or whoever else. They would say "no there's not an audience for that." There is, it might just be a bit smaller but that's still a valid audience. (Pip 2017)

Like Herring he recognizes that there is a smaller audience, his core audience (the 20,000 to 30,000 who will listen to every episode (Pip 2017)), with whom he feels that he has built a degree of trust. An understanding about the integrity and probity of his show: "I've done enough and shown them enough quality that they have the trust to go 'I'll give that a listen' and that's kind of amazing" (Pip 2017).

Pip left an environment of controlled and targeted broadcasting to join one of open and unpredictable narrowcasting. By doing so he was freed from the

---

2   The sense of ownership Pip has over his podcast is demonstrated by how untroubled he is by those who are critical of his stammer: "I'm never offended by that, but I am a little bit 'you don't need to tweet me and let me know that my unbearable stutter is ruining your day, so you can't listen.' It's free anyway, just don't listen!" (2017).

necessity of appealing to the tightly defined demographic requirements of a media outlet. Broadcasters know who their audience is intended to be; a radio station is crafted to fit the perceived tastes and needs of a particular demographic. The narrowcaster exists outside external remits and can construct their audience to be whomever they wish, without any fixed idea of whom they are likely to be (until they need to source advertising). The focus of their process can be on the production of the content they wish to offer, working with the assumption that there is an audience that will be drawn to it, and without concern for demographic distinctions.[3]

The Facebook page of Podcast Movement, an annual conference that offers advice for up-and-coming producers, explains how to plan program content to draw the largest audience: "Use your listener analytics to help keep track of which topics and formats attract the most interest from your audience. Then use that to help shape the direction of future episodes" (Podcast Movement 2017). Advice of this nature proliferates in the many online "How to podcast" guides, but this is not how successful podcasters approach their work. Their approach is more organic and manifests trust in their relationship to their work, and in turn their audience's relationship to them. Alex Blumberg explains how the whole ethos of his commercial podcast network Gimlet Media is based around a passion for creating engaging stories. This is not a qualitative, data-backed approach; there are no focus groups or audience feedback mechanisms, but rather an understanding of the craft of story and of an audience's response:

> Anytime we tried to do things because we think "oh there's definitely a market for this" it doesn't work as well as when we just try to do something [with an attitude of] "here's a show that somebody really feels quite passionate about doing." That's what works, and that's when we get the audience and then the money can follow from that. (Blumberg 2017)

Independent media needs to find an audience. It needs to find an audience that is "committed to the industrial, aesthetic, ethical and sociopolitical ideals of that media" (Bennett 2014: 5), but it does not have to pander to that audience, or prejudge their tastes. Repeatedly, interviewees discussed how creating work for a specific audience would be "the kiss of death" (Cranor and Fink 2015) and would

---

[3] Podcaster Helen Zaltzman describes this process: "I think that happens in radio a lot where they have a specific demographic that they've often invented here so a demographic is a woman, she's single, she is thirty-five to forty years, she loves ABBA, she cries on a Friday night after she gets home from being out with her friends. It's so reductive, and also you are missing a lot of people who might enjoy the same content by making those assumptions" (2016).

have led to "failure" (Zaltzman 2016). They speak of having faith that there will be an audience "out there" for their work. That if a show is released and runs for long enough, "they will come" (Wayland 2016). This allows for niche, and hyper-niche, programming. These are shows that deploy a taxonomy that is so deeply arcane, so intensely private that no one outside of their target audience would understand the references or terminology. Podcasts can do this unapologetically because no one outside of their listening community is going to hear them—no one is going to flick a dial on the car radio or set their alarm to hear a podcast about dentistry techniques, golf equipment, or the lives of porn stars unless they chose to. Hybridized shows and seemingly impossible formats can be trialed and can find audiences at the lower reaches of the long tail of listening. The leftwing *Chapo Trap House* podcast can produce a series of episodes that combine comedic observations about the Antifa movement structured around the 1980s role-playing game *Call of the Cthulhu* not because an algorithm or marketing group told them that there was a confluence of these interests, but because they intuited that there would be an audience (however small) who would enjoy picking their way through a tangled web of in-references and knowing jokes. This insight is possible not just because they understand their audience, but because they are the audience. They are making shows for themselves as much as others. There is an "am" in "Pro-am"; it is a portmanteau of producer and amateur, and this is what independent podcasters begin by being, amateurs or enthusiasts; audience members as well as creators.

(3) Lo-fi equals hi-engagement: *My Dad Wrote a Porno*

The format of *My Dad Wrote a Porno* is both disarming and enticing in its simplicity. Jamie Morton sits at a kitchen table reading from a self-published pornographic novel that was written by his father, and as he does so he is mocked by his college friends, James Cooper and Alice Levine. The first episode was released in September 2015, and since then its forty-five episodes have been downloaded over ninety million times (Morton 2017). It is an exemplar of how an independent production can rise seemingly from nowhere to the top of the industry. It should be noted that though the show's production techniques are stripped down and its producers work free from corporate oversight, it cannot be considered an amateur production. The creative team all had previous careers in the media; as a director (Morton), executive (Cooper), or presenter (Levine). They came to the project with a broad comprehension of the requirements of the form (Cooper 2017), and a wish to benefit from the freedom podcasting offered them in terms of both their creative approach and technical considerations.

Morton, Cooper, and Levine wanted to produce something that was easy to create a "homemade passion project" (Cooper 2017) that could be put out regularly without overheads or complex requirements (Levine 2017). The shows were, and still are, recorded in one of their kitchens, "after cooking each other dinner and with a glass of wine" (Morton 2017). They have refused offers to work in studios for fear that a cleaner, sonically controlled environment would sterilize the show's sense of intimacy and mutual rapport. Levine, familiar with the logistics of studio recording from her work at BBC Radio One, recognizes that they would risk "some of the atmosphere that we get because we're relaxed, and we're at home . . . I think for what you would gain with sharpness of audio, you'd maybe lose in atmosphere" (2017). Their intention is that the audience feel as if they are the fourth member of the group, sat at a table with friends: "that natural camaraderie is a nice thing, and people see themselves, and their friends in it" (2017). The presenters can speak honestly and personably, without having to "psyche themselves up" or prepare a performative mask before recording. As the show grows, this sense of intimacy has to be protected in order to maintain the illusion that the listener is the fourth member of a tightly knit group, rather than the two million and fourth (as they are based on current download figures).

Podcasting's roots, and even its name, lie in the method of its delivery. An interest in the technology of production and distribution was identified by Markman as one of the principle draws for Pro-am producers (2012). Podcasting in its earlier iterations was associated with both technical communities of listeners and producers. Aaron Mahnke, the presenter of *Lore*, describes being put off by the idea of moving into podcasting because he felt it was not suitable for his work, believing that it consisted of "men sitting round talking to each other about iPhones" (2017). The emphasis and expectations of the medium have changed to the extent that a pseudo "punk" ethic, of actively denying technical prowess, prevails. Herring, Pip, and Mahnke all speak of their lack of understanding of how RSS feeds or any of the mechanics of podcast distribution work. Mahnke and Jeffrey Cranor and Joseph Fink (the creators of *Welcome to Night Vale*) discuss how they began making their respective shows using "cheap USB microphones" and editing on "free software packages," and of having not upgraded their equipment and facilities significantly since (Mahnke 2017; Fink and Cranor 2015).

Lo-fidelity recording can be perceived as being more authentic and more intimate, as if the technologies associated with high-production values create a barrier between the presenter and their audience. Once works have been passed through audio processors, cleaned, and edited, they can be felt to have lost an essential quality of immediacy and honesty. These naturalistic sonic qualities are present when Alan Buxton introduces his show while he walks his dog in the fields of Norwich, or in Mur Lafferty's *I Should be Writing* where she offers writers advice while speaking into a headset and moving around her home, continually presenting, as she boils the kettle or answers the front door. These are moments of raw sound, presented as actuality, almost as found sound, at powerful contrast to the constructed audio of conventional broadcast presentation. Bennett notes that "the emphasis on self-representation and DIY cultures in independent media brings independent media in close proximity to their audiences" (2014: 22). There is a tendency to distrust anything that is over produced, or produced in any way at all, a feeling that to do so is to "sell out." Zaltzman observes that "a lot of people believe that editing is lying . . . and 'authentic' has to seem scrappy" (Zaltzman 2016).

The simplified aesthetic of podcasting allows productions to be made cheaply, rapidly, and without specialist knowledge. Production teams can be stripped down and costs reduced; this allows more fringe and niche content to be created for smaller audiences, and more time spent developing projects. Dana Chivvis describes moving from working as a producer on *This American Life* to *Serial* as being a liberating experience (Chivvis 2016) because she no longer had to work with a large production team. She was able to become her "own boss," finding the pace the story needed to be told not just on air, but in how the logistics of the reporting were organized. *Serial's* success was in part a product of a small team of reporters allowing themselves the time and space to invest deeply in a story. It was also the result of releasing the podcast at exactly the right time.

(4) Right product right time: *Lore*

Aaron Mahnke was a self-published author when he began presenting *Lore*. He had written a sequence of five factual essays—all set in New England—that he didn't know how to release, and was on the brink of disposing of them when he decided to turn them into audiobooks. "I fell back on my love of audiobooks, and I envisioned them almost like a self-published audiobook of four or five essays.

Even while doing the recording I still wasn't thinking 'podcast'. I wasn't thinking of being 'user-friendly'. I just wanted to give people a folder full of MP3 files" (Mahnke 2017). At this point his aims, approach, and attitude were concurrent with those of the Pro-am producer, his intention being to "keep making the show that I would listen to if I wasn't making it" (Mahnke 2017). Generating an income would have been an unexpected bonus: "It's podcasting right? I mean very few people earn a living doing this sort of thing. They earn a couple hundred dollars a month in small sponsorships, and a lot of podcasts are too niche to be able to grab a sponsor that fits a lot of their audience" (Mahnke 2017).

Lore's success was not instantaneous. It was released in March 2015 and on the first day there were nine downloads, and within a month that rate had increased to 150 a day. Shortly after the show went viral:

> I was on vacation with my wife and family; we were at my in-laws, and I was checking my downloads that evening like I always did. Around 8 p.m. I would always go in and check to see what my stats were for the day, and instead of 150 it was 350, and I thought "well that's odd" and I tried to figure out. I went on social media and looked for hash tags and people talking about the show, and there was nothing. The next day there were 2000 downloads, and the day after that it was 8500. (Mahnke 2017)

By August 2015 the audience had grown to such an extent that he was able to sell advertising and give up his day job as a graphic designer. A month later "the TV offers came in, and then the book offers." *Lore* has been serialized on Amazon Video, a trilogy of books is to be released, and Mahnke is now in control of a media franchise.

The original success of *Lore* can be ascribed to its format. It features simple stripped down, but highly crafted, storytelling—the reading of historical tales, of real-world ghost stories, and whodunits. Mahnke's presentation is measured and engaging. Each episode is structured to set up a mystery and leave the listener with a moral that can be learned from the tale. Mahnke released *Lore* without any plans, there was no target audience—"I made a show for myself" (Mahnke 2017)—or precedent that he was following. The project's profile benefited from being given a "featured" slot on the iTunes store front page, but other than that, it appeared to be an organic, word of mouth success:

> It's tough because I don't know what's made *Lore* so popular. I mean other than subject matter, I try to put out quality audio and I do try to write my best. But what if there is something in the tone? What if there is something in what the

software does that makes it all work? Maybe that sounds superstitious. From the moment I started, I have just been trusting my gut. (Mahnke 2017)

The reason why Mahnke cannot adequately conceptualize why *Lore* was initially so successful is because there is a host of influences at play that are outside of his control. Factors of circumstance and timing. Releasing a show just at the correct moment to attract attention, to capitalize on a social change or the release of new technology is key to the success of a podcast. Ira Glass credits the success of *Serial* to "a lucky congruence of a bunch of new, really good podcasts, but also the fact that the technology has changed [and] made for a lot of new people finally hearing podcasts" (cited in Berry 2015a: 171). Within a year of *Serial*'s launch *Distraction Pieces* (launched October 2014), *Lore* (March 2015) and *My Dad Wrote a Porno* (September 2015) were released into a digital media movement undergoing a surge in public interest. Terry Miles and Paul Bae's *The Black Tapes*, a fictional reworking of *Serial* as a paranormal horror story, was launched in May 2015. They had developed the project prior to Koenig's success and were able to release it at the moment when public attention for *Serial* peaked. Two years later their home-produced show has been downloaded thirty million times. Their timing was both immaculately precise and extremely fortunate; they were able to present to the market exactly the right project at exactly the right time.

Without the support of a marketing budget, a press team, or a wealth of contacts, the independent podcaster is reliant on the congruence of innumerable factors that are beyond their control. This is an organic process that unfolds in the digital sphere; Nahon and Hemsley describe media virality as being a "naturally occurring, emergent phenomenon facilitated by [an] interwoven collections of websites" (2013: 2). It helps to have a base audience, or a profile to gain attention in the days and weeks following launch. Alice Levine and Scroobius Pip had media profiles, Mahnke was a dedicated blogger, self-published author, and informal podcaster when he launched *Lore*. Richard Herring refers to his very first show as "only" having an audience of "about 10,000" on launch; he is dismissive of this number, which is small when compared to the audience he would have attracted at the height of his television career, but it is far more than most podcasters will ever achieve.[4]

---

[4] Even *The Odditorium*, the podcast I launched from Brighton in spring 2015, that sweet spot of the "Golden Age," was able to attract 4,000 downloads in its first week because it was associated with a live spoken word club that had built up a following over 15 years.

What is common to these stories from podcasting's "Golden Age" is that independent producers have found success by working instinctively, and by trusting an innate sense of what their work should be. They have not been distracted by technical considerations but have focused on creating work that is unmediated, impulsive, and authentic. They have then released this work with initially little planning and consideration, but have been astute, and sometimes fortunate, in their timing:

> It has to be a combination of things doesn't it? It has to be luck, timing, the market that you're in, and what's gone before you, and what comes after. All of those things, your idea, it's really hard to pinpoint what makes that happen. (Levine 2017)

Warnings from the golden age: The neoliberal shark tank

When discussing the economic and industrial frameworks of podcasting it is important to avoid survivorship bias, to ask not why certain podcasts succeed (because as noted the reasons for success can be both tangential and coincidental), but why others fail. The economics of independent podcasting, which are built around the freemium of model of distribution, favor the minority who have been successful and leave the majority with nothing in return for their time and their efforts. The long-tail economics of the web dictate that there are hundreds of thousands of podcasts that have not gone viral, that have been abandoned, or that are being made for an audience of friends and family.

The relationship to others, the urge to produce work that benefits a community of listeners, is key to why podcasters keep podcasting (Markman 2012). The process of creating a production is isolating, and each show is set up as an individual enterprise that must then enter into free-market competition. Podcasting could be read as a manifestation of the commodification of the individual practitioner, an example of neoliberalism at its most extreme. Richard Herring likens this working environment to one that he encountered when building his career as a comedian:

> That's the way competition works, that's how everything works. It's the same with stand up, there's too many stand ups but you know that just means you have to push yourself, be more original, and be more creative which is a good thing. It's supply and demand, you've got to work out how you're going to get people to listen to you. (Herring 2016)

While there are costs associated with the processes of production, oversupply and ease of distribution have driven the commercial value of the product down to zero, with shows being reliant on the secondary income streams of advertising, merchandising, and crowdfunding. These sources of revenue are only triggered when a project has a particularly large audience, with an associated dedicated fan base. This creates a winner-takes-all economy with only a very small number of shows considered economically viable. Podcasting is a hungry format; the Apple Podcast charts, the focal point of the form's discoverability, are based entirely on the numbers of new subscribers.[5] New listeners are what matters, not existing listeners. There is a constant striving for new material, a fight for what little publicity is available and only an elite few shows can take a hiatus or be reliant on their back catalog of work.

Selling your authenticity

Robert Krulwich interrupts an episode of *Radiolab* to stiffly read text about an electronic banking service; Jonathan Mitchell introduces *The Truth* with a vignette where he and his young daughter discuss the benefits of a brand of women's shavers; Nick Van Der Kolk signs off an emotionally jarring episode *Love + Radio* by telling the listener how comfortable it is to wear underpants fashioned from silver mesh. There is a balance in podcast production between the financial necessity of featuring advertising and creative integrity. It is one that producers rarely appear comfortable making. Although pre-recorded slots are still used, the preferred format, that bakes in the content and prevents the audience skipping through to the next section, is to have the presenter personally endorse a product (Rosin 2016). This is described as "native advertising" and can consist of an interview with a representative of the sponsor, a user endorsement, or a section where the host discusses the uses and benefits of a product.

Native advertising represents a trade-in where the producer is selling not just their audience's listening time, their "ear time," but also their trust. This is a finite resource that is one of the most important commodities that they have. There is an implied contract between the independent podcaster and their listener, an understanding that they are saying what they are saying, because they chose to.

---

[5] For a discussion of how the iTunes charts are calculated, and their import to the discoverability of podcasts, see Chapter 7, "*Blood Culture*: Gaming the Podcast System."

No one else has paid them, asked them, or made them say the words that they speak. The moment they speak from a script that they have been given, then that contract is broken, and their authenticity begins to drain away. In response podcasters perform verbal and conceptual contortions to delineate the veracity of *their* content and to demark what they have been paid to say.

One response to this dilemma is to treat the sponsored segment as being a "necessary evil," and to assume that the audience are able to pick up audio and verbal signals that this is the case. Radiotopia's Van Der Kolk and Mitchell dutifully deliver their messages, even claiming to have slept on a Casper Mattress or cooked a Blue Apron meal, but they do so without the energy or finesse with which they present their unsponsored content. Jad Abumrad speaks of wrestling with the decision of how to position *Radiolab*'s paid segments, and of being uncomfortable with the blurring of the boundary between "the person reading the ad and the person giving the [podcast] information" (Abumrad 2016). His and Krulwich's ads are recorded on phones, often in public spaces, and read straight from the script. Their advertised content is demarcated through lo-fi "bad audio" and a sense of distain in how it is presented. A more extreme version of this response is for the presenter to mock the product, and thus remove themselves from the process of having to sell it. Richard Herring invites salespeople onto his show to pitch their wares, which he then mocks in front of his audience. Helen Zaltzman was encouraged by her contacts at Audible to "slightly take the piss" out of their work because it "doesn't damage the product at all" and "makes it feel more part of the show" (Zaltzman 2016).

These conflicts can be avoided by presenters who chose to only promote products that they can either endorse on a personal level or resonate directly with their audience. Kaitlin Prest and Mitra Kaboli's *The Heart,* a podcast about sex and relationships, was sponsored by a sex toy chain of shops. Scroobius Pip claims to be only willing to discuss and recommend products that he actively uses. In limited cases advertising content can be incorporated into the flow of a show in a manner that heightens the experience. Central to Paul Bae and Terry Miles's *The Black Tapes* is the artifice that the presenter, and Alex Reagan, is an actual reporter working for a real-world production company (Pacific Northwest Stories). The audience can find this company on the web; the claim is that they create other podcasts and Bae and Miles deny that the show is a work of fiction. When Reagan pauses her investigations into demonology and the occult, and endorses mail services, sock brands, or website hosting services she is breaking the flow of the narrative, but is heightening the verisimilitude of the experience. Reagan is a fictional character endorsing real-world products, and in so doing, the imagined storyworld of the series is blended with the real. This creates another means by which the listener may actively suspend their disbelief. Comedian Adam Buxton composes and performs jingles for his sponsors that overstate the benefits of their products, and satirize the language and conventions of marketing forms. This allows him to appear to be "above" the uncomfortable process of actually selling something, while providing his clients with highly effective earworms that serve to heighten awareness of their brand.

Advertisers are not investment funders, they will only be drawn to projects that either already have an audience or ones that they believe, through the involvement of a celebrity or a recognized media franchise, can guarantee one (Wayland 2017; Dryden 2017). There are tensions between the creative freedom of the producer and their client's willingness to associative their products with particular content. Radiotopia's Julie Shapiro admits that the involvement with sponsors entails a "dampening down of experimentation" (Shapiro 2016) and Alex Blumberg, the CEO of Gimlet Media, specifies that shows tackling difficult themes such as "depression or death would be tough to sell [to advertisers]" (Blumberg 2017). Both Richard Herring and *My Dad Wrote a Porno's* James Cooper had difficulties finding sponsors willing to risk placing material on shows that push the boundaries of taste and decency. These pressures can influence producers to produce work that avoids controversy, driving podcasting toward safer, less extreme, and less diverse middle ground.

Podcasting as a form has been accused of being fearful of challenging its audience, of lacking an "avant-garde" or an urge to be "weird" and disorientating (Verma 2017b). Content is accused of having fallen into "to a handful of predictable genres or categories (e.g., interviews, news, talk, game shows, comedy, drama), each with roots in radio" (Bottomley 2014). There are no shows where "part of the experience of listening is to be knocked askew, assaulted, and otherwise disturbed, even as you're enthralled" (Weiner 2014). Podcasters cannot risk producing work that is focused just on sound, and not on gathering audience (Van Der Kolk 2015); in a podcast world of limitless choice; such shows would function as works of auto-destructive art. Independent producers need to maintain their audience because they are their source of funding, they cannot risk losing them. The very freedom that is granted by independence from the structures and concerns of networked, mass-market media is simultaneously limited by that freedom. They find themselves caught in what Julie Shapiro terms "a very tangled kind of desire" where they wish to "do more and be creative and innovate" but they are tied by the pragmatic realities of keeping their show running (Shapiro 2016).

The most precarious of the Precariat

The open web is not necessarily a utopian space; as Hesmondhalgh notes, "We need to be especially on guard when assessing claims that the internet and the World Wide Web have democratized culture" (2013: 314). There are class, social, and educational divides; Brake found that Pro-am producers "have higher sociodemographic status than the broader internet-using populations they come from" (2013: 592). Access to technologies used to be a barrier to entry but (as discussed in Chapter 6, "A Utopian Moment: *Podium.me*, Diversity and Youth Podcasting") this has been lifted by the ubiquity of mobile devices that can record, edit, and distribute media content. The challenge is now not how to become a podcaster, but how to remain a podcaster. As Shapiro observes, "It isn't hard starting a podcast, what is difficult is keeping it running" (2016).

The unpaid and unwaged realities of podcasting's freemium economy create an environment where producers are often working without fiscal support. The "sweat collateral" invested in any start-up project is considerable; time must be taken to develop a format, produce content, build websites, manage and test the RSS, and seek and build an audience. All without any guarantee of a return on investment. As Leadbeater and Oakley note, independent production can provide choice, autonomy, and satisfaction but it also involves constant uncertainty, insecurity, and change (1999: 15). The independent producer must work without support, and without stability; they must recognize this as part of their process and be able to operate with, and respond positively to, the pressures involved. Peck argues that "discourses of urban creativity seek to normalize flexible labor-market conditions, lionizing a class of workers that can not only cope with, but positively revel in, this environment of persistent insecurity and intense, atomized competition" (2005: 742). To work like this requires an understanding of what the media is and what can be achieved (Bourdieu 1969). To take the risks and invest the time required to gain success in the freemium economy requires a degree of fiscal and emotional support that is available to only the most fortunate.

Independently producing a podcast is not just a job. The drive of many podcast producers is personal; they are producing work that represents an attempt to "gain self-realization" through expressing themselves to an audience. This represents, as McRobbie notes, part of the "utopian thread embedded in this wholehearted attempt to make-over the world of work into something closer to a life of enthusiasm and enjoyment" (2002: 521). There exists highly personal association with their labor, and the products of their labor, leaving them vulnerable to conditions of self-exploitation. They are producing work in the most precarious of working environments, and burdened with pressure and anxieties about maintaining their situation. Stories of long hours, over work, and exhaustion are common among even the most successful of producers (Mahnke 2017; Miles 2017). In the later period of 2017 Megan Tan has stepped away from her successful Radiotopia show *Millennial*, Jad Abumrad has taken a break from *Radiolab*, and Kaitlin Prest and Mitra Kaboli have put *The Heart* into hiatus. The economics of podcasting favor productions that are produced with low overheads and in high volume, work that can be released cheaply and easily, which in turn can lead to creative burn-out.

What the Pro-am revolution has done is reconfigured "work" as play, and this in turn has devalued independent producer's labor to the extent that it is now rendered almost worthless. They are creating content to be played on Apple and Android devices, made available through the iTunes store, listened to on Bose and Beats earbuds. They do this without any guarantee of financial recompense for their efforts while Apple and Alphabet have become not just two of the most highly valued companies in the world, but quite possibly two of the richest corporations in history.

The power of networks

The freemium economy transfers the risks of the market through a networked hierarchy of manufacturers and distributors to the individual creative workers. Production networks allow these risks to be shared across multiple projects and with other producers. By gathering shows into an associated brand, podcast networks can assist creators and alleviate some of the starker choices that must be made between creative independence and fiscal security. Podcast networks can provide a degree of protection similar to that offered by a union (Greenhalgh 2017), but they can also represent a threat to the independence of podcasters. Industry observer Nick Quah highlights the aggressive strategies of large networks, such as Panoply and Midroll, whom he describes as having performed a "land grab" between them as they sign up each and every successful show they can find (2016a).

A podcast network can offer the independent producer a degree of stability. A group of shows can pool resources and knowledge, share technical talent and content, and spread costs. They can aggregate their audience and diversify their reach, allowing them to present more attractive packages to advertising clients. They can engage in mutually beneficial cross-project marketing. Berry ascribes part of the success of *Serial* to its association with *This American Life*, "a well-known, much loved, and highly respected brand" (2015b: 174). This "*TAL* effect" has also served as a positive influence on other podcasts: for instance, Jonathan Mitchell's drama *The Truth* began to gain audience traction after an episode, "Tape Delay," was distributed by *This American Life*. Networked podcasters will vouch for their peers' shows, and they will play extracts or release entire episodes as part of their RSS stream. This will cross-fertilize audiences, and serve to spread their product, while highlighting their position as part of a network. This can have the same negative connotations that are associated with native advertising; being part of a network challenges the independence and authenticity of a show's identity.

If "public radio is ready for capitalism," as Ira Glass opined (quoted in Greiff 2015), then it is also risking the connection it has with the public. The debates related to public service broadcasting are long and intricate, and will not be unpacked here, but it should be recognized that the remit of commercial-funded media network is to accrue profit, rather than act in fulfillment of any broader societal mission. There is a tendency for podcast producers to avoid association with commercial media and its considerations. They emphasize the "down-to-earth" nature of their productions and present them as projects driven by passion rather than profit. Advertising revenues proceeds from crowd funding and operating budgets are hidden. There is a focus upon self-representation, on DIY culture, that Bennett believes "brings the audience closer" (2014: 22). Sarah Koenig and Dana Chivvis assert that they produced the first series of *Serial* from a basement, rather than framing it as part of a hugely successful radio franchise. In an unguarded moment Jad Abumrad introduced the "Oliver Sipple" episode (2017) of *Radiolab* by appealing for funding support and explaining how some episodes can cost over $100,000 to make. Tellingly he drew the comparison between this budget and that of a "small independent movie." In so doing he was careful to maintain a relationship to indie culture, and with what terms Hesmondhalgh defines as an "opposition to popular culture" and an association with "a do-it-yourself attitude" (1999: 53).

The Radiotopia podcast network, which is run by the Public Radio Exchange (PRX), alleviates these pressures by allowing its producers to maintain a significant degree of control over the management of their productions. The network runs effectively as a collective. Risk is distributed, costs are spread, and funding (garnered from grants, advertising, and funding drives) is shared between shows. The network was not set up to foster new talent, but rather to provide support and a platform for those who have known some success, and have some experience in audio production. Executive producer Julie Shapiro describes how they wish to work with "very entrepreneurial-minded independent-spirited producers that want to own their own shows, do their own things, and are ready to do all of the work that comes with that, and we help along the way when we can, but the producers really carry the bulk of the production and getting their shows out" (2016). What Radiotopia offers is unusual: producers are able to fully own their intellectual property, maintain creative freedom and benefit from editorial support. Quah observes that this is a "pretty sweet deal for shows already on the up and up that are looking to outsource some processes, like advertising sales and technology support, but on the whole want to maintain firm creative control" (2017a).

Shows that are part of Radiotopia benefit from association with a tightly curated brand. In the three years since its launch by Roman Mars in 2014, the network had expanded its roster of podcasts from seven to only fifteen. The link by demographic appeal is clearly, though not explicitly, defined. Michael Newman notes that "the oppositional stance that defines indie culture is one key to its status as a source of distinction, a means by which its audience asserts its superior taste" (2009: 22). With its finely crafted storytelling, wry presentation, and precise marketing strategies Radiotopia "serves as a taste culture perpetuating the privilege of a social elite of upscale consumers" (2009: 17). Through a combination of astute marketing, gifted production, and impeccable timing Radiotopia has managed to establish itself as a source of authentic high-quality podcast production. Its selection of shows is the audio equivalent of the indie movie house, drawing to it an audience that is educated, urban and, most likely, solvent. The network's operating model is only possible because its brand is strong, and its range of shows limited. If it diversifies too far then those brand associations will be lost. If it does not, then without investment capital to bolster the project, it risks being lost in the expanding, and increasingly monetized "sea of free audio" that is the podcasting industry.

Gimlet Media—Where public radio meets capitalism

Gimlet Media is a disorientating entity. The company sits on the boundary between public radio and commercial production. They freely deploy the tropes and tricks of the "Golden Age" of podcasting: from the self-reflective reporter, to the finely crafted factual narrative, to the "vocal fry" of the presenter.[6] Gimlet garbs itself in the trappings of the indie podcaster while simultaneously broadcasting the fact that they are an investor-funded, profit-driven organization. No attempt is made to hide the millions of dollars of capital that has been raised by its founders Alex Blumberg and Matt Lieber. The first season of one of its most successful podcast, *StartUp*, was dedicated to openly documenting this process. They are in the business of producing crafted, story-driven audio and are attempting to make a profit as they do so. Gimlet Media is a practical example of the repurposing of the ethos of public radio for capitalism.

The origin story of Gimlet has been documented in granular detail, not only across the course of the first season of *StartUp* but also as basis for the comedy TV series *Alex, Inc.* The strap-line for which is: "Alex is in his mid-30s with a wife and two kids. He makes the crazy decision to quit his good job and dive into the brave new world of starting a business." The licensing of his company's start-up story is indicative of the success of Blumberg and Lieber's business model, wherein the ownership of show rights lies with the company and not the producer. The expansion of the company has confounded its founders' expectations; they raised $1.5 million in capital investment in the spring of 2014, prior to the post-*Serial* explosion in podcasting. They did not foresee how rapidly audiences, and the numbers of competitor podcasts, would expand. The podcasting industry has accelerated, advertising revenues have grown, the company raised a further $15 million investment in 2016 and in 2017 Gimlet's staff numbered over seventy: "Everything is happening fast, which is great for us" (Blumberg 2017). The challenge to Blumberg as company CEO is to maintain

---

[6] Vocal fry is a mode of speaking where the ends of words are drawn out with a low, almost "creaky" voice. It has become associated with female speakers, and with podcasters, being the subject of debate (Grose 2015), defense ("Freedom Fries," *This American Life* 2015), and satire (Sibler 2017).

the creative quality of the content that the network produces, while satisfying investors and simultaneously predicting how the industry will develop.

Gimlet's mission is to produce and monetize engaging audio content. Like Radiotopia they are interested in sourcing and developing existing talent, though Gimlet focuses more on adopting promising personnel rather than programs that are already successful. Gimlet rarely take an existing show and rebrand it as being part of the network; Blumberg is looking for a "sweet spot" where people are "passionate about what they are building, but they're a little bit tired of doing something in isolation" (2017). The aim is to take "podcasters who have known some success and providing them with the means and framework to develop their craft and build a project from a financially stable base" (Blumberg 2017). Blumberg places a great deal of emphasis on the stability that Gimlet offers its creative staff; when interviewed he mentioned several times that they were benefiting from healthcare, sick pay, holiday time, and a regular salary. At the heart of their model there is a transaction that sees the network ameliorate the producer's risks of working in the open market in return for their signing over nearly all of the benefits of that market.

With the podcasting industry expanding rapidly, Blumberg sees competition for talent, as opposed to audience, as being paramount. From their Brooklyn base at the epicenter of the podcasting revolution, they are able to draw the best new podcasters to them while also having access to the experience and guidance of some of the most experienced producers in American radio. Blumberg learned his craft under Ira Glass, something that gives him "a pretty unique advantage"; his offer to nascent podcasting talent is that Gimlet can provide similar mentorship and opportunities for collaboration.

Blumberg is not involved in the editorial decisions of individual shows, at least not on a regular basis. Presenters are paired with producers who together manage productions and their associated budgets. Each show must prove itself to be financially viable; Blumberg believes that the company has a duty to provide engaging and provoking material to the public without being in the service of the public. With the majority of funding being drawn from advertising and licensing, the success of a project in terms of audience demand is paramount:

> If a show does not get to that level of audience eventually, then we will shut it down, and we have shut down shows before. We need shows that can find an audience, and maintain an audience. When they do that they have more resources, but if we can't find an audience we can't keep a show going. (Blumberg 2017)

The most high-profile show that Gimlet has canceled, to date, was Starlee Kine's *The Mystery Show*. Running to just six episodes *Mystery Show* was critically lauded, declared Best New Podcast by Apple in 2015, and the episode "Belt Buckle" listed as Number 1 in *The Atlantic's* list of the best podcast episodes of 2015. It was described by Blumberg himself as "one of the most amazing podcasts I have ever had the privilege of being associated with" (Blumberg 2016), though he said this during an episode of *StartUp* where he was discussing the show's cancellation. *The Mystery Show* was styled as an investigation into mysteries that "couldn't be resolved with a search engine alone." It entailed Kine engaging in a forensic level of investigation into what appears to be the most trivial of conundrums. Why was Britney Spears photographed holding a friend's unsuccessful novel? Exactly how tall is the actor Jake Gyllenhaal? What is the story behind an elaborately designed belt buckle that was found in the streets of Phoenix thirty years ago? Kine engaged the listener in these investigations and then introduced them to characters far beyond the remit of each show's initial premise. It was surprising, revealing, at times moving, and costly to produce. In April 2016 the second season was dropped and several months later Kine voiced her disappointment on the website Medium:

> Alex told me the show was unsustainable. I was out. I lost my staff, my salary, my benefits, my budget and my email address. *Mystery Show* is the only show this has happened to at Gimlet. Just a few months prior, iTunes voted it Best Podcast of the Year. (Kine 2016)

Gimlet had responded by releasing an announcement that praised *The Mystery Show* while describing it as "an ambitious production" and noting that "Starlee has an uncompromising vision for the show, which is what makes it so great" (cited in Dale 2016), but which also, presumably, made it so expensive. These factors were deemed to have combined to make the show "unsustainable to produce and publish on a consistent basis" and it had to be withdrawn. This decision made the network's identity, as a venture capital backed enterprise, more explicitly evident than any episode of *StartUp* ever could. Blumberg had used that show to present Gimlet's inception as the story of his struggle to realize a dream, of a faltering, honest, and slightly shy man having to interface with the world of post-digital finance, of lift-pitches, and the demands of capitalistic enterprise. It was an exposition of the company's origins that possessed at once a "radical, authentic transparency" (Quah 2016b), and a controlled and sugarcoated versioning of the truth. The cancellation of *The Mystery Show* demonstrated that Gimlet could not, and would not, back a project if it was not able to prove itself economically viable. No matter that the show drew critical praise, was featured on network TV talk shows, and had a dedicated, and very vocal, fanbase. Its format was inflexible, its release schedule too infrequent, and its methods too expensive. Gimlet can afford to produce a show like *Reply All* because it releases episodes regularly, and can offset the costs of an international investigation, such as that featured in the "Long Distance" episodes, with cheaper studio-bound episodes where Blumberg visits to chat with the hosts about net news and gossip. The cancellation of *The Mystery Show* represented a turning point, a moment that Nick Quah believed involved Gimlet confronting a fundamental tension that it had never properly resolved:

> The company actively cultivates a feeling of goodwill associated with being small, scrappy, and independent—a carryover, one would imagine, from its public radio DNA—while at the same time enjoying the advantages of being an empire-building, venture-backed, for-profit business. The company has, in a lot of ways, never really had to publicly confront the burdens, traps, and responsibilities that come with being big and venture-backed, and now it's doing just that. (Quah 2016b)

In the summer of 2016, shortly after the cancellation of *The Mystery Show*, the company launched Gimlet Creative, its "branded podcast division," where content is produced in direct association with major corporations. Thus far shows have included *The Venture* with Virgin Atlantic, *The Secret of Victory* with Gatorade, and *Open for Business* with eBay. Their business model has grown from its roots; it is no longer seeking an indie audience for whom they develop exclusive and elite content. The assumption appears to be that as podcasting grows, then a new, more mainstream audience will be drawn in. They will be less concerned about the putative "authenticity" of the presenters, and will accept product placement and branding as part of the listening experience. For this model to be effective the audiences for podcasting must continue to expand, and the source of the bulk of that audience, the Apple podcast and iTunes store, must be open and free to access:

> In terms of Apple being a dominant force to fear, anything is possible. They could destroy the industry with one careless step . . . they are a behemoth, any move [they] make sends ripples everywhere, and they've also almost singlehandedly created all this. (Blumberg 2017)

Living under the giant

In 2006 Berry described the emergent podcasting environment as being one in which "there is no 'gatekeeper' controlling who can and who cannot transmit in this space" (2006: 147). Prior to the growth of podcasting, access to the means of distribution of audio media was limited. In the UK, Ofcom (or previously the Radio Authority) controlled the airwaves and, in the field of speech radio, the BBC controlled both the budgets and the route to accessing an audience. Producers had to work with the whims of a small coterie of commissioning editors, responding to the gnomic requirements of commissioning documents and compressing their ideas into proposals that had to possess a Haiku-like brevity. Podcasting had the potential to wipe these corporate and practice-based frameworks away, to create a horizontal media space where all were potentially equal, where there were no longer any gatekeepers to production, to distribution, or to reaching the audience. This is still the case, theoretically anyone can distribute their audio via RSS, but for their work to be discoverable they will have to interface with, and be approved by, a podcast aggregator. For their work to gain traction and build an audience, they will have to be accepted by and gain "featured" status on the Apple iTunes store, the source of 80 percent of podcast traffic (Walch 2017). It has not been possible to interview Apple as part of this research, and they have not replied to any of our approaches, something that is indicative of their operational methodologies. They are a "black box" company, one whose long-term goals are oblique, and the intentions of their podcast policy are not apparent. They have built the podcast industry, they control that industry but no one that we interviewed is entirely sure why.

It is not just the independent producer that is reliant on Apple's largesse for their position in the market. The monolithic gatekeepers of traditional media, the public radio broadcasters from the United States and the BBC, acknowledge the extent of their dependency. Former Radiolab executive producer Ellen Horne discusses the "huge role" Apple plays in supporting individual shows (Horne 2015) and Alan Hall admits that the long-term success of the *Short Cuts* series that he produces for the BBC can in part be ascribed to there being "someone at iTunes who liked us, and stuck Josie [the presenter] and the show on the [front page] banner, and it made a profound impact" (Hall 2016). The BBC's Mark Friend, Controller of Radio and Music Multiplatform, is responsible for the largest podcast network (in terms of output) in the world, and yet he complains of the difficulties discoverability pose:

> You've got hundreds of thousands of active podcast feeds, and very little curation. I think it's quite hard to find things you're not really looking for, and that is where gatekeepers come in because if you look at the iTunes front page, you see a bunch of podcast icons, and that's far less difficult to manage than "the Internet." (Friend 2016)

That podcasts could offer an egalitarian mode of delivery of audio media, freed from gatekeepers, and empowering to the independent producer was an illusion. As King observes, "There is no such thing as absolutely true independence, in the sense of any form of cultural production that is one-hundred percent lacking in dependence on anything of any sort" (in Bennett 2014: 5). Every podcaster is at some level working for Apple, Samsung, or whoever has manufactured their audience's phones and devices, the things that enable their audience to listen to their material for free.

Communication is community

What independence offers podcasters is a degree of creative freedom, but autonomy as an end goal will be neither achievable nor reflective of the greatest strengths of their medium. Lee points out that to focus singularly on independence is to subscribe to a culture of capitalism that values flexibility and eschews "dependency" (2011). There is a sense of shame at having to defer to others, and workers in the new capitalism must accept that the "key to success is the ability to let go of one's past, to constantly go with the flow of ceaseless change, and to accept impermanence" (Lee 2011: 490).

The podcasting market could be read as a neoliberal shark tank, wherein over 350,000 separate entities fight over audience and funding, but interviews with the producers and presenters themselves belie this interpretation. Repeatedly they describe an environment that is supportive, bonded by a love of the medium and a wish that those involved will at once gain and learn from one another. Levine, presenter of *My Dad Wrote a Porno*, describes the podcast community as a "really nice world where you're able to connect with like-minded people" (2017). Mahnke peppers his discussion with references to the friendships he has built with other podcasters. Pip compares the podcast industry to the traditional radio: "I always felt with radio it was always competitive, Capital [Radio] hate Radio 1, and Radio 1 hate XFM and so forth, and it's all this competition. Whereas with podcasts it seems to be everyone wants more, everyone wants everyone to succeed . . . and it feels like a family" (Pip 2017). These highly successful independent podcasters are mirroring the responses of amateur producers when they were surveyed by Markman in 2012: "Participants mentioned the relationships they had formed, the networking opportunities they discovered, and very frequently, the sense that they were part of a community of listeners, guests, content providers, and other podcasters" (2012: 557).

A generosity of spirit is possible while the field is expanding and there is a mutual benefit to building audience and growing both the form and its associated community. Alex Blumberg openly admits that Gimlet Media does not have competitors "right now" because "we're just trying to get more and more people to listen to podcasts" (Blumberg 2017). This sense of community may pass. Prosumer producers may not be primarily motivated by money (Markman 2012; Berry 2016b) but investor backed networks are. Their mission does not sync with the nonhierarchical, grassroots media that Berry wrote about in 2006, they have an entirely different understanding of the form. When asked how his network intended to compete in an environment where so many were able to give their work away for free Blumberg was perplexed by the question: "Who is putting all their money and time into it for free?" he asked (Blumberg 2017).

This response is indicative of a fissure that is growing within podcasting, between the highly produced, funded, and publicized shows whose production belies their public radio roots, and the 350,000 shows that Rob Walch of the global podcasting hosting service Libsyn describes as representing the very heart of a UGC form (2017). In 2014 those two elements existed close enough for there to be synergistic relationship between the unfunded and funded producer. The revolution of September 2014 both stimulated podcasting and propelled it forward, and in so doing began to process of sundering the professional and amateur elements apart. At the time of writing the impact of this bifurcation has yet to be realized. It is unclear whether it will still be possible for an independent producer with some cheap equipment, a great idea, and a lot of passion to strike it lucky and sell out the opera house. Maybe that is not what is important about podcasting and for podcasters; fiscal and popular success was perhaps just an unexpected by-product of a particular set of circumstances that existed for a few years within this nascent medium. Perhaps thousands of people are putting their time and money into podcasting for free because this is a form that provides them with a voice, and offers them creative freedom and the chance to become part of a thriving community of independents.

Afterword

There is an audacity in writing a "book" about "podcasting"—freezing a medium so fluid, malleable, and evolving in the fixed and immutable medium of ink on paper. What we have attempted to create in these pages is not a document *of the medium* but a document *of a moment of change* in that medium, of a revolution that began in 2014 and is still unfolding as this Afterword is being written. We are pleased with the range of approaches and interpretations this book takes to podcasting and hope they open doors to a myriad of other fruitful methods which might be applied to generate diverse and compelling readings of some the major currents of our moment and beyond. While significant and noteworthy changes continue apace, particularly in the areas of money and metrics, to attempt to capture and update all of them here would have been a Sisyphean labor—this work will have to be left to other books and authors, and other forms like blogs, reviews, and articles. We only hope that we have contributed to a workable foundation for this collective project.

That said, there are some happenings and ideas that have developed over the three-year course of our research worth mentioning here because they suggest new sets of questions and further research opportunities. These include:

1. Some specific podcasts (and podcast genres) clearly replicate, mutate, and reproduce. A raft of shows have grown up in the shadow of industry behemoths like *Radiolab*, *Serial*, and *99% Invisible*. While some are copies and some are hybrids, they are all generally leaner and lighter than their progenitors (and some are as significant). What might this mean for podcasting's future?

2. Video dreams seem to tempt, or taunt, successful podcasters in the same way they have tempted and taunted successful radio producers from *The Hitchhiker's Guide to the Galaxy* to *This American Life*. Do the specifics of the medium outlined in this book mean that attempts to crossover are likely to be misguided or even doomed? To what extent is *Alex, Inc.*, in spite of its lackluster reviews, a harbinger of future projects? Will the TV industry begin actively testing ideas first in podcast form, and what might

this mean for narrative media more broadly? Fans still queue for *Welcome to Night Vale*, but with the TV licensing deal now finalized whether the show maintains its sense of authenticity and its fans a sense of engagement depends on how the move to visual space is realized.

3. Podcasts discussed in this book have already taken significant (for some perhaps permanent) pauses. These include *The Heart*, *Black Tapes*, *Radiolab*, and *We're Alive*; even *Serial* took until September of 2018 to release its third season. But to what extent should this be a concern for producers and production houses? As we noted in the introduction, podcasting is a longitudinal form and the influence and ability to retain and generate audiences remain long after production dormancy. *Blood Culture* is testament to this; the series continues to garner listeners and bubbles around the iTunes Arts chart without any significant efforts to promote it. Occasionally people text Justine for a job at Meta and once in a while one of them rings Livi's phone.

4. Why has podcast drama not yet had its breakthrough moment? Followers, producers, and academics have yet to settle on a name for the form and it seems to remain a niche interest, though a significant one with passionate devotees. Meanwhile, the remarkable rise of the role-play podcast opens up new and exciting performative possibilities. How might these inflect the future of podcast drama?

5. While the youth-access podcast *Podium.me* has grown significantly since our research began, similar projects have not proliferated in the way we anticipated. More troublingly, the internship economy and the gig economy that follows it seem to be worsening in intensity. Is this a permanent trajectory and if so should we just recognize and valorize youth-access podcasts for the social and nonvocational contributions they make?

6. Podcasting is at once becoming more diverse (in terms of the voices that are being heard and presented) and more homogenized (in terms of those garnering recognition). *The New York Times*, the BBC, *Slate*, Wondery, and the ever-expanding Gimlet Media and Radiotopia houses are sucking up all the oxygen of publicity and beginning to dominate the podcasting ecosystem. What will this mean for the "experiential diversity" we noted as a feature of the podcast listening and making of young people like those we surveyed?

7. What, if any, are the future alternatives to Apple's de facto role as podcasting's tastemaker? A significant change in the podcast ecosphere since our research began has been the development (by virtually every English-language national public broadcaster) of podcast review programs—podcasts that exist only to review and promote other podcasts. Might this suggest an effort by public broadcasters to reclaim for themselves the position of arbiters of "quality" media, or is this phenomenon simply an organic answer to Zorn's plea (mentioned in our introduction) for a broader and deeper culture of well-define audio arts criticism?

8. What are we to make of the fact that more and more radio programs are simply being repackaged, with very few changes, as podcasts? How does this complicate some of the central arguments of this book about the uniqueness of the podcast medium? To our ears many of the specifically podcasting characteristics (particularly those that deal with tone, attachment and engagement) are now feeding back into the way many non-current-events radio programs are being made. In simpler terms: "radio" is coming to sound more "podcast."

The questions raised by these enquiries may well be answered soon as podcast studies continues to grow, as will many others we cannot predict. It remains an incredibly dynamic, diverse, and often contradictory medium: While the form often feels at risk of being overrun with celebrity, branded content, and networked shows, podcasting still offers a platform for smaller voices, allowing the spare-room producer to create work that sits alongside the biggest of media companies, and provides an opportunity for communities to form among and between its creators and their listeners. As Helen Zaltzman noted, this community has not been characterized by the "poisonous culture [that] there is around YouTube where the commenting is lethal" (2016). There has yet to be the podcasting equivalent of Gamergate, there is no podcasting Pepe the Frog, discourse around shows is rarely characterized by violence or racial invective, and no foreign government has yet been shown to have used a podcast to sway an election. To date the podcasting revolution has invited media change in human and empathetic directions, it has reinvigorated the field of speech radio, allowed beautiful, moving, and innovative audio to be produced, and has provided a range of fresh, unusual, and previously unheard voices a platform from which they can be heard. Let the revolution continue.

References

"20 and Undecided" (2016), [Podcast] *Podium.me*, May 10. https://www.acast.com/podiumreallife/20andundecided (accessed October 10, 2016).

"A Red Dot" (2015), [Podcast] *Love + Radio*, September 24. https://itunes.apple.com/gb/podcast/love-radio/id84389707?mt=2 (accessed July 17, 2017).

Abel, Jessica (2015), *Out on the Wire: The Storytelling Secrets of the New Masters of Radio*, New York: Broadway Books.

Abumrad, Jad (2016), interview by Martin Spinelli, Brooklyn, New York, October 26.

Abumrad, Jad (2017), email correspondence to Martin Spinelli, January 19.

"Adnan Syed's Setback" (2016), [Podcast] *Crime Writers On...*, December 29. http://www.crimewriterson.com/listen/2016/12/29/no-bail-for-adnan-syed-serials-mistake-homecoming-feels-at-home (accessed January 16, 2018).

"American Football" (2015), [Podcast] *Radiolab*, WNYC Studios, January 29. http://www.radiolab.org/story/football/ (accessed February 14, 2016).

Anderson, Benedict (1991), *Imagined Communities: Reflections on the Origin and Spread of Nationalism*, London: Verso.

Andreassen, Cecilie Schou, Ståle Pallesen, and Mark D. Griffiths (2017), "The Relationship between Addictive Use of Social Media, Narcissism, and Self-esteem: Findings from a Large National Survey," *Addictive Behaviours*, 64: 287–93.

Bae, Paul and Terry Miles (2017), interview by Lance Dann, Skype, July 6.

Baker, Brendan (2016), interview by Martin Spinelli, Chicago, Illinois, July 8.

Barone, Joshua (2017), "Audible Creates $5 Million Fund for Emerging Playwrights," *The New York Times*, May 30. https://www.nytimes.com/2017/05/30/theater/audible-creates-5-million-dollar-fund-for-emerging-playwrights.html (accessed January 24, 2018).

Barthes, Roland (1992), *The Grain of the Voice: Interviews, 1962-1980*, Berkeley, CA: University of California Press.

Barthes, Roland (1974, 2009 reprint), *S/Z*, trans. Richard Miller, New York: John Wiley & Sons.

BBC (1999), *BBC Radio 4 Commissioning Guidelines 1999*, London: BBC.

BBC (2017), *Commissioning Brief No: 31242: Drama on 3 2017*, London: BBC.

BBC Department for Culture, Media & Sport (2016), "A BBC for the future: a broadcaster of distinction," May. https://www.gov.uk/government/uploads/system/uploads/attachment_data/file/524863/DDCM_A_BBC_for_the_future_linked_rev1.pdf (accessed January 24, 2018).

Beck, Alan (1998), "Point-of-Listening in Radio Plays," *Sound Journal* [Online]. https://www.kent.ac.uk/arts/soundjournal/beck981.htm (accessed January 30, 2017).

Benkler, Yochai (2006), *The Wealth of Networks*, New Haven, CT: Yale University Press.

Bennett, James (2014), "The Utopia of Independent Media," in James Bennett and Niki Strange (eds.), *Media Independence: Working with Freedom or Working for Free?* London: Routledge.

Bernstein, Charles (1998), *Close Listening*, New York: Oxford University Press.

Berry, Richard (2006), "Will the iPod Kill the Radio Star," *Convergence: The International Journal of Research into New Media Technologies*, 12(2): 143–62.

Berry, Richard (2015a), "Considering Podcasting Evolution," *The Radio Journal*, 14 (1): 7–22.

Berry, Richard (2015b), "A Golden Age of Podcasting? Evaluating Serial in the Context of Podcast Histories," *Journal of Radio & Audio Media*, 2 (2): 170–8.

Berry, Richard. (2016a), "Part of the Establishment: Reflecting on 10 Years of Podcasting as an Audio Medium," *Convergence: The International Journal of Research into New Media Technologies*, 22 (6): 661–71.

Berry, Richard (2016b), "Podcasting: Considering the Evolution of the Medium and Its Association with the Word 'Radio'," *The Radio Journal International Studies in Broadcast and Audio Media*, 14 (1): 7–22.

Birch, Hayley and Emma Weitkamp (2010), "Podologues: Conversations Created by Science Podcasts," *New Media & Society*, 12 (6): 889–909.

"*Blood Culture*, Episode One" (2017), [Podcast] *Blood Culture*, Resonance FM, April 27. https://blood-culture.com/audio (accessed February 15, 2018).

Blum-Ross, Alicia. (2015), "Filmmakers/Educators/Facilitators? Understanding the Role of Adult Intermediaries in Youth Media Production in the UK and the USA," *Journal of Children and Media*, 9 (3): 308–24.

Blumberg, Alex (2016), *Alex Blumberg on "Mystery Show"* [Soundcloud Audio], https://soundcloud.com/gimletmedia/alex-blumberg-on-mystery-show (accessed February 1, 2018).

Blumberg, Alex (2017), interview by Lance Dann, Skype, October 10.

"Boars, Gore and Swords S06E06" (2016), Scott, Red and Ivan Hernandez, May 29. http://boarsgoreandswords.com/2016/05/29/6x06-meet-the-tarlys/ (accessed February 6, 2018).

Bonini, Tiziano (2014), "The 'Second Age' of Podcasting: Reframing Podcasting as a New Digital Mass Medium," *Quaderns del CAC*, 41 (18): 21–30.

Bonini, Tiziano and Belén Monclús (2015), *Radio Audiences and Participation in the Age of Network Society*, New York: Routledge.

Borel, Brooke (2015), "The Problem with Science Journalism: We've Forgotten What Really Matters Most," *The Guardian*, December 30. https://www.theguardian.com/media/2015/dec/30/problem-with-science-journalism-2015-reality-kevin-folta (accessed January 24, 2018).

Bottomley, Andrew J. (2015), "Podcasting, Welcome to Night Vale, and the Revival of Radio Drama," *Journal of Radio & Audio Media* 22 (2): 179–89.

Bourdieu, Pierre (1969), "Intellectual Field and Creative Project," *Social Science Information*, 8 (2): 89–119.

Bourdieu, Pierre (1993), *The Field of Cultural Production*, New York: Columbia University Press.

Boynton, Robert (2005), *The New New Journalism: Conversations with America's Best Nonfiction Writers on Their Craft*, New York: Vintage.

Brake, David R. (2013), "Are We All Online Content Creators Now? Web 2.0 and Digital Divides," *Journal of Computer Mediated Communication*, 19 (3): 591–609.

Brecht, Bertold (1932), "Der Rundfunk als Kommunikationsapparat inBlätter des Hessischen Landestheaters, Darmstadt, No. 16, July 1932" in Jon Willet (ed.) (1964), *Brecht on Theatre*, New York: Hill and Wang.

Bridge Ratings (2017), "Podcasting Best Practices: The Study," *Bridge Ratings*, August 26. http://www.bridgeratings.com/podcasting-best-practices-the-study (accessed January 24, 2018).

Bull, Michael (2004), "Automobility and the Power of Sound," *Theory, Culture and Society*, 21 (4–5): 243–59.

Bull, Michael (2005), "No Dead Air! The iPod and the Culture of Mobile Listening," *Leisure Studies*, 24 (4): 343–55.

Bull, Michael (2007), *Sound Moves: iPod Culture and Urban Experience*, New York: Routledge.

Bull, Michael and Les Back (2003), "Introduction: Into Sound," in Michael Bull and Les Back (eds.), *The Auditory Culture Reader*, 1–24, Oxford: Berg.

Burum, Ivo and Stephen Quinn (2015), *MOJO: The Mobile Journalism Handbook*, London: Focal Press.

Byk, Camilla (2015), interview by Martin Spinelli, London, 11 December.

Byk, Camilla (2016), interview by Martin Spinelli, London, 24 May.

Capote, Truman (1966), *In Cold Blood*, New York: Random House.

Carr, David (2014), "Serial, Podcasting's First Breakout Hit, Sets Stage for More," *The New York Times*, November 23, https://nyti.ms/1vfPqFK (accessed January 24, 2018).

Chaudry, Rabia. (2016), *Adnan's Story: The Case That Inspired the Podcast Phenomenon Serial*, London: Century.

Chivvis, Dana (2016), interview by Martin Spinelli, New York, July 5.

Clark, Roy Peter (2001), "The Line between Fact and Fiction," *Creative Nonfiction* 16, https://www.creativenonfiction.org/online-reading/line-between-fact-and-fiction (accessed January 24, 2018).

Clough, Patricia Ticento and Jean Halley (eds.) (2007), *The Affective Turn: Theorizing the Social*, London: Duke University Press.

Collins, Michael J. (2016), "Pod People: Brave New Worlds of Digital Audio Drama," *Alluvium* 5 (4). http://dx.doi.org/10.7766/alluvium.v5.4.01 (accessed January 24, 2018).

Coppa, Francesca (2014), "Participations: Dialogues on the Participatory Promise of Contemporary Culture and Politics," panel with S. Banet-Weiser, N. Baym, D. Gauntlett, J. Gray and H. Jenkins, *International Journal of Communication*, 8: 1069–88.

Cranor, Jeffrey and Joseph Fink (2015), interview by Lance Dann, Skype, September 11.

Crenshaw, Kimberlé (1989), "Demarginalizing the Intersection of Race and Sex: A Black Feminist Critique of Antidiscrimination Doctrine, Feminist Theory and Antiracist Politics," reprinted in Anne Phillips (ed.) (1998), *Feminism and Politics*, New York: Oxford University Press, 314–43.

Crissell, Andrew (1986), *Understanding Radio*, London: Methuen.

Crissell, Andrew (1994), *Understanding Radio*, 2nd ed., London: Routledge.

Crissell, Andrew (2002), *An Introduction to British Broadcasting*, 2nd ed., London: Routledge.

Crook, Timothy (1999), *Radio Drama: Theory and Practice*, London: Routledge.

Dale, Brady (2016), "Gimlet Has Dropped Starlee Kine's Podcast, 'Mystery Show,'" *Observer*, June 10. http://observer.com/2016/10/gimlet-mystery-show-starlee-kine/ (accessed January 24, 2018).

Dann, Lance (2015), "Only Half the Story: Radio Drama, Online Audio and Transmedia Storytelling," *Radio Journal: International Studies in Broadcast & Audio Media*, 12 (1–2): 141–54.

Das, Ranjana (2010), "Digital Youth, Diversity and Heterogeneity," *Journal of Media Practice*, 11 (3): 293–99.

Davidson, Roei and Nanthaniel Poor (2015), "The Barriers Facing Artists' Use of Crowdfunding Platforms: Personality, Emotional Labor, and Going to the Well One Too Many Times," *New Media & Society*, 17 (2): 289–307.

Davies, Pete (2014), "Downloads, Listens, Listeners," *Medium.com*, December 12, https://medium.com/@pete/downloads-listens-listeners-and-about-those-podcast-numbers-73a5ee3e2fca (accessed May 17, 2017).

Deahl, Dani (2017), "Three Men in Thailand Reportedly Ran a Clickfarm with Over 300,000 SIM Cards and 400 iPhones," *The Verge*, June 12. https://www.theverge.com/2017/6/12/15786402/thai-clickfarm-bust-iphones (accessed January 24, 2018).

Douglas, Susan (2004), *Listening In: Radio and the American Imagination*, Minneapolis: University of Minnesota Press.

Dryden, John (2017), interview by Lance Dann, phone, April 28.

Duffett, Mark (2015), *Understanding Fandom*, New York: Bloomsbury Academic.

Edison Research (2017), "The Infinite Dial," http://www.edisonresearch.com/wp-content/uploads/2017/03/The-Infinite-Dial-2017.pdf (accessed January 24, 2018).

Edmond, Maura (2015), "All Platforms Considered: Contemporary Radio and Transmedia Engagement," *New Media & Society*, 17 (9): 1566–82.

"*Engaged* Magazine" (1998), [Radio Program] Prod. Stewart, Rachael and Martin Spinelli, Resonance 104.4FM. http://epc.buffalo.edu/sound/file-list.html#e; (accessed January 9, 2018).

"Exonerated" (2017), [Radio Documentary] BBC Radio Four, January 4, 11:00. http://www.bbc.co.uk/programmes/b084wzjx (accessed January 20, 2017).

Fincham, Kelly (2014), "These Views Are My Own: The Private and Public Self in the Digital Media Sphere," in Zion, Lawrie and David Craig (eds.), *Ethics for Digital Journalists: Emerging Best Practices*, New York: Routledge.

Fiske, John (1992), "The Cultural Economy of Fandom," in Lisa A. Lewis (ed.), *The Adoring Audience: Fan Culture and Popular Media*, London and New York: Routledge.

Florini, Sarah (2015), "The Podcast 'Chitlin' Circuit': Black Podcasters, Alternative Media, and Audio Enclaves," *Journal of Radio & Audio Media*, 22 (2): 209–19.

Frank, Arthur (2016), "Knowing Other Peoples Stories: Empathy, Illness, and Identity," *Concentric Literary and Cultural Studies*, 42 (2): 151–65.

"Freedom Fries" (2015), [Podcast] *This American Life*, January 23. https://www.thisamericanlife.org/radio-archives/episode/545/if-you-dont-have-anything-nice-to-say-say-it-in-all-caps (accessed February 1, 2018).

Friend, Mark (2016). Interview by Martin Spinelli, London, June 22.

"Fu*k Love" (2014), [Podcast] *The Heart*, February 5. http://www.theheartradio.org/events/fuk-love (accessed October 14, 2016).

Ganesh, Janan (2016), "Podcasts Create Golden Age of Audio," *Financial Times* online, March 5. https://www.ft.com/content/cd1b444a-e160-11e5-9217-6ae3733a2cd1 (accessed February 7, 2018).

Garfield, Lianna (2015), "Why Podcasts Like the *Heart* Are Intimate," *Business Insider*, November 8. http://uk.businessinsider.com/why-podcasts-like-the-heart-are-intimate-2015-10?r=US&IR=T (accessed January 24, 2018).

Goldstein, Jessica (2014), "The Complicated Ethics Of 'Serial,' The Most Popular Podcast Of All Time," *Think Progress*, November 21. https://thinkprogress.org/the-complicated-ethics-of-serial-the-most-popular-podcast-of-all-time-6f84043de9a9 (accessed January 24, 2018).

Greenhalgh, Fred (2016), interview by Lance Dann, Los Angeles, April 2.

Greenhalgh, Fred (2017), interview by Lance Dann, Skype, June 30.

Greiff, Felicia (2015), "Ira Glass: 'Public Radio is Ready for Capitalism,'" *AdAge*, April 30. http://adage.com/article/special-report-tv-upfront/ira-glass public-radio-ready-capitalism/298332/ (accessed January 24, 2018).

Grose Jessica (2015), "From Upspeak To Vocal Fry: Are We 'Policing' Young Women's Voices?" *NPR*, June 23. https://www.npr.org/2015/07/23/425608745/from-upspeak-to-vocal-fry-are-we-policing-young-womens-voices (accessed January 24, 2018).

Hall, Alan (2016), interview by Lance Dann, South London, July 5.

Hall, Lee (1997), "Spoonface Steineberg," [Radio Program] BBC Radio Four, January 27.

Hardt, Michael (2007), "Forward: What Affects Are Good For," in Clough, Patricia Ticineto and Jean Halley (eds.), *The Affective Turn: Theorizing the Social*, London: Duke University Press.

Harrington, Walt (1997), *Intimate Journalism: The Art and Craft of Reporting Everyday Life*, London: Sage.

Hart, Jack (2012), *Storycraft: The Complete Guide to Writing Narrative Nonfiction*, Chicago: University of Chicago Press.

Hearns-Branaman, Jesse Owen (2014), "Journalistic Professionalism as Indirect Control and Fetishistic Disavowal," *Journalism*, 15 (1): 21–36.

Heffernan, Virginia (2007), "The Myth of the Omniscient Narrator, and Other Stories," *The New York Times* online, March 22. http://www.nytimes.com/2007/03/22/arts/television/22heff.html (accessed October 10, 2016).

Hendy, David (2000), *Radio in the Global Age*, Cambridge: Polity Press.

Hendy, David (2007), *Life on Air: A History of Radio Four*, Oxford: Oxford University Press.

Hendy, David (2014), *Noise: A Human History of Sound and Listening*, London: Profile Books.

Heppermann, Ann (2015), interview by Martin Spinelli, Brooklyn, New York, October 30.

Herring, Richard (2016), interview by Lance Dann, London, November 18.

Hesmondhalgh, David (1999), "Indie: The Institutional Politics and Aesthetics of a Popular Music Genre," *Cultural Studies*, 13 (1): 34–61.

Hesmondhalgh, David (2013), *The Cultural Industries*, 3rd ed., London: Sage.

Hess, Amanda (2016), "The Story So Far: Fiction Podcasts Take Their Next Steps," *The New York Times*, November 11. https://www.nytimes.com/2016/11/13/arts/fiction-podcasts-homecoming.html (accessed January 24, 2018).

Hilliard, Robert (2009), *Dirty Discourse: Sex and Indecency in Broadcasting*, 2nd ed., Hoboken, NJ: Wiley-Blackwell.

Hills, Matt (2002), *Fan Cultures*, London: Routledge.

Hills, Matt (2013), "Fiske's 'Textual Productivity' and Digital Fandom: Web 2.0 Democratization Versus Fan Distinction?" *Participations: Journal of Audience and Reception Studies*, 10 (1): 130–53.

"*Homecoming* S01E01, Mandatory" (2016), [Podcast] Gimlet Media, October 16. https://gimletmedia.com/episode/1-mandatory/ (accessed January 24, 2018).

Horkheimer, Max and Theodor Adorno (1973), *The Dialectic of Enlightenment*, London: Penguin.

Horne, Ellen (2015), interview by Martin Spinelli, Newark, New Jersey, October 27.

"How to Argue" (2017), [Podcast] *Love + Radio*, February 11. http://loveandradio.org/2017/02/how-to-argue/ (accessed March 15, 2017).

"How to Become a Princess" (2015), [Podcast] *The Heart*, May. 5 http://www.theheartradio.org/season1/howtobeaprincess?rq=princess (accessed October 19, 2016).

"How to Look at Boobs" (2016), [Podcast] *Podium.me*, February 4. https://www.acast.com/podiumreallife/howtolookatboobs (accessed December 19, 2016).

Imison, Richard (1991), "Radio and Theatre: A British Perspective," *Theatre Journal*, 43 (3): 289–92.

"Jad's Brain" (2012), [Podcast] *How Sound* #35, PRX, November 7. https://beta.prx.org/stories/87353 (accessed February 27, 2017).

Jenkins, Henry (2006), *Convergence Culture*, New York and London: New York University Press.

Kafka, Peter (2017), "Apple Is Going to Let Podcast Creators—and Advertisers— See What Listeners Actually Like," *Recode,* June 10. https://www.recode. net/2017/6/10/15774936/apple-podcast-analytics-wwdc (accessed June 16, 2017).

"Kaitlin + Mitra, Part 1" (2015), [Podcast] *The Heart*, October 25. http://www. theheartradio.org/season2/kaitlinandmitra-pt1?rq=kaitlin%20mitra; iTunes (accessed May 24, 2017).

"Kaitlin + Mitra, Part 2" (2015), [Podcast] *The Heart*, October 27. http://www. theheartradio.org/season2/kaitlinandmitra-pt2; iTunes (accessed May 24, 2017).

Kang, Jay Caspian (2014), "White Reporter Privilege," *The Awl*, November 13. https:// theawl.com/white-reporter-privilege-541a743ad90d (accessed May 24, 2017).

Karatzogianni, Athina and Adi Kuntsman (eds.) (2012), *Digital Cultures and the Politics of Emotion, Feelings, Affect and Technological Change*, London: Palgrave/Macmillan.

Kine, Starlee (2016), "*The Mystery Show*," *Medium,* October 6. https://medium.com/ @StarleeKine/hi-everyone-2c140c11488c (accessed October 24, 2018).

Kramer, Mark and Wendy Call (2007), *Telling True Stories: A Nonfiction Writers' Guide*, New York: Plume.

Krulwhich, Robert (2012), "From Robert Krulwich on Yellow Rain," [Blog] Radiolab. org, September 30. http://www.radiolab.org/story/240899-robert-krulwich-yellow-rain/ (accessed March 21, 2017).

Kumanyika, Chenjerai (2015), "The Whiteness Of 'Public Radio Voice,'" *BuzzFeed*, January 27. https://www.buzzfeed.com/chenjeraikumanyika/the-whiteness-of-public-radio-voice?utm_term=.trQRd529M#.ouRzMRB25 (accessed June 19, 2017).

Lacey, Kate (2013), *Listening Publics: The Politics and Experience of Listening in the Media Age*, Cambridge: Polity.

Lacey, Kate (2014), "Smart Radio and Audio Apps: The Politics and Paradoxes of Listening to (Anti-) Social Media," *Australian Journalism Review*, 36 (2): 77–90.

Larson, Sarah (2015), "*Serial*, Podcasts, and Humanizing the News," *The New Yorker*, February 20. http://www.newyorker.com/culture/sarah-larson/serial-podcasts-humanizing-news (accessed March 31, 2015).

Leadbeater, Charles and Paul Miller (2004), *The Pro-Am Revolution: How Enthusiasts Are Changing Our Society and Economy*, London: Demos.

Leadbeater, Charles and Kate Oakley (1999), *The Independents Britain's New Cultural Entrepreneur*, London: Demos.

Lee, David (2011), "The Ethics of Insecurity: Risk, Individualization and Value in British Independent Television Production," *Television & New Media*, 13 (6): 480–97.

Lenhart, Amanda (2015), "Social Media and Friendships" in the report "Teens, Technology and Friendships," Pew Research Center. http://www.pewinternet. org/2015/08/06/chapter-4-social-media-and-friendships/ (accessed May 9, 2017).

Lind, Seth (2016), email correspondence with Martin Spinelli, September 1.

Littleton, C (2010), "HBO Lays a Big-bucks Bet on 'Boardwalk,'" *Variety*, August 7. http:// variety.com/2010/tv/features/hbo-lays-a-big-bucks-bet-on-boardwalk-1118022673/ (accessed January 24, 2018).

Lønstrup, Ansa (2012), "Listening to Voice and Polyphony in *Radiolab*," *SoundEffects*, 2 (1): 127–36.

Loviglio, Jason (2005), *Radio's Intimate Public: Network Broadcasting and Mass-Mediated Democracy*, Minneapolis: University of Minnesota Press.

Lyne, Charlie (2016), "Cast Party: Podcast Giants Take to the Stage in Excruciating Style," *Guardian*, September 20. https://www.theguardian.com/film/2016/feb/20/cast-party-movie-review (accessed January 24, 2018).

Maggs, Dirk (2009), interview by Lance Dann, phone, November 16.

Maggs, Dirk (2018), interview by Lance Dann, Skype, January 5.

Mahnke, Aaron (2017), interview by Ella Gray Thomas, Skype, April 19.

Malik, Sarita (2008), "'Keeping it Real': The Politics of Channel 4's Multiculturalism, Mainstreaming and Mandates," *Screen*, 49 (3): 343–53.

Malikhao, Patchaneen and Jan Servaes (2011), "The Media Use of American Youngsters in the Age of Narcissism: Surviving in a 24/7 Media Shock and Awe—Distracted by Everything," *Telematics and Informatics*, 28 (2): 66–76.

Markman, Kris M. (2012), "Doing Radio, Making Friends, and Having Fun: Exploring the Motivations of Independent Audio Podcasters," *New Media and Society*, 14 (4): 547–65.

Markman, Kris M. (2015), "Considerations—Reflections and Future Research. Everything Old Is New Again: Podcasting as Radio's Revival," *Journal of Radio & Audio Media*, 22 (2): 240–43.

Marshall, David P. (1997), *Celebrity and Power: Fame and Contemporary Culture*, Minneapolis: University of Minnesota Press.

Mayer-Schönberger, Viktor (2009), *Delete: The Virtue of Forgetting in the Digital Age*, New York: Princeton University Press.

McCain, Jessica and Keith W. Campbell (2018), "Narcissism and Social Media Use: A Meta-Analytic Review," *Psychology of Popular Media Culture*, 7 (3): 308–27.

McHugh, Siobhan (2016), "How Podcasting Is Changing the Audio Storytelling Genre," *The Radio Journal: International Studies in Broadcast and Audio Media*, 14 (1): 65–82.

McKee, Robert (1997), *Story: Substance, Structure, Style, and the Principles of Screenwriting*, London: Methuen.

McKinney (2015), "First Survey of Serial's Listeners Sheds Light on the Serial Effect," June 25. https://www.prnewswire.com/news-releases/first-survey-of-serials-listeners-sheds-light-on-the-serial-effect-300104734.html (accessed March 23, 2017).

McMurtry, Leslie Grace (2016), "'I'm Not a Real Detective, I Only Play One on Radio': Serial as the Future of Audio Drama," *The Journal of Popular Culture*, 49 (2): 306–24.

McRobbie, Angela (2002), "Clubs to Companies: Notes on the Decline of Political Culture in Speeded up Creative Worlds," *Cultural Studies*, 16 (4): 516–31

Mengiste, Maaza (2017), "How 'S-Town' Fails Black Listeners," *Rolling Stone*, April 13. http://www.rollingstone.com/culture/how-s-town-fails-black-listeners-w476524 (accessed April 27, 2017).

Milutis, Joe (2006), *Ether: The Nothing that Connects Everything*, Minneapolis: University of Minnesota Press.

Mitchell, Jonathan (2015), interview by Martin Spinelli, New York, October 26.

Morris, Jeremy Wade and Eleanor Patterson (2015), "Podcasting and Its Apps: Software, Sound, and the Interfaces of Digital Audio," *Journal of Radio & Audio Media*, 22 (2): 220–30.

Mortimer, Jeremy (2016), interview by Lance Dann, North London, July 5.

Morton, Jamie, James Cooper, and Alice Levine (2017), interview by Ella Thomas, London, April 28.

"Movies in Your Head" (2004), [Podcast] *The Heart* (*Audio Smut*), June 23. http://www.theheartradio.org/audio-smut/moviesinyourhead (accessed April 27, 2017).

Murtha, Jack (2016), "WNYC Is Leading Public Radio's Transition to Public Podcasting," *Columbia Journalism Review*. http://www.cjr.org/the_feature/wnyc_public_radio_podcast.php accessed 24/01/2017 (accessed April 27, 2017).

Nahon, K. and Hemsley J. (2013), *Going Viral*, Cambridge, Malden, MA: Polity Press.

Naylor, Hattie (2005), "Wooden Heart," [Radio Program] BBC Radio Four, March 31.

Neumark, Norie (2006), "Different Place Different Times: Exploring the Possibilities of Cross Platform Radio," *Convergence: The International Journal of New Media Technologies*, 12 (2): 213–24.

Newman, Michael Z. (2009), "Indie Culture: In Pursuit of the Authentic Autonomous," *Alternative Cinema Journal*, 48 (3): 16–34.

Nyre, Lars (2015), "Urban Headphone Listening and the Situational Fit of Music, Radio and Podcasting," *Journal of Radio & Audio Media*, 22 (2): 279–98.

O'Baoill, Andrew (2009), "Broadcasting in an On-demand World: Creating Community Radio in the Era of Podcasting and Webcasting," PhD diss., Chicago: University of Illinois.

O'Keeffe, Anne (2006), *Investigating Media Discourse*, London: Routledge.

Ojebode, Ayobami (2009), "Media Diversity With and Without a Policy: A Comparison of the BBC and Nigeria's DBS," *Journal of Radio & Audio Media*, 16 (2): 216–28.

"Oliver Sipple" (2017), [Podcast] *Radiolab*, WNYC Studios, September 21. http://www.radiolab.org/story/oliver-sipple/ (accessed September 24, 2018).

Patterson, Eleanor (2016), "This American Franchise: This American Life, Public Radio Franchising and the Cultural Work of Legitimating Economic Hybridity," *Media, Culture & Society 2016*, 38 (3): 450–61.

Peck, Jamie (2005), "Struggling with the Creative Class," *International Journal of Urban and Regional Research*, 29 (4): 740–70.

"Pilot" (2012), [Podcast] *Welcome to Night Vale*, June 15. https://soundcloud.com/nightvaleradio/1-pilot-1 (accessed January 24, 2018).

Pinsker, Joe (2015), "Why So Many Podcasts Are Brought to You by Squarespace," *The Atlantic*, May 12. https://www.theatlantic.com/business/archive/2015/05/why-so-many-podcasts-are-brought-to-you-by-squarespace/392840/ (accessed January 24, 2018).

Pip, Scroobius (2017), interview by Ella Gray Thomas, London, April 28.

Podcast Movement's Facebook page, https://www.facebook.com/PodcastMovement/ (accessed September 23, 2017).

"Podcasting: The First Ten Years" (2014), [Radio Program] BBC Radio Four, May 22. http://www.bbc.co.uk/programmes/b03zdkk5 (accessed January 24, 2018).

Prest, Kaitlin (2015), interview by Martin Spinelli, Brooklyn, New York, October 30.

Quah, Nick (2016a), interview by Martin Spinelli, New York, October 26.

Quah, Nick (2016b), "Hot Pod: Gimlet Risks Its Image as Scrappy and Transparent by Mishandling a Show Cancellation," *NiemanLab*, October 11. http://www.niemanlab.org/2016/10/hot-pod-gimlet-risks-its-image-as-scrappy-and-transparent-by-mishandling-a-show-cancellation/ (accessed January 24, 2018).

Quah, Nick (2017a), "If Your Favorite Podcast Gets a New Host, Is It Still Your Favorite Podcast?" *NiemanLab*, November 28. http://www.niemanlab.org/2017/11/if-your-favorite-podcast-gets-a-new-host-is-it-still-your-favorite-podcast/ (accessed January 24, 2018).

Quah, Nick (2017b), "The Future of Podcasting Is Strong but the Present Needs to Catch Up," *Hot Pod* 111, March 14. http://www.niemanlab.org/2017/03/the-future-of-podcasting-is-strong-but-the-present-needs-to-catch-up/ (accessed January 24, 2018).

Quirk, Vanessa (2015), "Guide to Podcasting," *Tow Centre for Digital Journalism*, December 7. http://towcenter.org/research/guide-to-podcasting/ (accessed January 24, 2018).

Radio Radio (2003), [Radio Series] Prod. Martin Spinelli, Resonance 104.4FM. http://www.ubu.com/sound/radio_radio/ (accessed January 9, 2018).

"Radiolab," *Wikipedia*. https://en.wikipedia.org/wiki/Radiolab (accessed January 24, 2018).

Ragusea, Adam (2015), "Three Ways Podcasts and Radio Actually Aren't Quite the Same," *Current*, July 13. http://current.org/2015/07/three-ways-podcasts-and-radio-actually-arent-quite-the-same/ (accessed January 24, 2018).

Rattigan, Dermot (2002), *Theatre of Sound: Radio and the Dramatic Imagination*, Dublin: Carysfort Press.

Ritzer, George, and Nathan Jurgenson (2010), "Production, Consumption and Prosumption: The Nature of Capitalism in the Age of the 'Digital Prosumer'," *Journal of Consumer Culture*, 10 (1): 13–16.

Roberts, Amy (2014), "The 'Serial' podcast: By the numbers," CNN, December 23. http://edition.cnn.com/2014/12/18/showbiz/feat-serial-podcast-btn/index.html (accessed June 21, 2017).

Rodero, Emma (2012), "Stimulating the Imagination in a Radio Story: The Role of Presentation Structure and the Degree of Involvement of the Listener," *Journal of Radio & Audio Media*, 19 (1): 45–60.

Rodger, Ian (1982), *Radio Drama*, London: Macmillan.

Rosin, Larry (2016), interview by Martin Spinelli, Somerville, New Jersey, October 31.

Ross, Andrew (2009), "On the Digital Labor Question," filmed at Vera List Center for Art and Politics at The New School, September 29. http://dev.autonomedia.org/node/13277 (accessed February 1, 2018).

Ross, Andrew (2004), *No-Collar: The Humane Workplace and Its Hidden Costs.* Philadelphia, PA: Temple University Press.

Rowley, Tom (2014), "The New Radio Station for—and Made by—Teenagers," *The Telegraph*, April 15.

Sawyer, Miranda (2016), interview by Martin Spinelli, London, March 17.

Schudson, Michael (2001), "The Objectivity Norm in American Journalism," *Journalism* 2 (2): 149–70.

Schulz, Karen (2017), "On Air and On Error: This American Life's Ira Glass on Being Wrong," *Slate*, June 7. http://www.slate.com/blogs/thewrongstuff/2010/06/07/on_air_and_on_error_this_american_life_s_ira_glass_on_being_wrong.html (accessed May 18, 2017).

Sconce, Jeffrey (2002), "Irony, Nihilism and the New American 'Smart' Film," *Screen*, 43 (4): 349–69.

"*Serial* S01E01, The Alibi" (2014), [Podcast] *Serial*, WBEZ Chicago, October 3. https://serialpodcast.org/season-one (accessed February 1, 2018).

"*Serial* S01E02, The Breakup" (2014), [Podcast] *Serial*, WBEZ Chicago, October 30. https://serialpodcast.org/season-one (accessed February 1, 2018).

"*Serial* S01E03, Leakin Park" (2014), [Podcast] *Serial*, WBEZ Chicago, October 10. https://serialpodcast.org/season-one (accessed February 1, 2018).

"*Serial* S01E04, Inconsistencies" (2014), [Podcast] *Serial*, WBEZ Chicago, October 16. https://serialpodcast.org/season-one (accessed February 1, 2018).

"*Serial* S01E05, Route Talk" (2014), [Podcast] *Serial*, WBEZ Chicago, October 23. https://serialpodcast.org/season-one (accessed February 1, 2018).

"*Serial* S01E06, The Case Against Adnan Syed" (2014), [Podcast] *Serial*, WBEZ Chicago, October 30. https://serialpodcast.org/season-one (accessed February 1, 2018).

"*Serial* S01E07, The Opposite of the Prosecution" (2014), [Podcast] *Serial*, WBEZ Chicago, November 6. https://serialpodcast.org/season-one (accessed February 1, 2018).

"*Serial* S01E08, The Deal with Jay" (2014), [Podcast] *Serial*, WBEZ Chicago, November 13. https://serialpodcast.org/season-one(accessed February 1, 2018).

"*Serial* S01E09, To Be Suspected" (2014), [Podcast] *Serial*, WBEZ Chicago, November 20. https://serialpodcast.org/season-one (accessed February 1, 2018).

"*Serial* S01E10, The Best Defence Is a Good Defence" (2014), [Podcast] *Serial*, WBEZ Chicago, December 4. https://serialpodcast.org/season-one (accessed February 1, 2018).

"*Serial* S01E11, Rumors" (2014), [Podcast] *Serial*, WBEZ Chicago, December 11. https://serialpodcast.org/season-one (accessed February 1, 2018).

"*Serial* S01E12, What We Know" (2014), [Podcast] *Serial*, WBEZ Chicago, December 18. https://serialpodcast.org/season-one (accessed February 1, 2018).

Shapiro, Julie (2016), interview by Martin Spinelli, Chicago, Illinois, July 8.

Sheppard, Emma (2016), "Podcasting: 'It Builds Trust, Credibility and Brand Loyalty,'" *The Guardian*, November 1. https://www.theguardian.com/small-business-network/2016/nov/01/podcasting-it-builds-trust-credibility-and-brand-loyalty (accessed January 24, 2018).

Shirky, Clay (2008), *Here Comes Everybody*, London: Lane.

Sibler, Maia (2017), "With Vocal Fry and Upspeak, these Podcast Hosts Parody the Policing of Women's Voices," *The Washington Post*, July 27. https://www.washingtonpost.com/lifestyle/style/with-vocal-fry-and-upspeak-these-podcast-hosts-parody-the-policing-of-womens-voices/2017/07/27/8888f40a-7226-11e7-8839-ec48ec4cae25_story.html?utm_term=.88934a76793d (accessed January 24, 2018)

"Space" (2004), [Podcast] *Radiolab*, WNYC Studios, June 25. http://www.radiolab.org/story/91520-space/ (accessed February 1, 2018).

Spinelli, Martin (1996a), "Radio Lessons for the Internet," *Postmodern Culture*, 6 (2). https://muse.jhu.edu/article/27562 (accessed February 1, 2018).

Spinelli, Martin (1996b), "LINEbreak public radio marketing material" folder, Box 1, Buffalo, New York, The Martin Spinelli Collection, available via The Poetry Collection of the University at Buffalo Libraries.

Spinelli, Martin (2006a), "Electric Line: The Poetics of Digital Audio Editing," in Morris, Adalaide and Thomas Swiss (eds.), *New Media Poetics: Contexts, Technotexts and Theories*, Cambridge, MA: MIT Press.

Spinelli, Martin (2006b), "Rhetorical Figures and the Digital Editing of Radio Speech," *Convergence: The International Journal of Research into New Media Technologies*, 12 (2): 199–212.

Spinelli, Martin (2009), "Masters of Sacred Ceremonies: Welles, Corwin, and a Radiogenic Modernist Literature," in Cohen, Debra R., Michael Coyle, and Jane Lewty (eds.), *Broadcasting Modernism*, Gainesville: University of Florida Press.

Stankievech, Charles (2007), "From Stethoscopes to Headphones: An Acoustic Spatialization of Subjectivity," *Leonardo Music Journal*, 17: 55–9.

Starkay, K., C. Barnett, and S. Tempest (2000), "Beyond Networks and Hierarchies: Latent Organisations in the UK Television Industry," *Organisational Science*, 11 (3): 299–305.

Sterne, Jonathan, J. Morris, M. B. Baker and A. M. Freire(2008), "The Politics of Podcasting," *The Fibreculture Journal*, 13 http://thirteen.fibreculturejournal.org/fcj-087-the-politics-of-podcasting/ (accessed January 24, 2018).

Stockfelt, Ola (2012), "A Sound…," *SoundEffects*, 2 (1): 113–26.

Stockfelt, Ola (2004) "Adequate Modes of Listening," in S. Frith (ed.), *Popular Music: Critical Concepts in Media and Cultural Studies*, London: Routledge, 375–391.

Sturrock, Christian (2015), "Mayday Maday," [Radio Program] BBC Radio Four, October 26.

Taylor, Devon (2017), "5 Questions with Homecoming's Eli Horowitz," *The Sarahs*, February 12. http://thesarahawards.com/article/2017/2/12/5-questions-for-homecomings-eli-horowitz (accessed January 24, 2018).

"The Bad Show" (2012), [Podcast] *Radiolab*, WNYC Studios, January 9. http://www.radiolab.org/2012/jan/09/ (accessed February 19, 2018).

"The Fact of the Matter" (2012), [Podcast] *Radiolab*, September 24, amended October 5. http://www.radiolab.org/story/239549-yellow-rain/ (accessed February 19, 2018).

"The Investigators" (2016), [Live Event Recording] *Welcome to Night Vale*, May 20. https://nightvale.bandcamp.com/album/the-investigators-live (accessed February 1, 2018).

"The Silver Dollar" (2014), [Podcast] *Love + Radio*, February 11. http://loveandradio.org/2014/02/the-silver-dollar/ (accessed February 19, 2018).

"The Storm: A Personal Story of Sexual Abuse" (2014), [Radio Documentary] Prod. Kirsti Melville, ABC Radio National, December 19.

"They're Made of Out of Meat" (2012), [Podcast] *The Truth*, March 20. http://www.thetruthpodcast.com/story/2015/10/14/theyre-made-out-of-meat (accessed February 1, 2018).

"Things" (2014), [Podcast] *Radiolab*, WNYC Studios, May 30. http://www.radiolab.org/story/things/ (accessed February 19, 2018).

"Time" (2005), [Podcast] *Radiolab*, WNYC Studios, February 25. http://www.radiolab.org/story/91584-time/ (accessed February 16, 2018).

Todorov, Tzvetan (1971), "The 2 Principles of Narrative," *Diacritics*, 1(1): 37–44.

Tow Centre (2015), "Guide to Podcasting," December 15. https://towcenter.org/research/guide-to-podcasting/ (accessed April 26, 2017).

Trilling, D. (2007), "Putting the Broad into Broadcasting," *New Statesman*, June 28. https://www.newstatesman.com/radio/2007/06/resonance-station-london-peel (accessed January 24, 2018).

Van Der Kolk, Nick (2015), [Comments On] "Noisecasting: Searching for Podcasting's Bleeding Edge," *The Timbre*. http://thetimbre.com/noisecasting-search-podcastings-bleeding-edge (accessed August 12, 2017).

Van Dijck, Jose and David Nieborg (2009), "Wikinomics and Its Discontents: A Critical Analysis of Web 2.0 Business Manifesto," *New Media & Society*, 11 (5): 855–74.

Verma, Neil (2017a), "The Arts of Amnesia: The Case for Audio Drama, Part One," *RadioDoc Review*, 3(1). http://ro.uow.edu.au/rdr/vol3/iss1/5/ (accessed February 14, 2018).

Verma, Neil (2017b), "The Arts of Amnesia: The Case for Audio Drama, Part Two," *RadioDoc Review*, 3(2). http://ro.uow.edu.au/rdr/vol3/iss1/6/ (accessed February 14, 2018).

Walch, Rob (2017), interview by Lance Dann, Skype, November 5.

Walker, Rob (2011), "On 'Radiolab', the Sound of Science," *The New York Times*, April 7. http://www.nytimes.com/2011/04/10/magazine/mag-10Radiolab-t.html (accessed February 19, 2018).

Ward, Stephen J. A. (2015), "The Magical Concept of Transparency," in Zion, Lawrie and David Craig (eds.), *Ethics for Digital Journalists: Emerging Best Practices*, New York: Routledge.

"Watching Me Watching You" (2016), [Podcast] *Radiolab*, WNYC Studios, October 26. http://www.radiolab.org/story/watching-you-watching-me/ (accessed January 24, 2018).

Wayland, K. C. (2016), interview by Lance Dann, Los Angeles, April 4.

Wayland, K. C. (2017), interview by Lance Dann, Skype, 23.

Webster, Tom (2016), "Podcast Consumer," Edison Research. http://www.edisonresearch.com/wp-content/uploads/2016/05/The-Podcast-Consumer-2016.pdfn (accessed January 24, 2018).

Weiner, Jonah (2014), "The Voices: Toward a Critical Theory of Podcasting," *Slate*, December 14. http://www.slate.com/articles/arts/ten_years_in_your_ears/2014/12/what_makes_podcasts_so_addictive_and_pleasurable.html (accessed January 24, 2018).

Weiss, Allen (1995), *Phantasmic Radio*, Durham, NC: Duke University Press.

Whitehead, Gregory (1992), "Out of the Dark Notes on the Nobodies of Radio Art," in Kahn, Douglas and Gregory Whitehead (eds.), *Wireless Imagination: Sound, Radio and the Avant-Garde*, London: The MIT Press.

Williams, Linda (1999), *Hard Core: Power, Pleasure, and the "Frenzy of the Visible."* Berkeley, CA: University of California Press.

"Wolf-whistling: Compliment or Crime" (2016), [Podcast] *Podium.me*, February 4. https://www.acast.com/podiumreallife/wolf-whistling-complimentorcrime- (accessed February 19, 2018).

Zaltzman, Helen (2016), interview by Martin Spinelli, London, September 5.

Zorn, Johanna (2016), "Fall Preview: Where art thou, Radio/Podcasting?—Third Coast International Audio Festival," *Medium.com*, September 26. https://medium.com/third-coast-international-audio-festival/fall-preview-wherefore-art-thou-radio-podcasting-84cfd7643c87#.wu2j1d35w (accessed January 24, 2018).

Index